ABOUT THE AUTHORS

Gary Robert Muschla received his B.A. and M.A.T. from Trenton State College and teaches at Appleby School in Spotswood, New Jersey. He has spent many of his 25 years in the classroom teaching mathematics at the elementary level. He has also taught reading and writing and has conducted writing workshops for teachers and students. A successful freelance writer, editor, and ghostwriter, he is a member of the Authors Guild and the National Writers Association.

Mr. Muschla has authored other resources for teachers, including: *Writing Resource Activities Kit* (The Center for Applied Research in Education, 1989), *The Writing Teacher's Book of Lists* (Prentice Hall, 1991), *Writing Workshop Survival Kit* (The Center, 1993), *English Teacher's Great Books Activities Kit* (The Center, 1994), and *Reading Workshop Survival Kit* (The Center, 1997).

Judith Muschla received her B.A. in Mathematics from Douglass College at Rutgers University and is certified K-12. She has taught mathematics in South River, New Jersey for the last 25 years. At South River High School she has taught math at various levels, ranging from basic skills through Algebra II. She has also taught at South River Middle School. While there, in her capacity as a Team Leader, she helped revise the mathematics curriculum to reflect the standards of the NCTM, coordinated interdisciplinary units, and conducted mathematics workshops for teachers and parents. She was recipient of the 1990-91 Governor's Teacher Recognition Program in New Jersey.

The *Geometry Teacher's Activities Kit* is the fourth book Gary and Judith Muschla have co-authored. They have also written *The Math Teacher's Book of Lists* (Prentice Hall, 1995), *Hands-on Math Projects with Real-Life Applications* (The Center, 1996), and *Math Starters! 5- to 10-Minute Activities to Make Kids Think, Grades 6-12* (The Center, 1999).

For Erin

ACKNOWLEDGMENTS

We would like to thank our supervisors James Pope, principal at South River High School, and William Skowronski, principal at Appleby School, and colleagues for their encouragement and support.

Our special thanks to Michelle Philpott, a colleague at Appleby School, whose comments and suggestions helped us to revise the manuscript.

Thanks also to Sonia Helton, Professor of Education at the University of South Florida, who helped us to focus our topics and ideas when the book was still in its initial stages.

We would also like to thank Susan Kolwicz, our editor, who once again, as she has with our other books, shared with us her insight, experience, and guidance, without which this undertaking would surely have been more difficult, if not impossible.

A special thank you to Diane Turso, our development editor, whose meticulous work caught our oversights before this manuscript went to print. We also wish to thank Tom Curtin, our production editor, and Dee Coroneos, our interior design/ formatter, for their efforts in putting the many pieces of this manuscript together.

Finally, thanks to our students, who are what teaching is all about.

ABOUT GEOMETRY INSTRUCTION

Geometry is a fundamental part of any mathematics program. Although students will often ask why they must learn geometry, the understanding of geometric concepts and relationships is vital to the study of other branches of mathematics, can strengthen one's ability of analysis, and sharpen problem-solving skills. A solid knowledge of geometry is essential to interpreting, understanding, and appreciating our world in which examples of geometry abound—from hexagonal snowflakes to the Golden Rectangle of art and architecture.

Despite being found just about everywhere, geometry is one of the most challenging subjects to teach. Because much of geometry is abstract, students have a hard time understanding many of the concepts, seeing relationships, and making connections to the real world. Yet, geometry is crucial for learning higher mathematics and students need to gain proficiency in it.

Providing students with meaningful activities designed to help them comprehend geometric concepts and visualize geometric figures can supplement the program of any geometry class. Because the activities that follow will reinforce and extend the ideas and skills taught in your classes, they will help you to enhance the learning experience of your students.

We trust that this book will be helpful to you in your teaching. We'd like to extend our best wishes to you and your students.

Gary and Judith Muschla

HOW TO USE THIS RESOURCE

The *Geometry Teacher's Activities Kit* is divided into seven parts, each of which covers a major area of geometry.

▲ Part 1, "The Language of Geometry," contains 26 activities that focus on fundamental concepts and skills. The activities of this section include basic vocabulary and figures; networks; tangrams; lines; segments; angles; transversals; optical illusions; and if-then statements.

▲ Part 2, "Polygons—The Foundations," has 19 activities that cover the basics of polygons. Some of the activities here include concave and convex polygons; symmetry; triangles; the Pythagorean Theorem; polyominoes; magic squares; and quadrilaterals.

▲ Part 3, "Polygons—Advanced" contains 25 activities that address advanced topics of polygons. The activities of this section include figurate numbers; attributes of triangles; Pascal's Triangle; interior angles; diagonals; right triangles; special right triangles; sine, cosine, and tangent ratios; congruency; similarity; Fibonacci Rectangles; attributes of quadrilaterals; and transformations.

▲ Part 4, "Circles," has 15 activities. Included here are magic circles; symmetry; inscribed polygons; tangents; the Archimedean Spiral; and trigonometric functions.

▲ Part 5, "3-D Figures," has 12 activities, covering topics such as pentominoes; cubes; prisms; nets; regular pyramids; Platonic solids; the creation of three-dimensional models; and rotations.

▲ Part 6, "Applications of Geometry," contains 12 activities that demonstrate ways geometry can be applied in the real world. The activities focus on working with scale; finding perimeter, area, surface area, and volume; and working with formulas.

▲ Part 7, "A Potpourri of Geometry," contains 21 activities. Among the activities of this part of the book are a student-designed geometry lesson; a geometry newsletter; geometry rebuses; a geometry comic strip; a student-created geometry game; geometry poems; an essay in support of geometry; geometry and Native American cultures; geometry in sports, nature, and architecture; and geometry on the Internet.

The titles of the activities focus on the topic or skill that the activities address. The table of contents, therefore, can be used as a skills/topic list, making it easy to find an activity suitable for your classes.

Each activity stands alone and is numbered according to the part of the book in which it appears. For example, Activity 1–18, "Optical Illusions and Parallel Lines," is the eighteenth activity in Part 1. Activity 3–16, "Fibonacci Rectangles," is the sixteenth activity in Part 3, and Activity 5–6, "Platonic Solids," is the sixth activity in Part 5.

Objectives, Special Materials, and Teaching Notes are included with the activities. All activities are accompanied by a reproducible worksheet that guides students through the activity. To ease implementation, worksheets bear the same number and title as the activity. Answer keys are also included with many of the Teaching Notes, although some activities have various possible answers or outcomes. In such cases, you should accept any reasonable efforts and results of your students.

We suggest that when you are considering an activity for your students, you read the Teaching Notes and refer to the student worksheet. This will help you determine whether the activity is appropriate for your class and will also allow you to select the method of implementation best suited to your students.

The activities in Parts 1 through 6 of the book generally proceed from basic to more challenging in difficulty. Thus, the activities at the beginning of a section are geared more to middle school geometry, while the activities toward the end of a section are designed for high school students. Prerequisite skills for challenging activities are listed in the Teaching Notes. Of course, students vary in their abilities and you should choose any activity that you feel will benefit your classes. Because the activities of Part 7, "A Potpourri of Geometry," are open-ended, they may be used with most middle and high school classes.

Many of the activities in this book are ideal for use with calculators and computers. Whenever an activity lends itself to such equipment, it is noted under Special Materials of the Teaching Notes. Many software programs are capable of drawing geometric figures, which can be quite useful in some activities. Some of these programs, such as *The Geometer's Sketchpad* (Key Curriculum Press, Inc., 1995), enable users to draw complex geometric figures rather easily. Whether or not to use technology, however, is a decision you must make based upon your program and teaching preferences.

We suggest that you use this book as a resource, selecting the activities that best supplement your geometry classes. Choosing problems that will challenge and excite your students will help you to make your classes effective and rewarding.

CONTENTS

Part 1

THE LANGUAGE OF GEOMETRY   1

Part 2

POLYGONS—THE FOUNDATIONS 73

Part 3

POLYGONS—ADVANCED   127

Part 4

CIRCLES   199

Part 1

THE LANGUAGE OF GEOMETRY

A CROSSWORD PUZZLE
OF THE LANGUAGE OF GEOMETRY

Objective: Students will create a crossword puzzle using a list of fundamental geometric terms. Students may work individually or in pairs to complete this activity.

Special Materials: rulers, graph paper; *optional*—computers with software capable of generating crossword puzzles, printers

TEACHING NOTES

Understanding fundamental terms and concepts is essential for students to study geometry with success. This activity can be used as either an introduction to basic terms in geometry or a review.

1. Prior to the activity, collect crossword puzzles from newspapers and magazines, which you may hand out to your students as examples. (Depending upon the abilities and experiences of your students, this may be unnecessary.)

2. Introduce the activity by explaining that students are to create a crossword puzzle of basic geometric terms. If you have sample puzzles, hand them out and give students a chance to note how the puzzles are designed.

3. Distribute copies of Worksheet 1–1 and review the guidelines with your students. Point out that there is a word bank; however, you may wish to add words based on the background and abilities of your student.

4. Hand out two copies of graph paper to each student or pair of students on which they may do their puzzles. They should use one copy to plan their puzzle and another for the final copy. Suggest that students do rough copies in pencil.

5. If students have access to computers with software that enables them to create crossword puzzles, you may suggest they do their puzzles on their computers. While most crossword puzzle software will generate the form of the puzzles, students still must enter the answers and clues.

6. Accept any reasonable puzzle. At the end of the activity, make copies of the puzzles and allow students to exchange and try to solve them.

1–1   A Crossword Puzzle of the Language of Geometry

Crossword puzzles can be fun and challenging. Create a crossword puzzle of geometric terms. The following suggestions will help you to create your puzzle.

1. Use the geometric terms below for the answers to your puzzle. Arrange them in the boxes on your paper so that there is one letter per box. Be sure to place the answers down and across, trying to have a roughly equal number of down and across answers.

2. Write lightly in pencil so that it is easier to erase any mistakes you might make. Keep revising the structure of the puzzle until you find a form you like.

3. Make sure that you spell all words correctly.

4. After you are satisfied with the appearance of your puzzle, write a small number in the first box of each answer. Number the answers consecutively, one set of numbers for the down answers and another set for the across answers.

5. On a separate sheet of paper, write clues for your answers. Be sure that your facts are correct. If necessary, check the glossary of your math text or a dictionary to be sure of the accuracy of your clues.

6. Double-check your work, and create a final copy of your puzzle on a new piece of paper. Draw heavy lines on the boxes of your answers to make your answers stand out. Write the clues below the puzzle or on a separate sheet of paper.

Use the following words for the answers in your puzzle:

© 2000 by The Center for Applied Research in Education

point	straight angle
ray	segment
perpendicular lines	parallel lines
	degree
protractor	plane
intersecting lines	ruler
	vertex
line	right angle
angle	midpoint

A GEOMETRY "WORD" PUZZLE

Objective: Students will identify visual representations and/or concepts relating to points, lines, segments, rays, planes, and space. Students should work individually to complete this activity.

Special Materials: none

TEACHING NOTES

Using precise language and referring to geometric figures correctly reduce errors and result in a better understanding of geometry. In this activity students will complete a puzzle by matching geometric words with the figures they represent.

1. Introduce this activity by explaining the importance of using accurate terminology when discussing geometry (or any subject for that matter). On an overhead projector or the board, draw a line and a segment. Ask students if there is a difference between the two, then explain that a segment is a part of a line, and a line continues infinitely. Emphasize that many people refer incorrectly to segments as lines.

2. Distribute copies of Worksheet 1-2 and review the instructions with your students. Emphasize that some words of the word bank may be used twice, while others may not be used at all. Each blank space for each answer is to contain a letter. When students are done completing the puzzle, they are to arrange the numbers and the letters above them in numerical order. Assuming their answers are correct, they will need to provide spaces between words for the meaning of geometrein to be clear.

Answer Key

1. point;   2. segment;   3. ray;   4. space;   5. parallel;   6. perpendicular;   7. collinear;
8. coplanar;   9. point;   10. line;   11. segment;   12. line;   13. midpoint;   14. length;
15. parallel;   16. skew

Geometrein: to measure the land

Name _____ Date _____ Section _____

1–2   A Geometry "Word" Puzzle

The word *geometry* is taken from the Greek word *geometrein*. To find the meaning of geome-trein, complete the sentences below. Choose your answers from the following words and place one letter in each space. Then take the letters above the numbers and arrange them in numerical order. Insert spaces between words and you will find the meaning of geometrein. **Note:** Some words may be used twice; some may not be used at all.

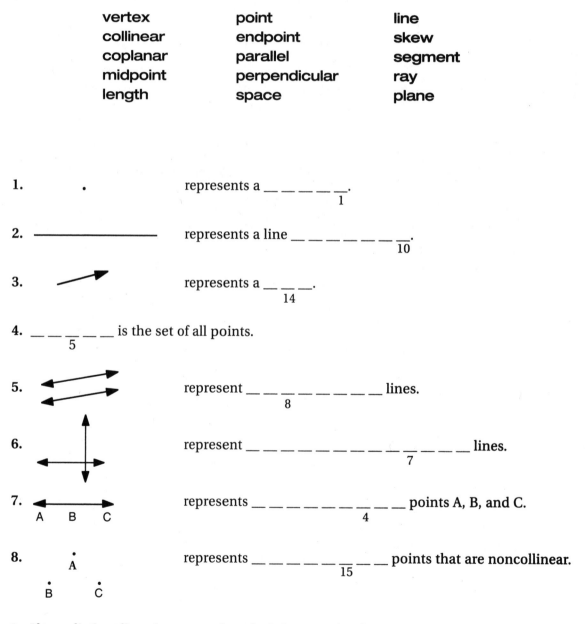

vertex	point	line
collinear	endpoint	skew
coplanar	parallel	segment
midpoint	perpendicular	ray
length	space	plane

1.   •   represents a $\underline{\ }\underline{\ }\underline{\ }\underline{\ }\underline{\ }$.
1

2. ————————— represents a line $\underline{\ }\underline{\ }\underline{\ }\underline{\ }\underline{\ }\underline{\ }\underline{\ }\underline{\ }$.
10

3.   represents a $\underline{\ }\underline{\ }\underline{\ }$.
14

4. $\underline{\ }\underline{\ }\underline{\ }\underline{\ }\underline{\ }$ is the set of all points.
5

5.   represent $\underline{\ }\underline{\ }\underline{\ }\underline{\ }\underline{\ }\underline{\ }\underline{\ }\underline{\ }$ lines.
8

6.   represent $\underline{\ }\underline{\ }\underline{\ }\underline{\ }\underline{\ }\underline{\ }\underline{\ }\underline{\ }\underline{\ }\underline{\ }\underline{\ }\underline{\ }\underline{\ }$ lines.
7

7.   represents $\underline{\ }\underline{\ }\underline{\ }\underline{\ }\underline{\ }\underline{\ }\underline{\ }\underline{\ }$ points A, B, and C.
4
A   B   C

8.   • A   represents $\underline{\ }\underline{\ }\underline{\ }\underline{\ }\underline{\ }\underline{\ }\underline{\ }$ points that are noncollinear.
15
• B   • C

9. If two distinct lines intersect, then their intersection is a $\underline{\ }\underline{\ }\underline{\ }\underline{\ }\underline{\ }$.
2

10. If two distinct planes intersect, then their intersection is a $\underset{9}{\_\,\_\,\_\,\_}$.

11. $\overline{AB}$ is a line $\underset{3}{\_\,\_\,\_\,\_\,\_\,\_\,\_}$.

12. 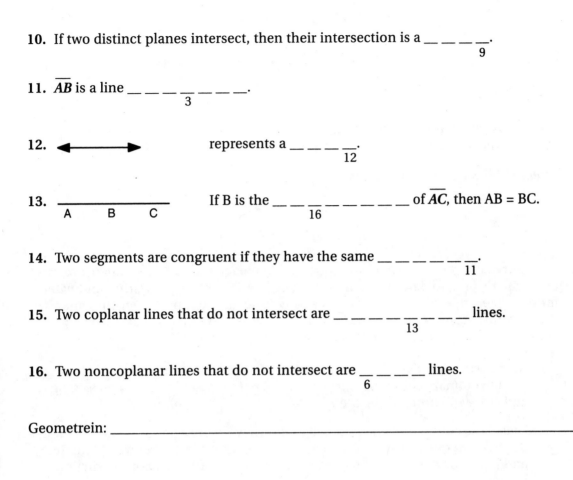 represents a $\underset{12}{\_\,\_\,\_\,\_}$.

13. $\overline{\underset{A \quad\ B \quad\ C}{}}$ If B is the $\underset{16}{\_\,\_\,\_\,\_\,\_\,\_\,\_\,\_}$ of $\overline{AC}$, then AB = BC.

14. Two segments are congruent if they have the same $\underset{11}{\_\,\_\,\_\,\_\,\_\,\_}$.

15. Two coplanar lines that do not intersect are $\underset{13}{\_\,\_\,\_\,\_\,\_\,\_\,\_}$ lines.

16. Two noncoplanar lines that do not intersect are $\underset{6}{\_\,\_\,\_\,\_}$ lines.

Geometrein: _____

A WORD GAME OF GEOMETRY

Objective: Students will identify various meanings and usages of the words *point*, *line*, and *plane*. Students should work individually to complete this activity.

Special Materials: dictionaries

TEACHING NOTES

Geometry is so prevalent in our culture and language that many geometric words are regularly used to describe common situations. The words *point*, *line*, and *plane*, for example, appear in conversations and writing all the time. When students use these words, however, few likely think of their "geometry" roots. This activity gives students a chance to consider how far-reaching geometry is in our society.

1. Introduce this activity by asking students to think of geometric words that are used in ordinary conversations. Words like *point*, *line*, *plane*, *square*, *rectangle*, and *circle* will probably be mentioned.

2. Distribute copies of Worksheet 1–3 and review the instructions with your students. *Point* out that some answers will be words closely related to point, line, and plane, or they might be phrases. Suggest that students consult dictionaries, which will be helpful.

Answer Key

1. point; 2. line; 3. pointless; 4. plane; 5. point; 6. plane; 7. planar; 8. line-up; 9. point; 10. pointer; 11. line of scrimmage (or scrimmage line); 12. point of view (or viewpoint)

Accept any reasonable student sentences.

Name _____ Date _____ Section _____

1–3 A Word Game of Geometry

We use geometric words and phrases every day in countless situations. This is an indisputable *point*. Use a dictionary and define the words *point*, *line*, and *plane*. Pay close attention to related words, for example, lineup and point-blank. Then fill in the blanks in the sentences below with *point*, *line*, *plane*, or a related word or phrase. The first one is done for you.

1. To be direct is to get to the <u>point</u>.

2. To march single file is to form a _____.

3. A meaningless or irrelevant comment is _____.

4. A carpenter's tool consisting of an adjustable blade for smoothing and leveling is called a _____.

5. The highest or culminating _____ is called the zenith.

6. Pairs of numbers are graphed on a coordinate _____.

7. A flat surface is also called a _____ surface.

8. The members of a baseball team who are chosen by the manager to start the game are in the _____.

9. A specific moment in time might be referred to as a _____.

10. A long tapered stick is called a _____.

11. In a football game, the opposing teams face each other at the _____.

12. The position from which you might view an event or situation is called your _____.

   Now write at least three sentences of your own using the words *point*, *line*, and *plane* or a related word or phrase.

_____

_____

_____

_____

_____

_____

TRACING NETWORKS

Objective: Students will apply the concepts of lines and points in a non-Euclidean setting and determine which networks are traceable. Students should work individually to complete this activity.

Special Materials: several different colored pencils or markers for tracing; *optional*—extra copies of Worksheets 1–4A and 1–4B

TEACHING NOTES

Students find the task of tracing networks interesting and view each tracing as a puzzle. Working with networks helps students to better understand the relationships between points and lines.

1. Introduce this activity by explaining that a network is a figure made up of line segments, which may be straight or curved, and the points where the line segments meet, which are called vertices.

2. There are two worksheets for this activity. The first, 1–4A, serves as an introduction and can be done as a class exercise to familiarize students with the concept of tracing a network. The second, 1–4B, is designed for students working alone.

3. If your students have little experience with networks and tracing, distribute copies of Worksheet 1–4A and review the rules for tracing a network. Doing the four examples as a class exercise will ensure that everyone understands the procedure. Using different colored pencils or markers will enable students to see the paths. Point out that the segments in a network may be straight or curved, but in Euclidean geometry segments must be "straight."

4. When you distribute Worksheet 1–4B, review the instructions with your students and instruct them to complete the examples.

Answer Key

Worksheet 1–4A—numbers 1 and 3 are traceable.
Worksheet 1–4B—all are traceable except numbers 3, 8, and 12.
Check students' networks for accuracy.

1–4A Tracing Networks

The figures below are called *networks*. They are made up of line segments (which may be straight or curved) and the points where the line segments meet. Each point is called a *vertex*.

A network is said to be *traceable* if you can start at a vertex and trace the figure following these rules:

▲ You do not lift your pencil from the paper.

▲ You do not retrace any part of the line.

Consider the following four examples.

1.

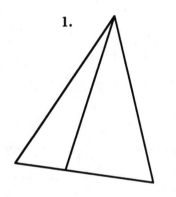

2.

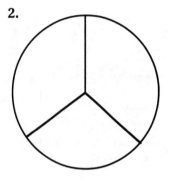

3.

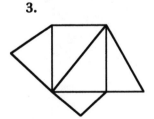

4.

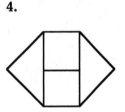

Which of the networks above are traceable? Show where you started the tracing and where you ended.

1–4B   Tracing Networks

Determine which of the following networks are traceable. If a network is traceable, show the vertex where the tracing could begin and end.

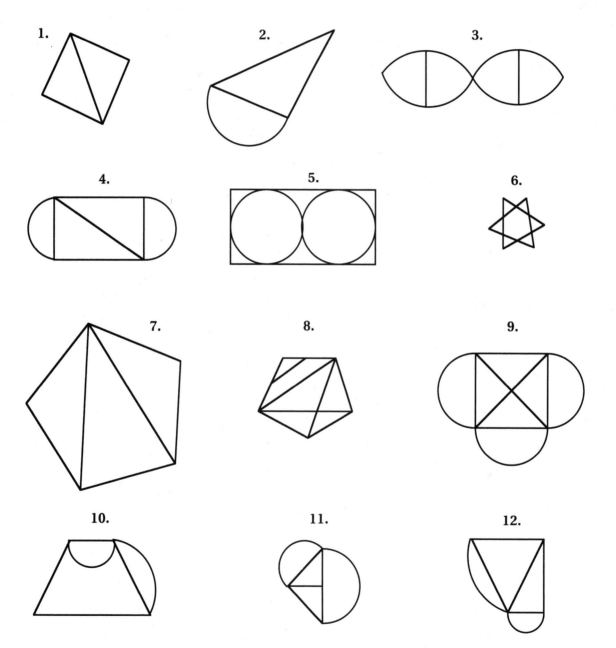

Draw a traceable network of your own. Exchange papers with a partner. Can your partner trace your network? If not, why not?

TRACEABLE NETWORKS AND TYPES OF VERTICES

Objective: Students will determine if a network is traceable by making and testing conjectures about the types of vertices in the network. Students should work individually to complete this activity.

Special Materials: none

TEACHING NOTES

Working with networks helps students to understand the kinds of vertices a network may have. This activity should be done only after students have completed Activity 1–4, "Tracing Networks," or if they have prior experience with networks.

1. Introduce the activity by briefly reviewing what a network is. Explain the meaning of line segments, which may be straight or curved, vertex, vertices, and the definitions of odd and even vertices to ensure that everyone understands the vocabulary necessary to complete the activity successfully.

2. Distribute copies of Worksheet 1-5 and review the instructions with your students. Explain that in mathematics a conjecture is a statement that must always be true. It is based on evidence of some sort. If a conjecture is not true, it must be redefined or abandoned.

Answer Key

	A	B	C	D	E	F	G	Number of Even Vertices	Number of Odd Vertices	Traceable
1.	O	E	E	O	E	E		4	2	yes
2.	O	O	E	E	E			3	2	yes
3.	E	E	E					3	0	yes
4.	O	E	O					1	2	yes
5.	E	E	E	E	E			5	0	yes
6.	O	E	O	O	E	O	E	3	4	no
7.	O	O	O	O	O	O		0	6	no
8.	O	O	O	O	E			1	4	no
9.	E	E	E	E	E	E		6	0	yes

Conjecture: A network is traceable if it has only even vertices or no more than two odd vertices.

1–5   Traceable Networks and Types of Vertices

The figures below are networks. They are made up of line segments (which may be straight or curved) and vertices (which are points where the segments meet). The vertices may be classified as even or odd.

▲ A vertex is odd if an odd number of segments meets at the point.

▲ A vertex is even if an even number of segments meets at the point.

Study the nine figures below. Vertices of each network are labeled with capital letters. Complete the chart that follows by:

1. Placing an "E" in the column if the vertex is even.

2. Placing an "O" in the column if the vertex is odd.

3. Placing the number of the even and odd vertices in the proper column.

4. Writing "yes" if the network is traceable.

5. Writing "no" if the network is not traceable.

Note: Boxes with X's cannot be filled in.

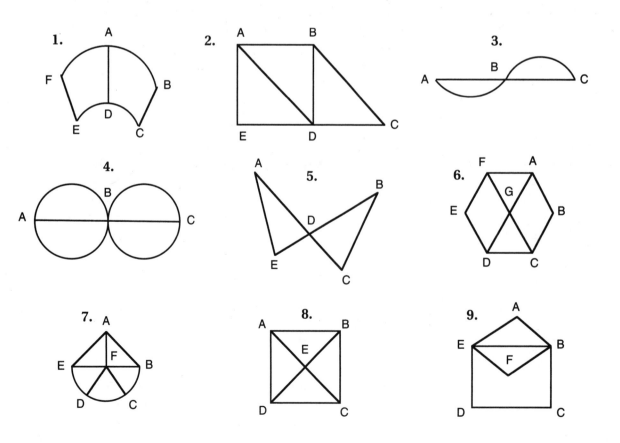

© 2000 by The Center for Applied Research in Education

Complete the chart.

	A	B	C	D	E	F	G	Number of Even Vertices	Number of Odd Vertices	Traceable
1.							X			
2.						X	X			
3.				X	X	X	X			
4.				X	X	X	X			
5.						X	X			
6.										
7.							X			
8.						X	X			
9.							X			

After examining the number and type of vertices, make a conjecture about the number of odd and even vertices and traceable networks.

_____

_____

_____

_____

_____

_____

CONSTRUCTING A TANGRAM

Objective: Following instructions written in the language of geometry, students will construct their own tangrams. Students should work individually or in pairs to complete this activity.

Special Materials: rulers, pencils, scissors, white drawing paper, or poster paper

TEACHING NOTES

Most students enjoy working with tangrams, which they find to be fun and challenging. Constructing tangrams in this activity is an instructive exercise in the language of geometry.

1. Begin the activity by explaining that a tangram is a Chinese puzzle that consists of a large square divided into five triangles, a square, and a parallelogram. These figures may then be reassembled into still different figures.

2. According to legend, the tangram puzzle originated in China when Tan, a Chinese nobleman, wished to present to his emperor a gift of an exquisite square tile. Unfortunately, before he could present it to the emperor, he dropped it and the tile broke into seven pieces—five right triangles (two small ones, two larger ones, and one in between), a square, and a parallelogram. Tan attempted to put the seven pieces back together again, but he could not. He did find, however, that he could make many other shapes with the seven pieces, including buildings, boats, and animals. Although no one knows exactly when tangrams originated, we do know that during the nineteenth century they became popular in the United States and Europe. They remain an interesting pastime among geometry enthusiasts today.

3. Hand out copies of Worksheet 1–6 and review the instructions with your students. Also distribute sheets of white drawing paper or poster paper, which students will use to make their tangrams. Caution students to follow the guidelines carefully and be precise with their measurements. At the end of the activity, review students' tangrams. You might wish to collect students' tangrams and store them in envelopes for later use. They fit nicely in standard business envelopes.

1–6 Constructing a Tangram

A *tangram* is a geometric puzzle thought to have been developed in China. The puzzle consists of two large congruent triangles, a medium-sized triangle, two small congruent triangles, a square, and a parallelogram. The pieces of a tangram can be used to create many interesting figures. Follow the instructions below to make a tangram and arrange the pieces into new figures.

1. Draw an 8-inch square on unlined paper. Starting at the the upper left-hand corner of the square, label each vertex clockwise and alphabetically where two line segments meet. Start with point A. Refer to the diagram below.

2. Draw segment $\overline{BD}$.

3. Find the midpoint of $\overline{AB}$. Label it E.

4. Find the midpoint of $\overline{AD}$. Label it F.

5. Draw $\overline{EF}$.

6. Find the midpoint of $\overline{EF}$. Label it G.

7. Draw $\overline{CG}$.

8. Find the intersection of $\overline{GC}$ and $\overline{BD}$. Label it H.

9. Find the midpoint of $\overline{HD}$ and label it J.

10. Draw $\overline{FJ}$.

11. Find the midpoint of $\overline{HB}$ and label it K.

12. Draw $\overline{GK}$.

13. Cut along the lines. You should have seven pieces, each of which is called a *tan*.

14. Assemble the tans and create other figures. Try to create a boat, a building, and an animal with your tans.

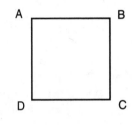

GEOMETRIC ART

Objective: Students will make a picture comprised of points, line segments, parallel lines, perpendicular lines, rays, and angles. Students should work individually or in pairs to complete this activity.

Special Materials: rulers, protractors, drawing paper, colored pencils, markers or crayons; *optional*—computers with software that has drawing components, printers

TEACHING NOTES

As they focus their efforts on learning during the typical geometry course, students seldom have time for fun. Because most courses are demanding, with numerous skills required to be taught within an inadequate amount of time, teachers often concentrate on material straight from texts. Certainly textbook exercises are essential to any geometry course, but sometimes it is important to let students work on an activity that is based on skills but is mostly creative.

1. Introduce the activity by explaining that geometry is vital to art. Look at any picture and it's likely you will see several examples of basic geometry, including points, line segments, and angles. Explain that students are to draw a picture on a topic or subject of their choice in which they highlight geometry. Emphasize that while neatness is important, you realize that most students are not "artists," and you are more interested in the geometric accuracy of their drawings than in artistic excellence.

2. Hand out copies of Worksheet 1–7 and review the instructions with your students. Be sure that they understand which items they are to include on their drawings. If you wish, let their creativity loose and suggest that they include other geometric figures such as triangles, quadrilaterals, circles, and semicircles in their pictures. Remind them that they are to label all examples of geometry in their work. If students have access to computers that have software with drawing capabilities, permit students to complete their pictures on their computers. Print out the finished pictures.

3. Upon completion of the activity, display the pictures of your students.

1–7 Geometric Art

Points and lines are fundamental to any drawing or sketch. Make a picture of a subject or topic of your choice and include the following examples of geometry: *points*, *line segments*, *parallel lines*, *perpendicular lines*, *rays*, and *angles*.

Be sure to label <u>at least one example of each of the above in your picture</u>. Before drawing your picture, define each of the following terms.

1. point _____

_____

_____

2. line segment _____

_____

_____

3. parallel lines _____

_____

_____

4. perpendicular lines _____

_____

_____

5. ray _____

_____

_____

6. angle _____

_____

_____

Activity 1–8

DRAWING INTERSECTIONS

Objectives: Students will draw diagrams of figures that have a specific number of points of intersection. Students should work individually or in pairs to complete this activity.

Special Materials: rulers, scrap paper

TEACHING NOTES

This activity seeks to reinforce the meaning of the word *intersection* and lets students explore the ways in which some geometric figures intersect. It also gives them practice working with points, lines, rays, and angles.

1. Introduce the activity by asking students to name some examples of intersections. Possible answers include a crossroad, a tic-tac-toe diagram, or a pattern of ceiling or floor tiles.

2. Distribute copies of Worksheet 1-8 and review the instructions with your students. You may wish to complete an example or two with them to ensure that everyone understands what to do. Suggest that they sketch figures on scrap paper first to find possible points of intersection, and then sketch their answers in the appropriate boxes on the worksheet.

Answer Key

Answers may vary; some possible answers are shown on the next page.

Activity 1–8   *(Cont'd)*

	Intersecting at 1 point	Intersecting at 2 points	Intersecting at 3 points
2 points	•		
2 lines			
3 lines			
2 rays			
3 rays			
2 angles			
3 angles			
2 lines and 1 angle			

1–8   Drawing Intersections

Complete the chart below and find at least one way (if possible) that the figures listed will *intersect* at one point, two points, and three points. (Note that some of the figures may intersect in several points.) Assume that all figures are in the same plane and all lines are straight lines. Sketch your answers in the appropriate box. If the figures do not intersect, leave the space blank.

Draw	Intersecting at 1 point	Intersecting at 2 points	Intersecting at 3 points
2 points			
2 lines			
3 lines			
2 rays			

Draw	Intersecting at 1 point	Intersecting at 2 points	Intersecting at 3 points
3 rays			
2 angles			
3 angles			
2 lines and 1 angle			

INTERSECTIONS AND UNIONS

Objective: Students will apply the concepts of intersection and union to geometric figures. Students should work individually or in pairs to complete this activity.

Special Materials: tracing paper, two different colored pencils per student

TEACHING NOTES

The concepts of *intersection* and *union* need to be reinforced so that students can better understand solving combined inequalities and graphing systems of equations and systems of inequalities. This activity provides experience with these concepts through the use of geometric figures. In this activity students are asked to find the intersection or union of geometric figures and name the figure that results. In the last four problems, students are given a geometric figure and must identify the intersections and unions from which the figure results.

1. Begin the activity by reviewing the meaning of intersection and union. An intersection is a set of which every member is a member of each of two or more other sets; a union is a set that consists of all members belonging to at least one of two or more sets.

2. Hand out copies of Worksheet 1–9 and review the instructions with your students. Depending on the abilities of your students, you may wish to do the first problem on the worksheet as an example. Tell students to place the tracing paper over the diagram and trace $\overrightarrow{AB}$ with one of their colored pencils. Then, without moving the tracing paper, choose a different colored pencil and trace $\overrightarrow{BC}$. The part of the diagram that has been traced twice—this part will have two different colors—is the intersection. The part that has at least one color is the union. Explain that the rest of the activity is done in this way, and note that several answers are possible for numbers 15 through 18.

Answer Key

1. $\overrightarrow{AC}$;   2. $\overrightarrow{BC}$;   3. $\overline{AC}$;   4. B;   5. B;   6. $\overleftrightarrow{AC}$;   7. $\angle EBC$;   8. $\angle DBE$;   9. B;   10. $\triangle FIJ$;
11. $\overline{IJ}$;   12. $\overrightarrow{FG}$;   13. J;   14. ϕ

For numbers 15–18 answers may vary; possible answers: **15.** $\angle HFG \cap \angle HFI$;
16. $\overline{IF} \cap \overline{IJ}$;   **17.** $\overrightarrow{IF} \cup \overrightarrow{IJ}$;   **18.** $\overrightarrow{FH} \cup \overrightarrow{FJ}$

1–9   Intersections and Unions

In this activity you will apply the definitions of *intersection* and *union* to geometric figures.

The *intersection*, represented by the symbol ∩, of two sets A and B is the set consisting of all the members that belong to both sets A and B. Consider the example $\overleftrightarrow{CEBF}$ below. Set A is the set of points in $\overrightarrow{EF}$ and Set B is the set of points in the segment $\overline{CB}$. The intersection is $\overline{EB}$, which is all the points that are in both the ray and the segment.

The *union*, represented by the symbol ∪, of two sets A and B is the set consisting of all members belonging to at least one of the sets A and B. In the diagram below, the union is $\overrightarrow{CF}$, which is all the points that are in at least one of the geometric figures.

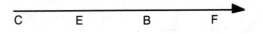

Now find the intersections and unions of all the geometric figures in the diagrams that follow.

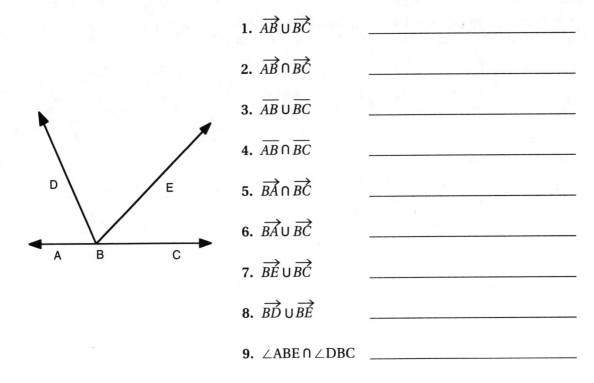

1. $\overrightarrow{AB} \cup \overrightarrow{BC}$ _____

2. $\overrightarrow{AB} \cap \overrightarrow{BC}$ _____

3. $\overline{AB} \cup \overline{BC}$ _____

4. $\overline{AB} \cap \overline{BC}$ _____

5. $\overrightarrow{BA} \cap \overrightarrow{BC}$ _____

6. $\overrightarrow{BA} \cup \overrightarrow{BC}$ _____

7. $\overrightarrow{BE} \cup \overrightarrow{BC}$ _____

8. $\overrightarrow{BD} \cup \overrightarrow{BE}$ _____

9. ∠ABE ∩ ∠DBC   _____

Diagram for problems 1 through 9.

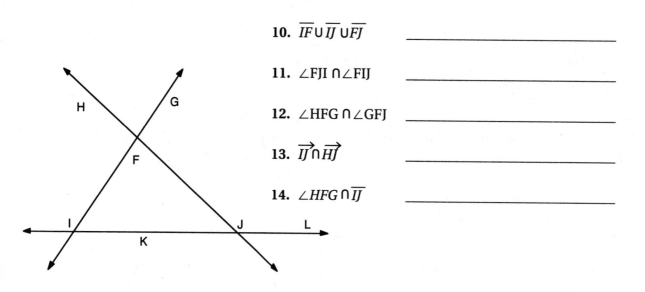

10. $\overline{IF} \cup \overline{IJ} \cup \overline{FJ}$ _____

11. $\angle FJI \cap \angle FIJ$ _____

12. $\angle HFG \cap \angle GFJ$ _____

13. $\overrightarrow{IJ} \cap \overrightarrow{HJ}$ _____

14. $\angle HFG \cap \overline{IJ}$ _____

Diagram for problems 10 through 18.

For problems 15 through 18, the answer is given. Several intersections or unions are possible. Provide at least one intersection or union for each answer.

15. $\overrightarrow{FH}$ _____

16. I _____

17. $\angle FIJ$ _____

18. $\overrightarrow{HJ}$ _____

WHAT DOES IT MEASURE?

Objective: Students will research and determine the purpose of various measuring devices of length (distance) and angles. Students should work individually to complete this activity; however, pairs are acceptable if research materials are limited.

Special Materials: dictionaries and encyclopedias; *optional*—computers with access to electronic references

TEACHING NOTES

Measuring angles and length or distance are essential skills in geometry. While most students are familiar with measuring angles with a protractor and length with a ruler, they may not be familiar with other instruments for measuring angles and distance. This activity enables them to learn about measurement instruments as varied as altimeters and yardsticks.

1. Prior to beginning the activity, decide how you wish students to conduct their research. If you have access to dictionaries and encyclopedias in your classroom, the activity can be managed easily in class. If you are like most math teachers, though, you probably don't have access to many reference materials. In this case, you might arrange library time for research. If students can use computers with which they can access reference sources, you may have students conduct their research in this manner.

2. Begin the activity by explaining that many kinds of instruments may be used to measure length and angles. Ask students to name some. Answers likely will include rulers, meter sticks, tape measures, and protractors. Emphasize that there are many others.

3. Distribute copies of Worksheet 1–10 and review the instructions with your students. Upon completion of the activity, discuss students' findings.

Answer Key

1. distance traveled;   **2.** angle of incline;   **3.** length;   **4.** horizontal and vertical angles;   **5.** depth of water;   **6.** ring size (distance around finger);   **7.** length;   **8.** altitude;   **9.** distance;   **10.** angles;   **11.** very small distances;   **12.** angular distance;   **13.** number of steps taken;   **14.** length;   **15.** length

1–10   What Does It Measure?

Following is a list of instruments used to measure length (distance) or angles. Using reference materials such as dictionaries and encyclopedias, find what each measures.

1. odometer: _____

2. clinometer: _____

3. ruler: _____

4. theodolite: _____

5. fathometer: _____

6. jeweler's stick: _____

7. meter stick: _____

8. altimeter: _____

9. trundle wheel: _____

10. protractor: _____

11. micrometer: _____

12. sextant: _____

13. pedometer: _____

14. tape measure: _____

15. yardstick: _____

MEASURING ANGLES WITH A PROTRACTOR

Objective: Students will measure angles with protractors. Students should work individually to complete this activity.

Special Materials: protractors

TEACHING NOTES

Being able to measure the degrees of angles with a protractor is a basic geometric skill. This activity provides students with practice for measuring angles with protractors.

1. Note that this activity includes two worksheets. Worksheet 1–11A provides instructions for measuring angles with a protractor, and Worksheet 1–11B presents students with angles they must measure.

2. Begin this activity by explaining that students will use protractors to measure angles. If students are unfamiliar with protractors, explain their function.

3. Distribute copies of Worksheet 1–11A and review the guidelines that detail how students should use their protractors for measuring. Have students measure the two angles. (Example one is 40° and example two is 120°.) Next hand out copies of Worksheet 1–11B and review the instructions with your students. Point out that correct answers will enable students to find the secret message.

4. If necessary, during the activity, monitor your students' use of their protractors to ensure that they are using them correctly. Caution students to be accurate in their measurements.

Answer Key

Worksheet 1–11A—**1.** 40°;　**2.** 120°
Worksheet 1–11B: **1.** 20;　**2.** 10;　**3.** 30;　**4.** 125;　**5.** 90;　**6.** 140;　**7.** 15;　**8.** 170;
9. 180;　**10.** 60;　**11.** 35

Message: Your measurements are right on.

Name _____ Date _____ Section _____

1–11A   Measuring Angles with a Protractor

A *protractor* is the instrument you need to measure an angle. Protractors may vary a little in their design, but they all have an arrow, a line, or a dot to represent the vertex of the angle you are measuring and a scale to measure the degree of the angle.

   Following are guidelines that will help you to measure angles accurately with your protractor.

1. Find the point of your protractor that represents the vertex and place it on the vertex of the angle you want to measure. The vertex is the point where the two sides of the angle meet.

2. Turn the protractor, keeping the vertex point of the protractor over the vertex of the angle, until one side of the angle is on the 0°–180° line of the protractor.

3. Look at the other side of the angle—the side that is not on the 0°–180° line of the protractor. Note the number at which this side crosses the scale of the protractor. (You may have to extend the side to cross the scale.)

4. If the angle is an acute angle (smaller than a right angle), read the lower scale. If the angle is an obtuse angle (more than a right angle), read the larger scale. If the angle is a right angle, the measure is 90°.

Directions: Now find the measures of the two angles below.

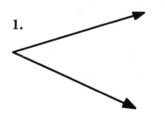

1.

2.

1–11B   Measuring Angles with a Protractor

Study the figure and find the measure of each angle below. Then arrange the angles from the smallest to the largest, copying the letters after each number. Write the letters on the line at the bottom of this sheet. If you find the correct measures and arrange the measures of the angles correctly, the letters will reveal a message.

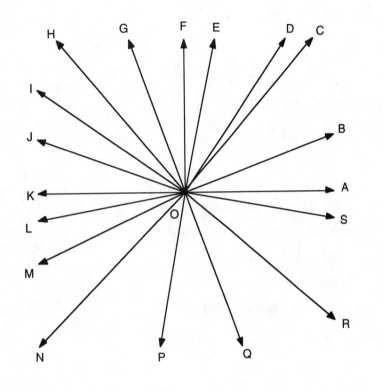

1. m∠AOB = _____ eas

2. m∠EOF = _____ yo

3. m∠JOH = _____ ure

4. m∠SON = _____ re

5. m∠KOF = _____ sa

6. m∠COL = _____ ri

7. m∠LOM = _____ urm

8. m∠DON = _____ gh

9. m∠GOQ = _____ ton

10. m∠POR = _____ nt

11. m∠IOG = _____ me

Message: _____

_____

FINDING MISSING ANGLES

Objective: Students will find the measures of angles in a diagram without using protractors. Students should work individually or in pairs to complete this activity.

Special Materials: none

TEACHING NOTES

When students are asked to find the measures of angles, most will think of using a protractor. In this activity, however, students will use diagrams and information that is provided to find the measures of angles. Instead of relying on an instrument, they will need to rely on their reasoning skills and knowledge.

To complete the activity successfully, students should know the following:

▲ A right angle measures 90°.

▲ Perpendicular lines form right angles.

▲ Congruent angles have the same measure.

▲ Vertical angles are congruent.

▲ A straight angle measures 180°.

▲ The sum of complementary angles is 90°.

1. Introduce the activity and explain that problems can often be solved through reasoning and the application of theorems. For example, the measure of angles can be determined from the measures of known angles in a diagram.

2. Distribute copies of Worksheet 1-12 and review the instructions with your students. Remind them to consider all the information related to a diagram. Also, caution them that in some cases not enough information is given, and the measure of the angle they are asked to find cannot be determined.

Answer Key

1. 120; **2.** 90, 90; **3.** NEI (not enough information); **4.** 45, 45; **5.** NEI; **6.** 70, 110, 70; **7.** 60, 60, 60; **8.** $m\angle 25 = 15$; NEI for other measures; **9.** 20, 40, 120; **10.** 90, 90; **11.** 28, 28, 62; **12.** NEI, NEI, 20, 30, 40

Name _____ **Date** _____ **Section** _____

1–12 Finding Missing Angles

Study the diagrams and the information, then find the measure of each missing angle. A good strategy is to label each diagram with the information you are given. This will help you to "see" possible clues that will help you to find the missing measures. Be careful. In some cases, not enough information is given to find the missing measures. For those problems, write NEI for "not enough information."

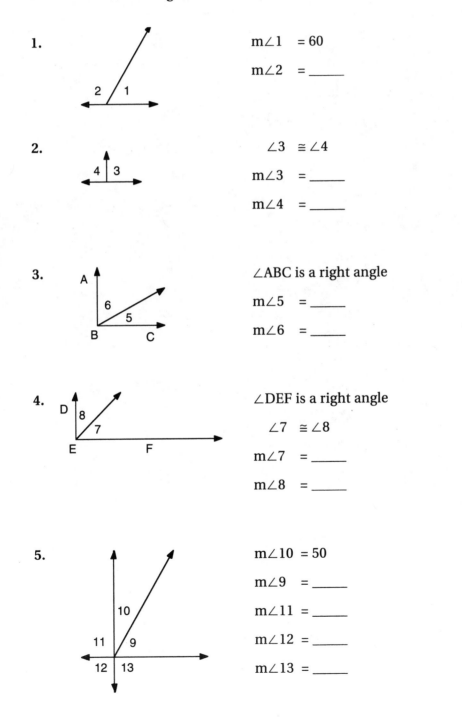

1.

m∠1 = 60

m∠2 = _____

2.

∠3 ≅ ∠4

m∠3 = _____

m∠4 = _____

3.

∠ABC is a right angle

m∠5 = _____

m∠6 = _____

4.

∠DEF is a right angle

∠7 ≅ ∠8

m∠7 = _____

m∠8 = _____

5.

m∠10 = 50

m∠9 = _____

m∠11 = _____

m∠12 = _____

m∠13 = _____

6.

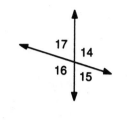

m∠14 = 110

m∠15 = _____

m∠16 = _____

m∠17 = _____

7.

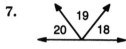

m∠18 = m∠19 = m∠20

m∠18 = _____

m∠19 = _____

m∠20 = _____

8.

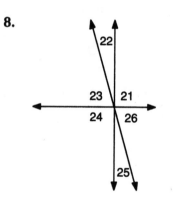

m∠22 = 15

m∠21 = _____

m∠23 = _____

m∠24 = _____

m∠25 = _____

m∠26 = _____

9.

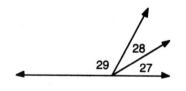

m∠28 = 2m∠27

m∠29 = 3m∠28

m∠27 = _____

m∠28 = _____

m∠29 = _____

10.

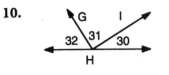

∠GHI is a right angle

m∠31 = _____

m∠32 + m∠30 = _____

11.

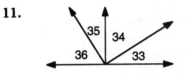

m∠34 = 62

∠34 and ∠35 are complementary

∠33 and ∠34 are complementary

m∠33 = _____

m∠35 = _____

m∠36 = _____

12.

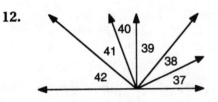

m∠39 = 40

m∠37 + m∠38 + m∠39 = 90

m∠37 + m∠38 + m∠39 + m∠40 = 110

m∠40 + m∠41 + m∠39 = 90

m∠37 = _____

m∠38 = _____

m∠40 = _____

m∠41 = _____

m∠42 = _____

USING ANGLES TO CREATE LINE DESIGNS

Objective: Students will draw and measure angles and line segments to create a design. Students should work individually to complete this activity.

Special Materials: protractors, rulers, different colored pencils, unlined paper; *optional*—computers with software capable of constructing angles, finding the midpoint of a segment, and drawing line segments; colored printer

TEACHING NOTES

Creating line designs is an interesting and enjoyable way to study angles. This activity can be used either as an introduction to angles or a review.

Note that two worksheets, 1–13A and 1–13B, are included with this activity. The first worksheet, 1–13A, provides the directions to create a line design. You might prefer to do this worksheet as a class exercise, or monitor students closely as they work. Worksheet 1–13B contains six designs students are to create individually. Depending on the abilities of your students, you may have students complete only Worksheet 1–13A, or assign only some of the designs on Worksheet 1–13B.

1. Distribute copies of Worksheets 1–13A and, if you prefer, 1–13B, and review the instructions with your students. Caution them that they must follow the procedures precisely if they are to construct the line designs correctly. Make sure they understand how to measure and divide the line segments. Encourage students to use colored pencils for their work as the color can make truly eye-catching designs.

2. If students have access to computers with software that has the capability of drawing angles and segments, have students use the technology to create their designs. Color printers can produce designs of high quality.

3. Review students' line designs at the end of the activity. Line designs make an interesting bulletin board, so you may wish to display the work of your students.

1–13A   Using Angles to Create Line Designs

By drawing an angle you can create your own line design simply by following the steps below. Be sure to follow the instructions carefully.

1. Use unlined paper and draw a 45° angle with sides 5 inches long.

2. Divide each side of the angle into 10 congruent (equal) segments. Each segment should be $\frac{1}{2}$ inch long.

3. Starting from the vertex of your angle, label the first segment of one side of the angle "1," the next segment of the same side of the angle "2," and so on up to 10.

4. Starting from the vertex of your angle, label the first segment of the other side of the angle "10," the next segment of the same side "9," and so on down to 1.

5. Use your ruler and draw lines that connect 1 to 1, 2 to 2, 3 to 3, and so on. Your design should look like the example shown below.

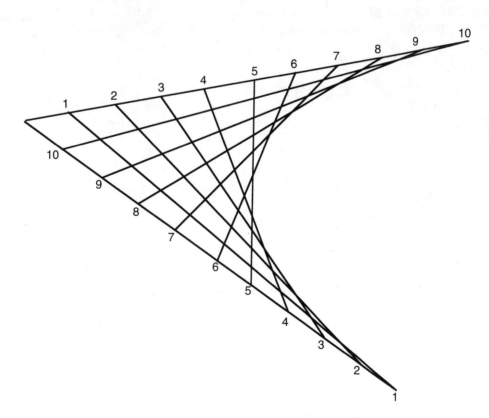

6. Notice that the interior of the angle seems to curve, but no curve is drawn.

1–13B   Using Angles to Create Line Designs

Use a separate sheet of paper and create line designs that have the following features:

1. A right angle that has 4-inch long sides and $\frac{1}{2}$ inch line segments.

2. A 120° angle that has 3-inch long sides and $\frac{1}{4}$ inch segments.

3. A 60° angle that has 4-inch long sides and $\frac{1}{2}$ inch segments.

4. A right angle divided into 3 congruent angles. Each side of each angle is 3 inches long, and each side is divided into 6 segments.

5. Three 120° angles having the same vertex. Each side of each angle is 3 inches long, and each side is divided into 6 segments.

6. Create a line design of your own. Choose any type of angle, or group of angles, any length for the sides, and any length of congruent segments.

ANGLES AND THE HANDS OF TIME

Objective: Students will draw, estimate, and classify angles. Students should work individually to complete this activity.

Special Materials: none

TEACHING NOTES

In our digital world, clocks with faces that show the hours are becoming obsolete. Some students are so used to telling time via digital displays that they have to think a moment when they check the time on an "old-fashioned" clock, as one student said. This activity gives students a chance to review telling time using the hour and minute hands of a clock, and also gives them practice estimating and classifying angles.

Hand out copies of Worksheet 1–14 and go over the instructions with your students. Make sure that your students understand the difference between the minute hand and hour hand. Also, make sure that students understand the definitions of acute, obtuse, right, and straight angles. You might prefer to do the first problem on the worksheet as a class exercise to ensure that students know what is expected.

Answer Key

Check students' drawings and accept reasonable approximations. Exact measurements are given here.

1. 82.5°, acute;   **2.** 90°, right;   **3.** 45°, acute;   **4.** 157.5°, obtuse;   **5.** 150°, obtuse;   **6.** 175°, obtuse;   **7.** 142.5°, obtuse;   **8.** 172.5°, obtuse;   **9.** 15°, acute;   **10.** 90°, right;   **11.** 110°, obtuse;   **12.** 180°, straight

1–14   Angles and the Hands of Time

In this activity you will be given various times expressed in digital form. You are to draw how each time will appear on a round clock. You are then to estimate the measure of the angle created by the hour and minute hands. After making your estimate, classify the angle as being acute, obtuse, right, or straight.

▲ An *acute* angle has a measure greater than 0° and less than 90°.

▲ An *obtuse* angle has a measure greater than 90° and less than 180°.

▲ A *right* angle has a measure of 90°.

▲ A *straight* angle has a measure of 180°.

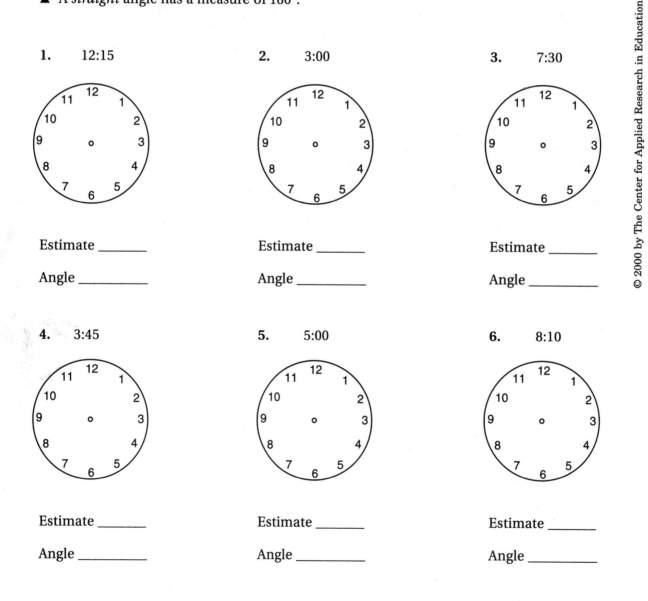

1.   12:15

Estimate _____

Angle _____

2.   3:00

Estimate _____

Angle _____

3.   7:30

Estimate _____

Angle _____

4.   3:45

Estimate _____

Angle _____

5.   5:00

Estimate _____

Angle _____

6.   8:10

Estimate _____

Angle _____

7.   1:45

8.   2:45

9.   6:30

Estimate _____

Angle _____

Estimate _____

Angle _____

Estimate _____

Angle _____

10.   9:00

11.   11:40

12.   6:00

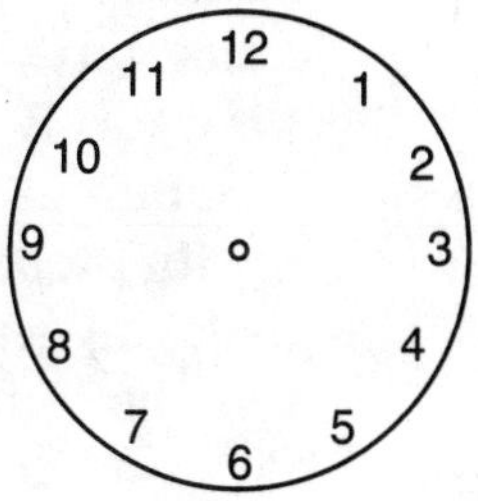

Estimate _____

Angle _____

Estimate _____

Angle _____

Estimate _____

Angle _____

FORMING STRAIGHT ANGLES

Objective: Students will measure angles and discover that the measure of a straight angle is 180°. Students should work individually for the first part of this activity and with a partner to complete the second part.

Special Materials: $8\frac{1}{2}$ inch squares, rulers, protractors, scissors, unlined paper

TEACHING NOTES

This activity is designed as a game in which students create polygons from a square. They then cut out the polygons, measure the interior angles of each polygon, and write the measure of the angles at the vertex. Students pair off, mix up their polygons, and randomly divide them. They compete against each other by attempting to use as many of their polygons as possible to form a straight angle. The winner of the game is the student who has the fewest polygons left. Since the polygons that students start with will be different, based on the way they divide their original square, it is unlikely any pairs of students will have identical pieces. The element of chance is an interesting aspect of this activity.

In preparing for this activity, you may wish to create $8\frac{1}{2}$ inch squares by simply taking standard $8\frac{1}{2}'' \times 11''$ pieces of drawing paper and cutting off $2\frac{1}{2}$ inches from the 11-inch side. Using a paper cutter makes the task easy. You might, of course, have students make the squares themselves at the beginning of the activity.

1. Introduce the activity by explaining to students that they will be playing a game, the purpose of which is to use the sides of polygons to form a straight line. Distribute copies of Worksheet 1–15 and review the instructions. Caution students to follow the guidelines carefully. You may also wish to review the steps for measuring angles with a protractor, especially which scale to use.

2. Once students have created their polygons, let them play the game! Students should conclude that the sum of the measures of the angles that form a straight line equals 180°. Another name for a straight line is a straight angle.

Name _____ Date _____ Section _____

1–15   Forming Straight Angles

In this activity, you will first work alone, then with a partner. While working alone, you will use a ruler to draw line segments and a protractor to measure angles. After cutting out polygons that you will have created, you will play a game with a partner in which you compete against each other to see who can use the most polygons to form lines. Be sure to follow the instructions carefully.

HOW TO MAKE POLYGONS

1. Start with an $8\frac{1}{2}$ inch square sheet of paper. Label each right angle with a right angle symbol, ⌐ , near the vertex.

2. Use your ruler to draw two line segments from one side of the square to the other. Make sure these segments do not intersect.

3. Draw a line segment from one side of the square to one of the line segments drawn in Step 2.

4. Repeat Step 3 four more times, making sure no line segments intersect.

5. You should have a square divided into eight parts. An example is shown below. Note that depending on where you drew your line segments, your diagram might be different.

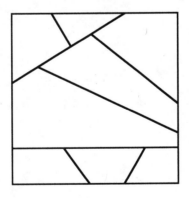

6. Cut along the line segments you have drawn. You should cut out eight polygons. Note that your polygons will probably not have the same shape as those of other students, because they may have drawn their segments differently.

7. Use a protractor to measure each angle in each polygon.

8. Write the measurement of each angle near the vertex of that figure.

How to Play the Game

You are now ready to play the game. Here's how!

1. Combine your polygons with the polygons of a partner and mix them up so that they are in a random pile.

2. Divide the pieces with your partner so that each of you has eight pieces.

3. Take turns placing a shape on your desk or table so that the angles of each figure form a line without overlapping.

4. If a player cannot make a straight line, without overlapping the pieces, he or she misses a turn.

5. After all attempts to use the polygons have been exhausted, the player with the fewest number of pieces remaining in his or her pile wins.

After playing the game, answer the following question. What can you conclude about two or more angles that form a straight line? _____

_____

_____

_____

Activity 1–16

THE ANGLES IN CONSTELLATIONS

Objective: Students will select three constellations, measure the angles and line segments between the stars that comprise them, and then redraw the constellations accurately on plain paper. Students should work individually or in pairs to complete this activity.

Special Materials: white drawing paper, protractors, rulers, science texts or other reference books that contain diagrams of constellations; *optional*—computers with Internet access through which diagrams of constellations may be researched and downloaded

TEACHING NOTES

Most students enjoy learning about constellations. "Seeing" the images represented by most constellations requires quite a bit of imagination. Because of this, many science and reference books outline the constellations with line segments. This provides the foundation for an activity combining geometry and astronomy. The activity lends itself well to an interdisciplinary unit.

Prior to assigning the activity, check for references students may use. Perhaps their science texts contain a chapter on astronomy that includes examples of constellations. If their science books don't contain information about constellations, you may reserve time in the school's library for your students to conduct research, or you may instruct them to find information at home. Online references are yet another option. Suggest that students use the key word "constellations" in any searches they conduct.

1. Introduce the activity by asking how many of your students have ever looked for constellations in the night sky. Most probably have. Ask what constellations they have seen; the most common answers will likely be the Big Dipper and Little Dipper. Explain that students will have a chance to learn more about constellations in this activity.

2. Distribute copies of Worksheet 1–16 and review the instructions with your students. Explain that they are to select at least three constellations, measure the angles and distances between the stars that make up the constellation, and then redraw the constellation on white paper. By constructing accurate angles and line segments, they should be able to create an accurate constellation. Discourage tracing; the focus of the activity should be the accurate construction of constellations using the measurements of angles and segments. Remind students to label their constellations.

3. At the end of the activity, review and/or display the work of your students.

1–16   The Angles in Constellations

Constellations are groups of stars that represent people, animals, or objects. Because it is sometimes hard to "picture" what a constellation represents, reference books often connect the stars of a constellation with line segments, or they may show a picture around the con-sellation.

For this activity, select three constellations, measure the angles of the stars that make them up, measure the length of the line segments that connect the stars, and then use these measurements to redraw the constellation. To create accurate constellations, follow these guidelines.

1. Use reference materials and select at least three constellations.

2. Start with any star that helps form the constellation. Measure the angle formed by this star and the next two stars on either side of it. The location of the star you started with is the vertex of the angle. Record this measurement on a separate sheet of paper.

3. Measure the line segments that connect these stars and record these lengths.

4. Draw the first star on your drawing paper. Recall the measure of the angle formed by this star and the other two stars. Use your protractor and lightly mark the rays that form this angle. Now recall the lengths of the segments you measured between these stars. Place the next two stars in their correct positions on the rays, based on the lengths of the segments. Repeat this process for the remainder of the stars that make up this con-stellation.

5. Repeat the entire process for other constellations. If you are accurate with your meas-urements, you should be able to reproduce the constellations you selected.

A PARALLEL SCAVENGER HUNT

Objective: Students will find examples of parallel lines and planes. Students should work individually to complete this activity.

Special Materials: reference books; *optional*—computers with Internet access

TEACHING NOTES

Many students view geometry in isolation and have trouble visualizing representations of geometric figures in everyday life. While students may recognize that circular clocks (especially when those clocks tell that the school day is done!) and rectangular windows (which forever draw their attention outside of your classroom) are geometric forms, they may not be aware of the many parallel lines and planes that make up their world.

1. Introduce this activity by reviewing with students the concepts of *parallel lines* and *planes.* Ask them to cite some examples. Some examples of parallel lines might include the lines on the sides of windows, ceilings, and floor tiles. Examples of parallel planes might include opposite walls or the ceiling and floor.

2. Hand out copies of Worksheet 1–17 and review the instructions with your students. Make sure students understand they may use various reference materials, and are to find as many examples of parallel lines and planes as they can for each category on the worksheet. Note the scoring, particularly the penalty for omitting a category. Remind students to list their examples on a separate sheet of paper according to category.

3. At the end of the activity, review students' lists and accept any reasonable answers. You might like to provide a prize of a homework pass for the students who compile the most extensive lists.

Name _____   Date _____   Section _____

1–17   A Parallel Scavenger Hunt

Representations of parallel lines and planes are everywhere. For this activity, you are to find as many examples of parallel lines and planes as you can for the following categories:

Architecture

Art

Your Home

Logos

Maps

Music and Musical Instruments

Nature

You may use any reference materials you find helpful, including books, encyclopedias, magazines, and the Internet. Use separate sheets of paper for your lists.

You will be awarded 2 points for each example of parallel lines and parallel planes you cite. You must provide at least one example of each for each of the categories above. Failure to provide an example of each in any category will result in a penalty of 5 points. Good hunting!

OPTICAL ILLUSIONS AND PARALLEL LINES

Objective: Students will be introduced to examples of optical illusions formed by parallel line segments. Students should work individually to complete this activity.

Special Materials: rulers

TEACHING NOTES

Most students find optical illusions interesting and challenging. While there are many categories of optical illusions, this activity focuses on two types that involve parallel lines.

1. Introduce the activity by asking students what an optical illusion is. Clarify any explanations you receive by stating that an optical illusion is a deceptive, visually perceived image. The image is not what it appears to be.

2. Hand out copies of Worksheet 1–18 and review the instructions with your students. Depending upon your students, you may prefer to work through the two examples as a class exercise. Be sure that students understand the difference between an illusion of contrast and illusion of interrupted extent. Emphasize that in most cases optical illusions can only be accurately perceived through measurement.

3. Most libraries contain numerous books on optical illusions. Displaying some of these books in your class is a good way to stimulate interest in this activity. Suggest that students find other optical illusions created by parallel lines.

Answer Key

1. Segment EF; a right angle; illusion of interrupted extent

2. All vertical line segments have the same length; the line segments that are not parallel intersect at a point; I; in everyday experiences lines appear to meet in the distance; illusion of contrast

3. The distance is the same; the distance is the same; it is unbroken by any other figure (i.e., it is "open space"); illusion of interrupted extent

4. Answers may vary between segment AB and segment GH; answers may vary between segment CD and segment EF; the extra marks at the end of the line segments create the illusion; all segments have the same length; illusion of contrast

1–18   Optical Illusions and Parallel Lines

"Seeing is believing" is an old saying. In most cases it's true. Sometimes, however, things are not what they appear to be.

Which of the two parallel line segments below is longer?

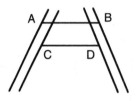

Measure them with your ruler. Were you right? If not, why might you have been wrong?

The sketch above is an example of an *optical illusion*—a visually perceived image that is deceptive. In the example, the segments on the sides move toward each other as they extend upward, giving the illusion that segment AB is longer than segment CD.

Optical illusions can trick you into seeing something that is misleading or false. While there are many kinds of optical illusions, the ones in this activity are created with parallel lines, or lines that appear to be parallel.

One common type of optical illusion is an *illusion of contrast*. In this illusion the position of surrounding lines or objects distorts figures. The example above is an illusion of contrast. The lines that are not parallel distort the distance from A to B and C to D.

Another type of illusion is an *illusion of interrupted extent* as in the example below. In this type of illusion, distance appears to shrink if a figure is broken.

Which of the three lines on the left is extended to the right? Use your ruler to verify that the second line is extended.

© 2000 by The Center for Applied Research in Education

Following are four figures that can play tricks on your eyes. Study them and then answer the questions to improve your ability to "see" things as they really are. Be sure to measure accurately.

1.

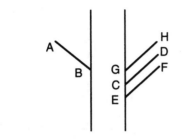

If segment AB was extended, what line segment would it intersect? _____ What type of angle would be formed?_____ What type of illusion is this? _____

_____

2.

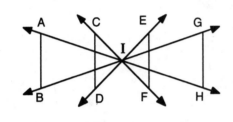

Which of the vertical line segments is the longest? _____ How is the illusion of length created? _____

_____

What point appears to be farthest away from you? _____ What makes this point seem far away? _____

_____

What type of illusion is this? _____

_____

3.

A	B	C	D	E	F

How does the distance from A to C compare with the distance from C to E?

_____ How does the distance from A to E compare with the distance from E to F? _____ Why does the distance from E to F appear to be longer than the distance from A to E? _____

_____

_____

What type of illusion is this? _____

_____

4.

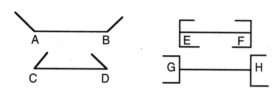

Which of the four line segments appears to be the longest? _____

Which line segment appears to be the shortest? _____ What creates this illusion?

_____

How do the lengths of the segments compare?

_____

What type of illusion is this? _____

_____

Activity 1–19

CALCULATOR DIGITS—
PERPENDICULAR AND PARALLEL SEGMENTS

Objective: Students will use deductive reasoning to determine which digit fits given clues using the language of geometry. Students should work individually to complete this activity.

Special Materials: none

TEACHING NOTES

Your students are no doubt familiar with calculators. The numbers on the display screen of a calculator—as well as the numerals of digital clocks, VCR displays, and similar electronic displays—are formed with parallel and perpendicular line segments. The reliance of these displays on parallel and perpendicular segments is the foundation of this activity.

Note that to complete this activity successfully, students should understand the following terms: right angles, parallel line segments, perpendicular line segments, linear pairs, lines of symmetry, congruency, rotations, and reflections. If necessary, review these terms with your students prior to the activity.

1. Introduce the activity by asking students to take out their calculators and randomly punch in some numbers. (If students don't have their calculators with them, you can use a single calculator as an example and walk around the room showing your students the display.) Instruct students to study the display and note how the numbers are formed. They should conclude that the numerals of a calculator display are formed with parallel and perpendicular segments. You might also mention that other digital displays form numerals in the same way.

2. Distribute copies of Worksheet 1–19 and review the instructions with your students. Emphasize that some clues have more than one answer.

Answer Key

1. 1; **2.** 7; **3.** 4; **4.** 0, 2, 3, 5; **5.** 6, 9; **6.** 8; **7.** 0; **8.** 2, 3, 5, 6, 8, 9; **9.** 3, 4, 6, 9;
10. 8; **11.** 0, 1, 3, 8; **12.** 2, 5; **13.** 6, 9; **14.** 4; **15.** 0, 1, 2, 5, 8

1–19   Calculator Digits—
Perpendicular and Parallel Segments

Calculators, digital clocks, VCRs and similar devices display the numbers from 0 to 9 as digits made up of perpendicular and parallel line segments. The digits 0 to 9 are pictured below. Identify the digits that satisfy each statement. There may be more than one answer for some statements, and some digits may be used more than once.

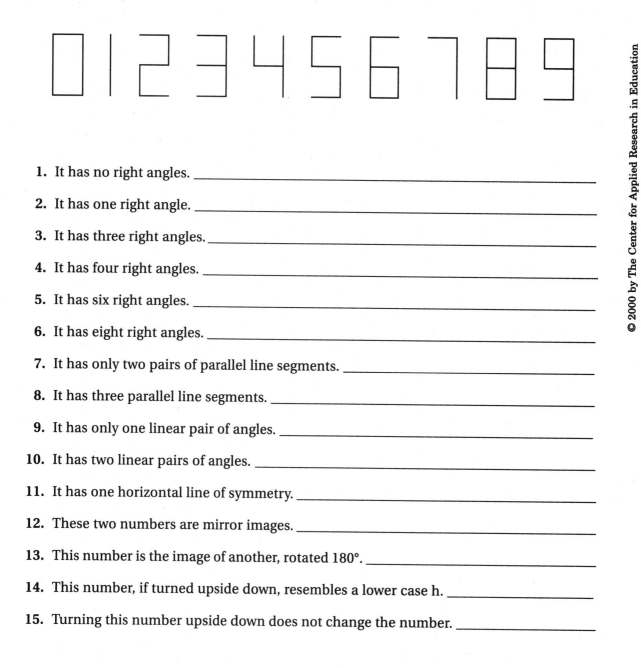

1. It has no right angles. _____

2. It has one right angle. _____

3. It has three right angles. _____

4. It has four right angles. _____

5. It has six right angles. _____

6. It has eight right angles. _____

7. It has only two pairs of parallel line segments. _____

8. It has three parallel line segments. _____

9. It has only one linear pair of angles. _____

10. It has two linear pairs of angles. _____

11. It has one horizontal line of symmetry. _____

12. These two numbers are mirror images. _____

13. This number is the image of another, rotated 180°. _____

14. This number, if turned upside down, resembles a lower case h. _____

15. Turning this number upside down does not change the number. _____

MONOPOLY® AND PERPENDICULAR AND PARALLEL LINES

Objective: Students will identify perpendicular and parallel streets using a map. Students should work individually to complete this activity.

Special Materials: none

TEACHING NOTES

Your students are probably familiar with the game of Monopoly® and have played it with family and friends. They may not know that the game was created by Charles Darrow, a salesman from Germantown, Pennsylvania, in 1930. During the Depression, Darrow, like many other people, was unemployed. Recalling earlier, happier times that he had spent vacationing in Atlantic City, New Jersey with his wife, he designed a board game using streets that he remembered from his trips to Atlantic City. At first Darrow produced the game by hand, making game pieces and the board himself. When he and his wife played it with friends, he would often present the game to the winner as a prize. It wasn't long before Darrow's game became popular and he could not produce enough to keep up with demand. In time Darrow sold the rights to his board game to Parker Brothers, who mass produced it and distributed it nationwide. Monopoly® is one of the most popular board games ever created.

Note that this activity has two worksheets, 1–20A and 1–20B. The first worksheet contains questions for the activity and the second contains a map of Atlantic City, New Jersey.

1. Introduce the activity by asking students if they have ever played Monopoly®. Share the story of Charles Darrow with them.

2. Distribute copies of Worksheet 1–20A and review the instructions with your students. Also distribute copies of Worksheet 1–20B and review the map of Atlantic City with your students. In particular, note the design of the city's streets, many of which are parallel and perpendicular line segments. You might like to mention that all of the streets on the worksheet are on the Monopoly® board and are still traveled in Atlantic City today. Also note that only streets necessary for this activity are included on the map.

Answer Key

1. parallel; 2. parallel; 3. parallel; 4. perpendicular; 5. parallel; 6. perpendicular;
7. parallel; 8. perpendicular; 9. parallel; 10. parallel; 11. perpendicular;
12. perpendicular

1–20A Monopoly® and Perpendicular and Parallel Lines

The streets that appear on the board game Monopoly® are named after streets in Atlantic City, New Jersey. Many of the streets of Atlantic City are parallel or perpendicular. Using a map of Atlantic City as a reference, complete each statement by writing "perpendicular" or "parallel" to make it true.

1. New York Avenue is _____ to Tennessee Avenue.

2. Indiana Avenue is _____ to North Carolina Avenue.

3. Atlantic Avenue is _____ to Pacific Avenue.

4. Connecticut Avenue is _____ to Oriental Avenue.

5. Baltic Avenue is _____ to Mediterranean Avenue.

6. St. James Place is _____ to Pacific Avenue.

7. Vermont Avenue is _____ to Pennsylvania Avenue.

8. North Carolina Avenue is _____ to Baltic Avenue.

9. Atlantic Avenue is _____ to Oriental Avenue.

10. Kentucky Avenue is _____ to Tenneesse Avenue.

11. Mediterranean Avenue is _____ to North Carolina Avenue.

12. Park Place is _____ to Pacific Avenue.

1–20B Monopoly® and Perpendicular and Parallel Lines

Use this map to answer the questions on Worksheet 1–20A.

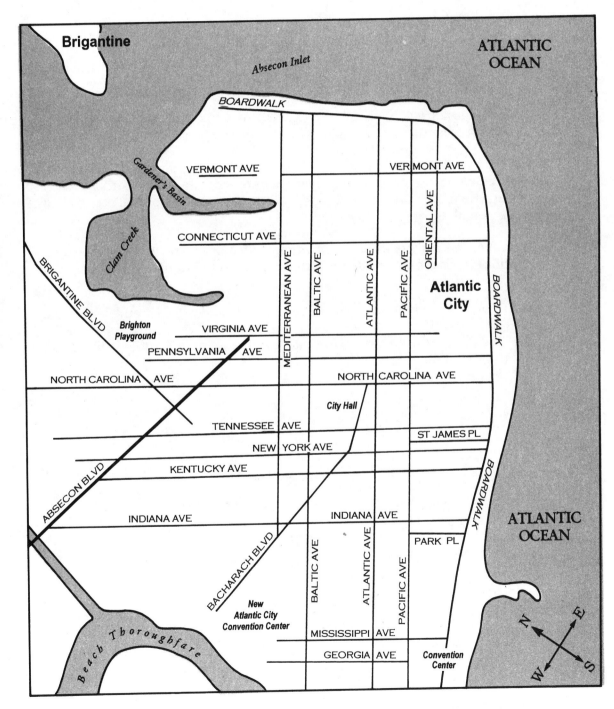

POSITIONING STREETS ON A MAP

Objective: Students will use the language of geometry and deductive reasoning to label streets on a map. Students should work in pairs to complete this activity.

Special Materials: none

TEACHING NOTES

Most students have used maps to locate places. In this activity, students are given clues and must construct a street map. The clues are expressed in the language of geometry.

Note that this activity includes two worksheets, 1–21A and 1–21B. The first worksheet contains instructions and clues students will follow to construct a street map of the town of East River. The second worksheet contains a partial map, which they are to complete.

1. Introduce this activity by explaining that students will create a map based on specific information. Caution them that they must follow the instructions they receive carefully.

2. Distribute copies of Worksheet 1–21A and Worksheet 1–21B and review the instructions with your students. (You might want to have extra copies of the map handy in case students make major errors.) Remind students to rely on the cardinal directions—north, east, south, and west—as reference points in the construction of their maps. Encourage them to be accurate in their work.

Answer Key

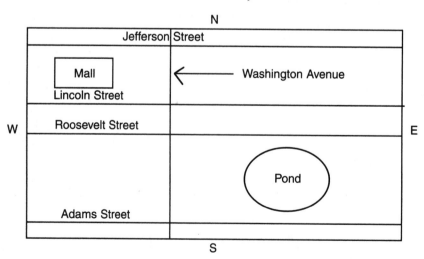

1–21A Positioning Streets on a Map

The town of East River has grown rapidly and the mayor has decided to have a map made of the town. He needs your help. Based on the instructions below, draw the streets on a map of East River.

As you draw your map, follow these guidelines:

▲ Draw and label all of the streets.

▲ Be sure that the streets extend from one side of the map to the other.

▲ Remember that streets do not run through the mall or the pond. (The mall and pond are positioned correctly.)

Here are your directions for drawing the street map of East River.

1. Washington Avenue is west of the pond but east of the mall.

2. Jefferson Street is north of the pond and the mall.

3. All streets (not avenues) are parallel to each other and perpendicular to the avenue.

4. A stop light is planned to be located at the intersection of Jefferson Street and Washington Avenue. The mall may be entered from either of these two streets.

5. The pond is north of Adams Street.

6. If you leave the mall via Jefferson Street, make a right at the intersection, make the second left onto Roosevelt Street, and then travel east, you will be directly north of the pond.

1–21B   Positioning Streets on a Map

Use the clues you were given on Worksheet 1–21A to complete the street map of East River.

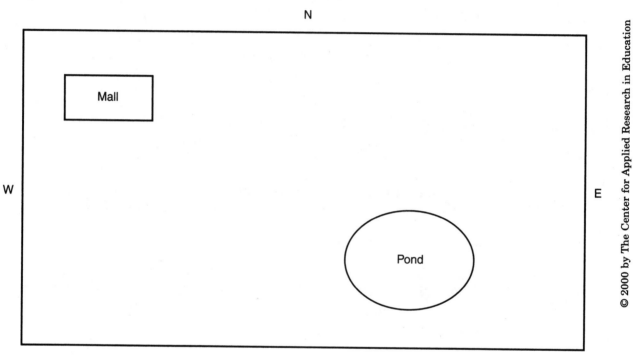

ANGLES AND TRANSVERSALS

Objective: Students will identify interior angles, same side interior angles, alternate interior angles, exterior angles, same side exterior angles, alternate exterior angles, and corresponding angles. Students should work individually to complete this activity.

Special Materials: none

TEACHING NOTES

This activity is designed to give students practice working with various interior and exterior angles. The concept of vertical angles and linear pairs is reinforced.

1. Introduce this activity by reviewing the concepts of angles, lines, and transversals. If necessary, also review the meaning of vertical angles and linear pairs.

2. Distribute copies of Worksheet 1–22 and review the instructions with your students. Remind students to study the diagram on the worksheet carefully as they complete the activity.

Answer Key

Each number represents the number of the angle on the illustration.

1. 1, 2; 1, 3; 1, 4; 1, 5; 1, 6; 1, 7; 1, 8; 2, 3; 2, 4; 2, 5; 2, 6; 2, 7; 2, 8;
   3, 4; 3, 5; 3, 6; 3, 7; 3, 8; 4, 5; 4, 6; 4, 7; 4, 8; 5, 6; 5, 7; 5, 8; 6, 7;
   6, 8; 7, 8

2. 3, 4; 3, 5; 3, 6; 4, 5; 4, 6; 5,6

3. 4, 5; 3, 6

4. 3, 5; 4, 6

5. 1, 2; 1, 7; 1, 8; 2, 7; 2, 8; 7, 8

6. 1, 7; 2, 8

7. 1, 8; 2, 7

8. 1, 5; 2, 6; 3, 7; 4, 8

9. 1, 3; 2, 4; 5, 7; 6, 8

10. 1, 2; 1, 4; 2, 3; 3, 4; 5, 6; 5, 8; 6, 7; 7, 8

Name ______________________ Date ____________ Section ______

1–22 Angles and Transversals

In the diagram below, l_3 is the *transversal* because it intersects two other lines. Refer to the diagram when answering questions 1–10.

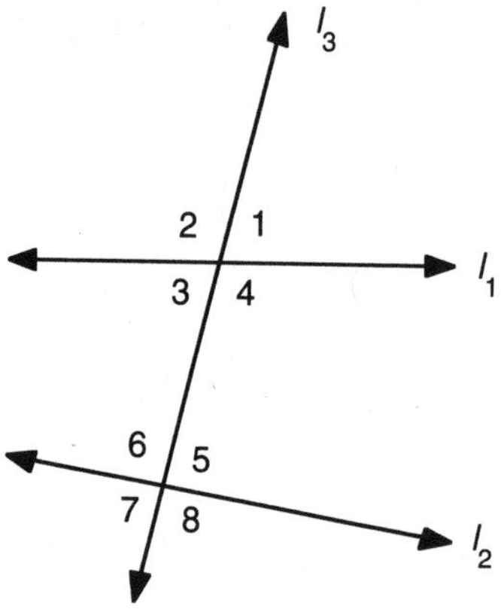

1. List all pairs of angles that are formed. ______________________

2. Which pair(s) of angles are "inside" of the space between l_1 and l_2? ____________
These are called *interior angles.*

3. Which pair(s) of interior angles listed in question 2 are on the same side of the transversal? ____________
These are called *same side interior angles.*

4. Which pair(s) of interior angles listed in question 2 are on opposite sides of the transversal? ____________
These are called *alternate interior angles.*

5. Which pair(s) of angles are "outside" of the space between l_1 and l_2? ____________
These are called *exterior angles.*

6. Which angles are alternate exterior angles? ____________

7. Which angles are same side exterior angles? ____________

8. *Corresponding angles* are two nonadjacent angles on the same side of the transversal. (One is an interior angle and the other is an exterior angle.) Which angles are corresponding angles? ____________

9. List all pairs of vertical angles. ______________________

10. List all linear pairs. ______________________

PARALLEL LINES AND TRANSVERSALS

Objective: Students will make and test five conjectures about pairs of angles formed when two parallel lines are intersected by a transversal: corresponding angles are congruent, same side interior angles are supplementary, alternate interior angles are congruent, same side exterior angles are supplementary, and alternate exterior angles are congruent. Students should work in pairs to complete this activity.

Special Materials: rulers, scissors, one sheet of looseleaf paper per student

TEACHING NOTES

Before assigning this activity, your students should complete Activity 1-22, "Angles and Transversals." In addition, students should be able to:

▲ Identify pairs of angles formed by two lines cut by a transversal.

▲ Identify vertical angles.

▲ Identify linear pairs.

▲ Apply the principle that vertical angles are congruent and angles that form a linear pair are supplementary.

1. If necessary, review the above prerequisite skills with your students.

2. Distribute copies of Worksheet 1-23 and review the instructions with your students. You may find it helpful to guide them through the initial steps of the activity. Also hand out a sheet of looseleaf paper to each student. Suggest that they use the top half of the paper for the first diagram. This will leave them room for number 7 and the second diagram.

Answer Key

6a. congruent; **b.** supplementary; **c.** congruent; **d.** supplementary; **e.** congruent

Note: answers to number 7 are the same as number 6. Accept any reasonable conjectures.

1–23   Parallel Lines and Transversals

In this activity you will work with a partner to make and test conjectures about angles formed if two parallel lines are intersected by a transversal. Follow the procedures below to draw the parallel lines and a transversal.

1. Take a sheet of looseleaf paper and choose two lines that are about two inches apart. Note that the lines on the paper are parallel. Using your ruler for accuracy, trace (pressing darkly) over these lines and make parallel segments about four inches long.

2. Label one line l_1 and the other l_2.

3. Use a ruler to draw a line that intersects the two parallel lines.

4. Label each angle as pictured in the diagram.

5. Use scissors to cut anywhere between l_1 and l_2. (l_1 and angles labeled 1 to 4 should be on one piece of paper, and l_2 and angles labeled 5 to 8 should be on the other.)

6. Reposition the lines and angles to find a relationship between pairs of angles. Remember, angles that align "on top of" each other are *congruent*, and two angles that form a linear pair are *supplementary*. Then answer the following questions with either the word "congruent" or "supplementary":

   a. How are corresponding angles related? _____

   b. How are same side interior angles related? _____

   c. How are alternate interior angles related? _____

   d. How are same side exterior angles related? _____

   e. How are alternate exterior angles related? _____

7. Place your diagrams aside. Repeat steps 1 to 6 with another pair of parallel lines and a transversal. Compare your answers. What conjecture can you make about a transversal that intersects two parallel lines?

   _____

   _____

   _____

   _____

   _____

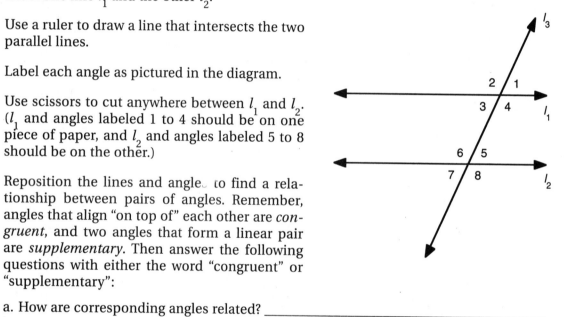

IF–THEN STATEMENTS

Objective: Students will write conditional statements in if–then form. They will also recognize the hypothesis and conclusion of a conditional, determine if a conditional is true or false, and provide a counter example to false statements. Students should work in pairs to complete this activity.

Special Materials: none

TEACHING NOTES

If–then statements are closely linked to the ability to reason and deduce consequences essential for proofs and determine a strategy to solve problems. This activity starts by explaining if-then statements, hypotheses, conclusions, and counter examples. The first six statements of the activity focus on real-life situations, and the final four are built on geometric concepts.

1. Begin the activity by reviewing basic if-then statements. Here is a simple example: "If it is cloudy and the humidity content of the air is high enough, then it will rain." Explain that this is how all if-then statements are composed, and note that we use them every day in all areas of life.

2. Distribute copies of Worksheet 1–24 and review the instructions with your students. If necessary, go over the example on the worksheet as a class activity, then instruct students to complete the worksheet.

Answer Key

1. If a being is a dog, then it is a mammal. If a being is a mammal, then it is a dog. The converse is false. A cat is a mammal.

2. If a person is on the basketball team, then he is over 5'10" tall. If a person is over 5'10" tall, then he is on the basketball team. The converse is false. Other students over 5'10" tall may have no interest in basketball and are not on the team.

3. If a student earns all A's on the quarterly report card, then he or she is on the honor roll. If a student is on the honor roll, then he or she earned all A's. The converse is true if all A's are necessary for achieving honor roll status. The converse may be false, depending on the qualifications for honor roll.

4. If a person is a licensed driver in New Jersey, then he is 17 years old or older. If a person is 17 years old or older, then he is a licensed driver in New Jersey. The converse is false. A person 17 years old or older may not have taken the driver's test.

Activity 1–24   *(Cont'd)*

Answer Key   *(Cont'd)*

5. If it is Washington's birthday, then it is February 22. If it is February 22, then it is Washington's birthday. The converse is true.

6. If a person is a Scorpio, then he or she was born between October 24 and November 21. If a person is born between October 24 and November 21, then he or she is a Scorpio. The converse is true.

7. If an angle is a right angle, then it measures 90°. If an angle measures 90°, then it is a right angle. The converse is true.

8. If two angles are vertical, then they are congruent. If two angles are congruent, then they are vertical. The converse is false. Angles may be congruent but not vertical.

9. If a figure is a ray, then it is part of a line. If a figure is part of a line, then it is a ray. The converse is false. A segment is part of a line.

10. If two lines intersect, then their intersection is a point. If there is a point, then two lines intersect. The converse is false. A point may exist in isolation.

Accept any reasonable if-then statements.

1–24   If–Then Statements

An *if-then statement* has two parts: a *hypothesis* (the clause that follows "if") and a *conclusion* (the clause that follows "then"). The entire if-then statement is called a *conditional*.

The statement "All professional football players are athletes" can be written as an if-then statement: If a person is a professional football player, then the person is an athlete. The hypothesis of the statement is "a person is a professional football player" and the conclusion is "the person is an athlete."

The *converse* of an if-then statement is formed by switching the hypothesis and conclusion. The converse of the above example is "If a person is an athlete, then the person is a professional football player." Of course, this is false, because professional baseball players, soccer stars, and Olympic hopefuls are also athletes. These examples of other types of athletes are known as *counter examples*. They show that the "if" part of the statement is true, but the "then" part is false. To prove that an if-then statement, or conditional, is false, you must give a counter example.

Write each statement below in if-then form on a separate sheet of paper. Then write the converse. If the converse is false, provide a counter example.

1. All dogs are mammals.

2. All members of the basketball team are over 5'10" tall.

3. All students who earn all A's on the quarterly report card are on the honor roll.

4. In New Jersey, all licensed drivers are at least 17 years of age.

5. George Washington's birthday is February 22.

6. A person is a Scorpio if he or she is born between October 24 and November 21.

7. All right angles are 90°.

8. All vertical angles are congruent.

9. A ray is part of a line.

10. Two lines intersect in a point.

Create two if–then statements of your own. Write one in which both the conditional and its converse are true. Write the other in which the conditional is true, but the converse is false.

SYMBOLS OF GEOMETRY

Objective: Students will review the symbols commonly found in geometry. Students should work individually to complete this activity.

Special Materials: none

TEACHING NOTES

Like most major areas in mathematics, geometry has its own set of symbols with which students must be familiar if they are to be successful in their study of the subject. Symbols are, in many ways, the language of geometry.

1. Introduce this activity by explaining that a symbol is a sign or mark that represents a thing or idea. Offer this example on the board or an overhead projector: Line segment AB can be written as *AB*. The short slash above AB is the symbol for line segment. Using symbols frees the individual from having to write out descriptions and explanations.

2. Hand out copies of Worksheet 1–25 and review the instructions with your students. Note that while most of the symbols on the worksheet pertain specifically to geometry, some, for example, < and >, are used in many areas of math. This does not lessen their importance to geometry, however.

Answer Key

Cymbals are part of a drumset.

1–25   Symbols of Geometry

Write the letter of the correct word or phrase in the blank before the symbol in the left column. When you are done, read down the column. A message will be revealed.

	Symbol		Word or Phrase
_____	$\overline{AB}$	B.	length of segment AB
_____	$\overrightarrow{AB}$	E.	intersection
_____	$\overleftrightarrow{AB}$	M.	empty set
_____	AB	S.	degree
_____	$\angle ABC$	U.	is approximately equal to
_____	$m\angle ABC$	Y.	ray AB
_____	°	P.	triangle ABC
_____	≠	R.	is perpendicular to
_____	⊥	T.	is similar to
_____	‖	A.	angle ABC
_____	$\triangle ABC$	A.	pi
_____	π	C.	segment AB
_____	≅	R.	is less than or equal to
_____	~	A.	is not equal to
_____	=	R.	is congruent to
_____	<	L.	measure of angle ABC
_____	>	O.	is equal to
_____	≥	M.	line AB
_____	≤	T.	union
_____	≈	D.	is greater than or equal to
_____	φ	E.	is parallel to
_____	∈	A.	is greater than
_____	∩	S.	is an element of
_____	∪	F.	is less than

THE GREEK ALPHABET

Objective: Students will write the names for the letters of the Greek alphabet. Students should work individually to complete this activity.

Special Materials: dictionaries and other reference books; *optional*—computers with Internet access or electronic reference sources

TEACHING NOTES

Many of your students are no doubt familiar with some letters of the Greek alphabet, especially those used for constants or variables. Most of your students probably know π as the ratio of the circumference to the diameter of a circle, or approximately 3.14. As students continue their study of geometry, letters of the Greek alphabet are used more frequently. Clearly this is a tribute to early Greek mathematicians such as Archimedes, Aristotle, Euclid, and Pythagoras, who advanced the theory and applications of geometry so many years ago.

1. Introduce this activity by explaining that the ancient Greeks produced many prominent mathematicians, many of whom provided great contributions to geometry. Many of the symbols we use in mathematics and geometry in particular are letters of the Greek alphabet.

2. Distribute copies of Worksheet 1–26 and review the instructions with your students. Note that they should use reference materials to find the names of the letters of the Greek alphabet. Suggest that they consult dictionaries under "alphabet." Many collegiate-edition dictionaries contain alphabets of different languages. Students may also use other references, such as encyclopedias, including on-line and electronic sources.

Answer Key

1. theta; **2.** eta; **3.** psi; **4.** xi; **5.** phi; **6.** pi; **7.** epsilon; **8.** lambda; **9.** upsilon; **10.** chi; **11.** iota; **12.** mu; **13.** nu; **14.** omega; **15.** omicron; **16.** beta; **17.** zeta; **18.** kappa; **19.** sigma; **20.** tau; **21.** rho; **22.** alpha; **23.** gamma; **24.** delta

1-26   The Greek Alphabet

Many formulas in mathematics use letters of the Greek alphabet as a constant or variable. One example is π, which is approximately equal to 3.14. That we still use these symbols is a tribute to the ancient Greeks who did so much to further the study of mathematics.

For this activity, write the name of the letter of the Greek alphabet in the space before the symbol. Consult reference sources.

1. _____ Θ
2. _____ H
3. _____ Ψ
4. _____ Ξ
5. _____ Φ
6. _____ Π
7. _____ E
8. _____ Λ
9. _____ Y
10. _____ X
11. _____ I
12. _____ M

13. _____ N
14. _____ Ω
15. _____ O
16. _____ B
17. _____ Z
18. _____ K
19. _____ Σ
20. _____ T
21. _____ P
22. _____ A
23. _____ Γ
24. _____ Δ

Part 2

POLYGONS—
THE FOUNDATIONS

POLYGON PREFIX SCAVENGER HUNT

Objective: Students will relate prefixes used in the names of polygons to everyday life. Students may work individually or in pairs to complete this activity.

Special Materials: dictionaries

TEACHING NOTES

This is an open-ended activity whose purpose is to reinforce the meaning of the names of polygons by connecting their prefixes to words of everyday life. The activity works well for enrichment.

1. Introduce the activity by reviewing with students that polygons are closed figures bounded by lines. Ask students to name some polygons. Their answers will probably include triangles, quadrilaterals, pentagons, etc. Explain that the names of many polygons are formed with a prefix. Triangle, for example, has the prefix *tri*, meaning three. An octagon has the prefix *octa*, meaning eight, and is an eight-sided polygon. The prefixes of polygons appear in many common words. Ask your students how many wheels a tricycle has. Three, of course. Ask them how many legs an octopus has. Eight. (Note that "octa" and "octo" both mean eight and are derived from the Latin *octo*.) The prefixes of polygons help to determine the meaning of the word.

2. Distribute copies of Worksheet 2–1 and review the instructions with your students. Be sure they understand the meanings of the various prefixes. Emphasize that they must record at least one word for each prefix and include its meaning.

3. If you decide to make this an activity to be completed in class, set a time limit of 20 or 25 minutes. That will give students time to find words and leave you enough time to review their lists and declare a winner or winners. Of course, you may ask students to work on the activity at home, which will give them the chance to find more words.

4. Accept any reasonable lists. You might like to offer a prize of a homework pass for the student or students who find the most words in the scavenger hunt.

2–1 Polygon Prefix Scavenger Hunt

A *prefix* is a syllable or group of letters placed at the beginning of a word that can alter or modify its meaning. A triangle is a three-sided figure that has three angles. The prefix is *tri* and the base word is *angle*. Prefixes are used to name polygons. The prefixes used to name polygons are also used to form many other words.

Following are prefixes, their meanings, and names of polygons. Using a dictionary, write as many words as you can that start with the prefixes below. Also write a brief meaning of the word; for example, tricycle: three-wheeled vehicle. Find as many words as you can for each prefix, but you must find at least one for each. Use a separate sheet of paper for your list.

tri—3—triangle

quad—4—quadrilateral

penta—5—pentagon

hexa—6—hexagon

hepta—7—heptagon

octa—8—octagon

nona—9—nonagon

deca—10—decagon

dodeca—12—dodecagon

poly—many—polygon

TANGRAMS AND POLYGONS

Objective: Students will use tangrams to form various polygons. Students should work individually or in pairs to complete this activity.

Special Materials: tangrams (or tangram pieces constructed in Activity 1–6), unlined paper

TEACHING NOTES

Tangrams can be used to form many figures. Because they permit students to manipulate pieces to construct different shapes, they should be a part of every geometry curriculum.

1. Introduce this activity by explaining that a tangram is a Chinese puzzle consisting of a square cut into five triangles, a square, and a parallelogram, which may be reassembled into various shapes. You may wish to review the background information on tangrams offered in the teacher notes of Activity 1–6.

2. Distribute copies of Worksheet 2–2 and review the instructions with your students. (If students have completed Activity 1–6 and you have saved their tangrams, you may hand them back to students for this activity. If you don't have tangrams, students can make them by following the instructions on Worksheet 1–6.) Note that students will be asked to form a triangle, quadrilateral, pentagon, hexagon, heptagon, and octagon with their tans. Be sure that students understand how many sides each of these figures has. After students form each polygon, they should outline the figure and label the parts. Tell students that several answers are possible.

Activity 2–2   *(Cont'd)*

Answer Key

Answers may vary. Following is one possible answer for each polygon.

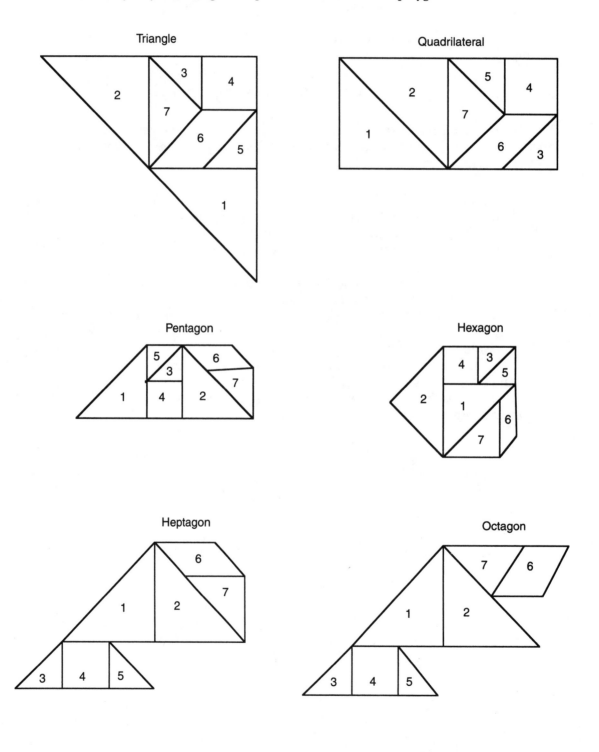

Triangle

Quadrilateral

Pentagon

Hexagon

Heptagon

Octagon

2–2   Tangrams and Polygons

In this activity, you will form a triangle, quadrilateral, pentagon, hexagon, heptagon, and octagon using the tans of a tangram. Before beginning, label each tan as follows:

▲ the two largest triangles, 1 and 2

▲ the two smallest triangles, 3 and 5

▲ the remaining triangle, 7

▲ the square, 4

▲ the parallelogram, 6

Labeling each tan in this manner will make it easier to refer to them.

Use all of your tans to form an example of each polygon below. (There is more than one shape for each.) Form your figures on unlined paper. After you have formed a polygon, trace around it and write the number of each tan in its position in the polygon. Label each polygon.

Triangle	Quadrilateral	Pentagon
Hexagon	Heptagon	Octagon

CONCAVE AND CONVEX POLYGONS

Objective: Students will form concave and convex polygons. Students should work in pairs or groups of three to complete this activity.

Special Materials: tangrams (or tangram pieces constructed in Activity 1–6), unlined paper

TEACHING NOTES

When students think of polygons, a variety of figures including triangles, quadrilaterals, pentagons, octagons, etc., may come to mind. Rarely do they think in terms of concave and convex. Although most of the polygons studied in a typical geometry class are convex, students should be aware that concave polygons exist and be able to differentiate between the two.

1. Introduce this activity by explaining to students that polygons may be either concave or convex. If necessary define the terms. *Concave* means to turn or bend inward. *Convex* means to turn or bend outward. Suggest that they remember the difference by recalling that concave polygons have a "cave," and one may walk into a cave. You may also like to review the background material regarding tangrams provided in Activity 1–6.

2. Hand out copies of Worksheet 2–3 and review the instructions and examples with your students. (If students have completed Activity 1–6 and you have saved their tans, distribute the tans. If you don't have tangrams, students can make them following the instructions on Worksheet 1–6.) Make sure that students understand how many sides the different polygons have and review the definitions if necessary. Remind them to label their tans and the figures they create. Caution them to follow the instructions carefully.

Activity 2–3   *(Cont'd)*

Answer Key

Answers may vary. Following is a possible answer for each.

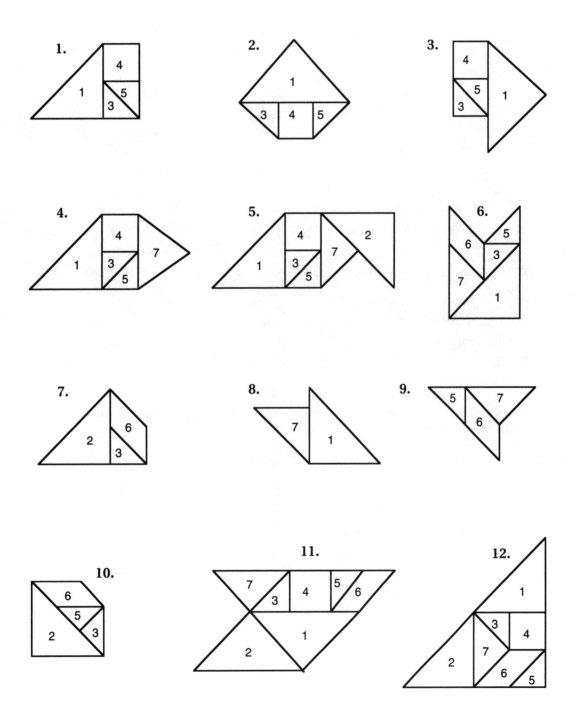

2–3   Concave and Convex Polygons

Polygons can be divided into two major types: *concave* and *convex*. A *concave* polygon bends or turns inward at some point; a *convex* polygon does not. In this activity you will form concave and convex polygons using tangrams.

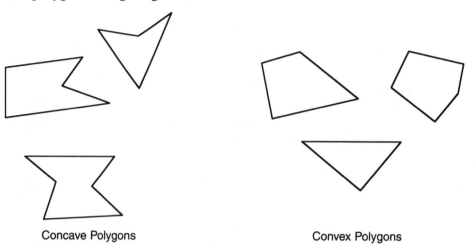

Concave Polygons   Convex Polygons

In order to be able to refer to the individual tans consistently, label them as follows:

▲ the two largest triangles, 1 and 2
▲ the two smallest triangles, 3 and 5
▲ the remaining triangle, 7
▲ the square, 4
▲ the parallelogram, 6

Use your tans to form the polygons below. Sketch each polygon on your unlined paper, and identify the placement of the tans you used.

1. Use tans 1, 3, 4, 5 to form a convex quadrilateral.

2. Use tans 1, 3, 4, 5 to form a convex pentagon.

3. Use tans 1, 3, 4, 5 to form a concave hexagon.

4. Use tans 1,3,4,5,7 to form a convex pentagon,

5. Use tans 1, 2, 3, 4, 5, 7 to form a concave hexagon.

6. Use tans 1, 3, 5, 6, 7 to form a concave pentagon.

7. Use tans 2, 3, 6 to form a convex quadrilateral.

8. Use tans 1 and 7 to form a concave pentagon.

9. Use tans 5, 6, 7 to form a concave quadrilateral.

10. Use tans 2, 3, 5, 6 to form a convex pentagon.

11. Use all tans to form a concave pentagon.

12. Use all tans to form a triangle. (All triangles are convex.)

THE SYMMETRY OF LOGOS

Objective: Students will create a poster that identifies types of symmetry in logos. Students should work in groups of three or four to complete this activity.

Special Materials: poster paper, scissors, glue or glue sticks, rulers, black pens, old magazines and newspapers

TEACHING NOTES

Symmetry is an important concept in geometry. Symmetry provides balance and beauty and is evident throughout the natural and manmade world. Because symmetry entices the eye, artists use it to capture the attention of viewers and add interest to their creations. An easy way to present symmetry to your students is through logos. Most logos have distinctive symmetry.

1. Prior to the activity, ask students to bring in old magazines and newspapers that they will use to find logos. You should also set aside materials you can give to students who don't have any. Perhaps your colleagues or your school's librarian can give you copies of old periodicals.

2. Introduce this activity by asking students to name and describe some logos with which they are familiar. Adidas with its three quadrilaterals; Tommy Hilfilger with the red, white, and blue rectangles; and the AT&T world with its varying shaded lines are some examples. Many companies use reflections, rotations, and translations in their logos. McDonald's famous arches are symmetrical through reflection; Texaco's star shows symmetry through reflection and rotation; and the three shields of a Buick are examples of symmetry by translation.

3. Distribute copies of Worksheet 2–4 and review the instructions with your students. Emphasize that students should select only logos that have some type of symmetry. Remind them that not only must they attach logos to their poster paper, but they must also identify the types of symmetry.

4. At the end of the activity, display the work of your students. Accept any logos in which the type of symmetry is correctly identified.

2–4   The Symmetry of Logos

A *logo* is a visual representation that establishes an identity. Companies and organizations use logos as a means to help people remember them. Most people only have to see two golden arches to think of McDonald's.

Because symmetry can make a picture more appealing and memorable, many logos use symmetry to make an impression. They may use symmetry in the following ways:

▲ Symmetry by *reflection*, in which a figure can be divided into two parts that are mirror images of each other.

▲ Symmetry by *rotation*, in which a figure coincides with its original position when turned about a point.

▲ Symmetry by *translation*, in which a figure coincides with its original position when it is moved to the right, left, up, down, or any combination of these directions.

▲ Symmetry through a combination of the above.

For this activity, your group will create a poster about logos. Follow the instructions below.

1. Compile several logos from old magazines and newspapers. If you recall any logos from memory, you may draw them. Use as many logos as you can. Be sure to select logos that have some type of symmetry.

2. Cut out the logos and attach them to your poster paper. Arrange them neatly and leave enough space between them so that you can provide information about the logo.

3. After attaching each logo to the poster paper, name the company or organization it represents, and identify the type of symmetry. It may be a reflection, rotation, translation, or a combination.

MAGIC TRIANGLES

Objective: Students will extend the concept of a triangle to number theory or math puzzles. Students should work individually to complete this activity.

Special Materials: none

TEACHING NOTES

Math puzzles are enjoyable and motivating for students. A magic triangle can spark interest in your class, especially for those students who like to use numbers rather than figures.

1. Introduce the activity by explaining that a magic triangle is a triangular arrangement of numbers in which the sums of the numbers along each side are the same.

2. Hand out copies of Worksheet 2-5 and review the instructions with your students. Note the examples of magic triangles and point out that the numbers are arranged as triangles. Explain that the numbers of any magic triangle must be consecutive or multiples of consecutive numbers. In each case the numbers at the vertices are the smallest numbers. Use the examples to discuss these properties.

Answer Key

Answers may vary; included is one possible solution for each problem.

1.	2.	3.
1	2	1
9 6	12 18	6 5
5 7	16 8	10 7
2 8 4 3	4 10 14 6	9 12
		2 8 4 11 3

Name _____ Date _____ Section _____

2–5   Magic Triangles

A *magic triangle* is a triangular arrangement of numbers in which the sum of the numbers along each side is the same. Each number placed along the side may be used only once. Three magic triangles are shown below.

```
          1                    2                    3
        6   5               12   10              18   15
       2  4  3             4   8   6            6   12   9

      Sum is 9            Sum is 18            Sum is 27
```

Notice that in each magic triangle the numbers are consecutive, as in the first example (1,2,3,4,5,6), or are multiples of consecutive numbers, as in the next two examples (2,4,6,8,10,12) and (3,6,9,12,15,18). Also notice that the smallest numbers are located at the vertices of the triangle.

Complete each magic triangle below.

1. Use the numbers from 1 to 9. The sum is 17.

```
              ___

           ___     ___

        ___           ___

     ___     ___     ___     ___
```

2. Use the multiples of 2 from 2 to 18. The sum is 34. Some numbers are included.

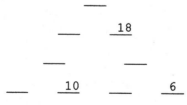

```
              ___

         ___        18

        ___          ___

     ___    10    ___    6
```

3. Use the numbers from 1 to 12. The sum is 28. Some numbers are included.

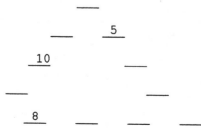

```
              ___

           ___    5

         10          ___

        ___            ___

     ___    8    ___    ___    ___
```

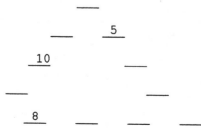

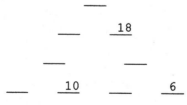

IT'S WORTH A "TRI"—CROSSWORD PUZZLE

Objective: Students will create crossword puzzles using the various types of triangles. Students may work individually or in pairs to complete this activity.

Special Materials: rulers, graph paper; *optional*—computers with software capable of generating crossword puzzles, printers

TEACHING NOTES

Students create a crossword puzzle about triangles in this activity. Not only may they use triangles that appear in a geometry text, but also examples of other triangles that occur in everyday life, such as the Bermuda Triangle.

1. Prior to beginning this activity, collect crossword puzzles from newspapers and magazines, which students may study as examples. (If students have done the crossword puzzle in Activity 1–1, they probably won't need any examples.)

2. Introduce the activity by explaining that students are to create a crossword puzzle about triangles. Ask students to name different kinds of triangles. Among their answers will probably be equilateral triangles, right triangles, and isosceles triangles. Ask them what other kinds of triangles they have heard about, that may not have much in common with geometry. Examples might include a love triangle (students who are fans of soap operas should get this one!), a work triangle, and of course the Bermuda Triangle.

3. Distribute copies of Worksheet 2–6 and review the instructions with your students. Emphasize that students must use all of the words designated by the triangles in their puzzles. They may use any or all of the others, and may include some that are not on the list. All words or phrases, however, must name some type of triangle.

4. If students have access to computers that contain software with crossword puzzle capabilities, you might have them do the activity on computers. Although the software will generate the configuration of the puzzle, students will still need to supply the answers and clues. Printed puzzles are quite nice.

5. Accept all reasonable puzzles. At the end of the activity, make a few copies of each puzzle and allow students to exchange puzzles and try to solve them.

2–6   It's Worth a "Tri"—Crossword Puzzle

Create a crossword puzzle about triangles. Use the words at the bottom of this page for the answers to your puzzle. You must use all of the words designated by the triangles, and may use any of the other words. You may also use any other "triangle" words you know. Following the guidelines below will help you design your crossword puzzle.

1. Place the answers in the boxes of graph paper so that one letter appears in a box. Arrange the letters down and across, and try to have a roughly equal number of down and across answers.

2. Write lightly in pencil so that it is easier to erase mistakes. Revise the structure of your puzzle until you are satisfied with its form.

3. Make sure you spell all words correctly.

4. After you are satisfied with the way your puzzle looks, write a small number in the first box of each answer. Number the answers consecutively, one set of numbers for the down answers and another set for the across answers.

5. On a separate sheet of paper, write clues, or definitions, for your answers. Consult your text or a dictionary, if necessary.

6. Double-check your work, and create a final copy of your puzzle on a new piece of paper. Draw heavy lines on the boxes of your answers to make your answers stand out. Put the clues below the puzzle or on a separate paper.

Use the following words for the answers in your puzzle. Remember, you must use the words designated by the triangles.

▲ acute triangle   harmonic triangle

▲ obtuse triangle   Pascal's Triangle

▲ right triangle   pedal triangle

▲ equiangular triangle   work triangle

▲ similar triangles   Bermuda Triangle

▲ equilateral triangles   love triangle

▲ isosceles triangle   Penrose Triangle

▲ scalene triangle   circumscribed triangle

▲ congruent triangles

▲ inscribed triangle

TRY YOUR HAND AT DRAWING TRIANGLES

Objective: Students will draw different types of triangles given at least two measurements. Students should work individually or in pairs to complete this activity.

Special Materials: 12″ × 18″ white drawing paper, rulers, protractors, crayons or markers; *optional*—computers with software capable of drawing triangles with specific measurements, printers

TEACHING NOTES

Drawing, naming, and classifying triangles has an important part in the study of geometry. Often students are able to state the definition of a term, but they don't fully understand the definition. Constructing a figure from instructions requires thorough understanding.

1. Introduce this activity by explaining to students that they will be asked to draw various types of triangles, given specific information. They will draw their triangles on white drawing paper, label them, and color them with crayons or markers, making a poster of triangles.

2. Distribute copies of Worksheet 2–7 and review the instructions with your students. Be sure they understand the attributes of the various triangles. Note that they are given only partial information about each triangle and that they must use their knowledge and reasoning skills to construct the triangle correctly. Caution students to arrange their triangles on their paper so that they have enough space to fit all of them.

3. If students have access to computers with software that has the capability to draw triangles according to specific measurements, let them do their work on their computers. This is an excellent way to implement technology in your classroom.

4. Display students' posters upon conclusion of the activity and discuss the various sizes and shapes of triangles that have been created.

Answer Key

Answers may vary; check students' posters for accuracy.

Name _____ Date _____ Section _____

2–7   Try Your Hand at Drawing Triangles

In this activity you will draw six triangles: an isosceles triangle, an equilateral triangle, a scalene triangle, a right triangle, an acute triangle, and an obtuse triangle. You are to name each triangle, label the measurements of its sides and angles, and color it. When you are done, you will have a poster of triangles.

The following information will help you draw the triangles accurately:

▲ *Isosceles triangles* have at least two congruent sides.

▲ *Equilateral triangles* have three congruent sides.

▲ *Scalene triangles* have no congruent sides.

▲ *Right triangles* have one right angle.

▲ *Acute triangles* have three acute angles.

▲ *Obtuse triangles* have one obtuse angle.

▲ In every triangle, the sum of the measures of the angles equals 180°.

Use the following information to construct the triangles. Remember to label the measures of all sides and angles.

1. Draw an isosceles triangle. One side is 5 inches and one angle is 70°.

2. Draw an equilateral triangle. One side is 4 inches.

3. Draw a scalene triangle. One angle measures 20° and another angle measures 85°.

4. Draw a right triangle. One side is 4 inches.

5. Draw an acute triangle. One side is 5 inches and another side is 7 inches.

6. Draw an obtuse triangle. One side is 6 inches and another side is 4 inches.

ANGLES OF TRIANGLES

Objective: Students will find the missing measures of the angles in a triangle. Students should work individually or in pairs to complete this activity.

Special Materials: none

TEACHING NOTES

This activity requires students to find the measures of angles in a triangle. To complete the activity successfully, students must understand the following:

▲ The sum of the measures of the angles in a triangle is 180°.

▲ Vertical angles are congruent.

▲ The measure of a straight angle is 180°.

Note that the activity contains two worksheets, 2–8A and 2–8B. Worksheet 2–8A provides examples that illustrate the process involved in finding the measures of angles. You may wish to do this worksheet as a class activity. Worksheet 2–8B is designed for students working on their own, using the same procedures.

1. Introduce the activity by explaining that deductive reasoning can be used to find the measures of some angles in a triangle, provided you have sufficient information. For example, since the sum of the measures of the angles of every triangle equals 180°, you can always find the measure of the third angle if you know the measures of the other two.

2. Distribute copies of Worksheet 2–8A and review the instructions with your students. Depending on your class, you may have your students complete the worksheet alone or as a class activity.

3. Hand out Worksheet 2–8B and review the instructions with your students. Explain that students should apply their knowledge of triangles to complete the worksheet.

Activity 2–8   *(Cont'd)*

Answer Key

Worksheet 2–8A—accept reasonable explanations: **a.** 66;   **b.** 114;   **c.** 75;   **d.** 105;
e. 105;   **f.** 10;   **g.** 85;   **h.** 56;   **i.** 37

Worksheet 2–8B:

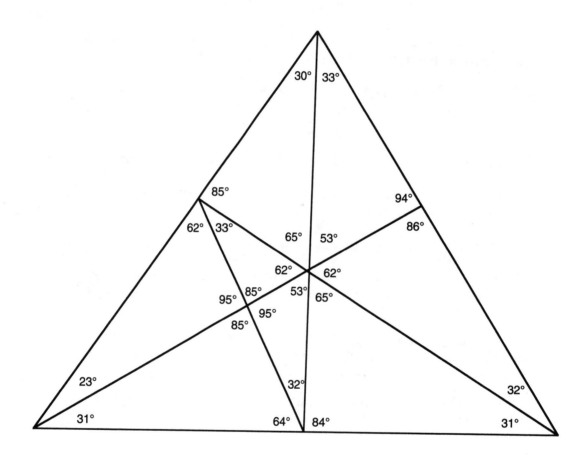

Name ______________________________ Date ____________ Section _____

2–8A Angles of Triangles

When you know some facts about specific triangles, you can often deduce other facts. This is particularly true of angles. Knowing the following facts can help you to find the measures of the angles *a* to *i* in the figure below.

- ▲ The sum of the measures of the angles in a triangle equals 180°.
- ▲ Vertical angles are congruent.
- ▲ The measure of a straight angle is 180°.

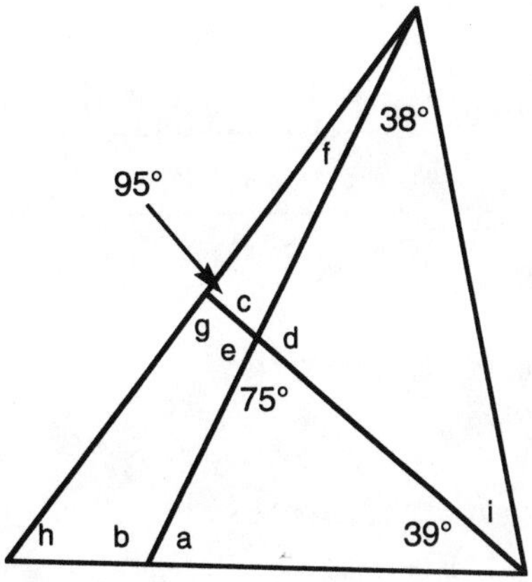

Answer the following.

1. The measure of ∠a is ______ because ______________________________

____

2. The measure of ∠b is ______ because ______________________________

____

3. The measure of ∠c is ______ because ______________________________

____

4. The measure of ∠d is ______ because ______________________________

____

5. The measure of ∠e is ______ because ______________________________

____

6. The measure of ∠f is _____ because _____

   _____

7. The measure of ∠g is _____ because _____

   _____

8. The measure of ∠h is _____ because _____

   _____

9. The measure of ∠i is _____ because _____

   _____

2–8B Angles of Triangles

Knowing some facts about specific triangles can help you to deduce other facts. Study the triangles below. Decide which measures of the angles you can find, then calculate these measures. Record your answer near the vertex. Follow the same procedure until you have found the measure of each angle. (Do not use your protractor.)

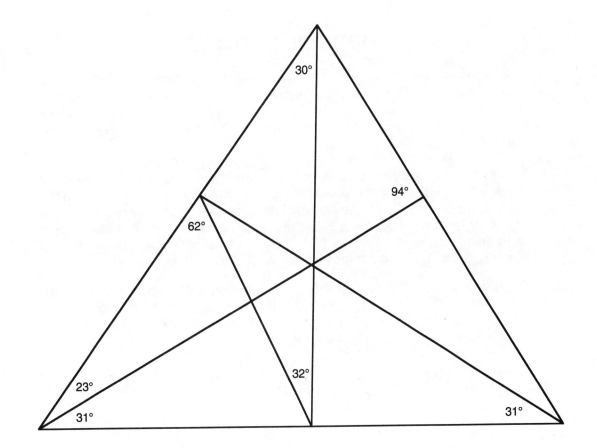

THE PYTHAGOREAN THEOREM

Objective: Students will find the missing leg or hypotenuse of a right triangle by using the Pythagorean Theorem. Students should work individually to complete this activity.

Special Materials: none; *optional*—calculators

TEACHING NOTES

The Pythagorean Theorem is perhaps one of the most important theorems in geometry, because it expresses a fundamental relationship between the legs and hypotenuse of a right triangle. This activity is designed to be an introduction to the Pythagorean Theorem and uses only whole numbers for the lengths of legs and the hypotenuse.

1. Introduce the activity by explaining that in the 6th century B.C., Pythagoras, a Greek mathematician and philosopher, discovered a relationship between the hypotenuse of a right triangle and the legs. Emphasize that the hypotenuse is the side opposite the right angle. The relationship, or Pythagorean Theorem, is expressed in the formula $a^2 + b^2 = c^2$. a and b represent the lengths of the legs of the right triangle and c stands for the length of the hypotenuse.

2. Distribute copies of Worksheet 2–9 and review the instructions with your students. Be sure that students understand the example and the use of exponents. Depending on your class, you may want to do the first problem as a class activity.

Answer Key

1. a = 6; **2.** a = 27; **3.** b = 21; **4.** c = 30; **5.** a = 18; **6.** a = 24; **7.** c = 15; **8.** a = 12;
9. a = 3; **10.** a = 9

2–9   The Pythagorean Theorem

The Pythagorean Theorem is a famous theorem in geometry. It is named after Pythagoras, the Greek philosopher and mathematician who lived in the 6th century B.C. The theorem describes a special relationship between the legs and hypotenuse of a right triangle and states that $a^2 + b^2 = c^2$. a and b represent the lengths of the legs of the triangle and c represents the hypotenuse.

In any right triangle, the *hypotenuse* is the side opposite the right angle. It is also the longest side. The *legs* are the other two sides. See the figure below.

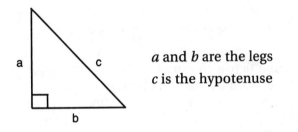

a and b are the legs

c is the hypotenuse

Find the lengths of the missing sides of the right triangles below.

1. b = 8,   c = 10

2. b = 36,   c = 45

3. a = 20,   c = 29

4. a = 18,   b = 24

5. b = 80,   c = 82

6. b = 45,   c = 51

7. a = 9,   b = 12

8. b = 35,   c = 37

9. b = 4,   c = 5

10. b = 40,   c = 41

POLYOMINOES

Objective: Students will form arrangements of trominoes, tetrominoes, and pentominoes. Students should work individually or in pairs to complete this activity.

Special Materials: construction paper cut into 2-inch squares (five squares per student), unlined paper; if students are to cut their own squares, you will also need scissors and rulers

TEACHING NOTES

A polyomino is a plane figure comprised of congruent squares connected to each other in a way that each square shares at least one side with one other square. This activity invites students to determine the possible arrangements of squares in a polyomino.

1. Prior to beginning the activity, you might want to make 2-inch squares from construction paper for your students. You will need at least five squares per student. An easy way to make the squares is to divide sheets of construction paper into 2-inch strips and cut the strips with a paper cutter. Then divide the strips into 2-inch squares and cut several strips at once. If you have the class time, students can cut sheets of construction paper into squares, using rulers and scissors.

2. Introduce this activity by discussing things made of squares—a checkerboard, floor tiles, dominoes, and bingo cards are some examples. Ask students to name more.

3. Distribute copies of Worksheet 2–10 and review the instructions with your students. Discuss the example and make certain that students understand why some arrangements of squares are polyominoes and others are not. Emphasize that "polyomino" is a general name, while monominoes, dominoes, and trominoes are special types of polyominoes.

4. Point out that rotations and reflections of an arrangement do not count as additional arrangements. For example, the two squares of a domino played horizontally is the same arrangement as the two squares played vertically. Remind students that once they have used their squares to find the arrangements of polyominoes, they are to sketch their findings on unlined paper.

Activity 2–10   *(Cont'd)*

Answer Key

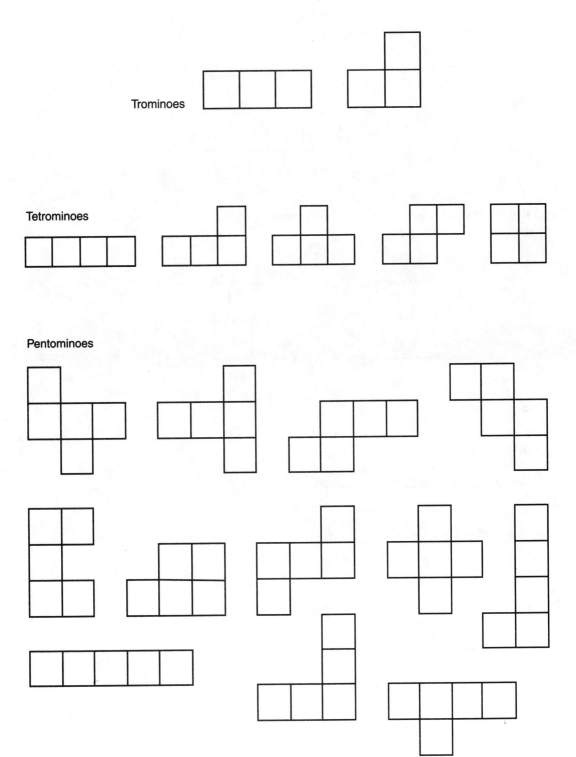

Trominoes

Tetrominoes

Pentominoes

2–10 Polyominoes

A *polyomino* is a plane figure made up of congruent squares that are connected to each other in a way that each square shares at least one side with one other square.
  Below are polyominoes made from four squares.

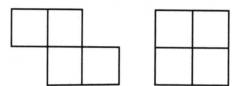

The two examples below are *not* polyominoes because not all the squares share a side with at least one other square.

There are different types of polyominoes. They are grouped according to the number of squares that are joined together.

  ▲ A *monomino* consists of one square.

  ▲ A *domino* consists of two squares.

  ▲ A *tromino* consists of three squares.

  ▲ A *tetromino* consists of four squares.

  ▲ A *pentomino* consists of five squares.

In this activity, you will use 2-inch squares to form the arrangements of polyominoes. After you have found the arrangements, sketch them on unlined paper.
  Because a monomino consists of only one square, there can be only one arrangement.

A domino, consisting of two squares, also has only one arrangement.

Find and sketch the arrangements of the following polyominoes.

1. Trominoes: 2 arrangements

2. Tetrominoes: 5 arrangements

3. Pentominoes: 12 arrangements

TETRIS SHAPES

Objective: Students will identify rotations of the Tetris shapes. Students should work individually to complete this activity.

Special Materials: none; *optional*—unlined paper, rulers, and scissors for students who may need to create the Tetris shapes so that they can manipulate them

TEACHING NOTES

Tetris is an electronic game that most students have played and many probably own. Despite its popularity, few students connect it to geometry.

1. Introduce this activity by asking your students how many of them have ever played Tetris. Most probably have, and they will likely be happy to explain the game for you. Share with your students some examples of geometry in Tetris. The game is played with seven shapes (illustrated on Worksheet 2–11) on a 9×20 grid comprised of 180 squares. One of the shapes is randomly generated by the computer, and the player must move the shape by rotating it, moving it to the left or right, and/or moving it to the bottom of the screen where it will fit a specific spot. The object of the game is to fill the grid entirely without leaving any open squares. As each row is filled, the completed row vanishes. The process continues and progresses to various levels. At each successive level, the computer generates the shapes at a faster pace.

2. Distribute copies of Worksheet 2–11 and review the instructions with your students. Explain that for this activity, students will be provided with completed rows similar to a Tetris screen, and they must explain which Tetris shape was used and if and how it was rotated. Note that the first seven do not require rotations. For students who might have trouble visualizing the shapes, you should provide blank paper, rulers, and scissors so that they may create a model and use that to determine the rotations. Also, make sure that students understand the difference between a clockwise rotation and a counterclockwise one. Note that in some cases more than one answer is possible.

Answer Key

2. G

3. E

4. A

5. D

6. B

7. F

9. F 90° counterclockwise or 270° clockwise

10. C 180° counterclockwise or 180° clockwise

11. A 90° counterclockwise or 90° clockwise

12. C 270° counterclockwise or 90° clockwise

13. F 270° counterclockwise or 90° clockwise

14. F 180° counterclockwise or 180° clockwise

15. G 180° counterclockwise or 180° clockwise

2–11   Tetris Shapes

In the computer game Tetris, a computer generates one of seven basic shapes. Each shape is illustrated below and labeled A through G for reference.

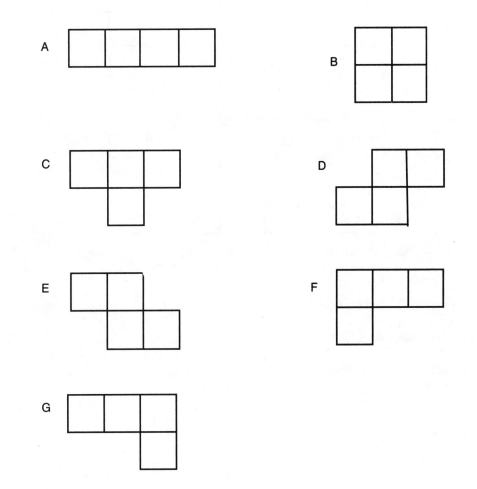

After a figure is generated, it may be rotated 90° clockwise (to the right) or 90° counterclockwise (to the left) or in multiples of 90°. It may also be moved or translated to the left or right and down. The object is to use Tetris shapes to fill complete rows at the bottom of the screen, leaving no squares open. The computer generates the shapes randomly, and the player must fit them into the correct place at the bottom.

In this activity, you are provided with a completed Tetris screen. Each shape on the grid is numbered 1 to 15. You must explain which Tetris shape labeled A to G was used to match each numbered shape. For some you must also determine how many degrees it was rotated and in what direction. You do not have to state the translations.

Problems 1 and 8 are completed for you. Do the other problems in a similar manner.

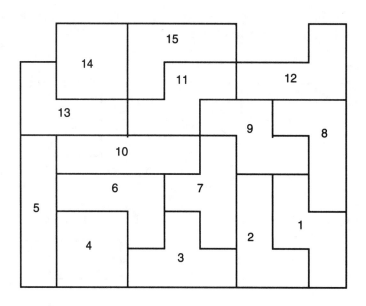

1. Shape 4 was obtained from Shape B.

2. Shape 6 was obtained from Shape _____

3. Shape 9 was obtained from Shape _____

4. Shape 10 was obtained from Shape _____

5. Shape 11 was obtained from Shape _____

6. Shape 14 was obtained from Shape _____

7. Shape 15 was obtained from Shape _____

8. Shape 1 was obtained by rotating Shape D 90° counterclockwise or 270° clockwise, or 90° clockwise or 270° counterclockwise.

9. Shape 2 was obtained by rotating Shape _____

_____

10. Shape 3 was obtained by rotating Shape _____

_____

11. Shape 5 was obtained by rotating Shape _____

    _____

12. Shape 7 was obtained by rotating Shape _____

    _____

13. Shape 8 was obtained by rotating Shape _____

    _____

14. Shape 12 was obtained by rotating Shape _____

    _____

15. Shape 13 was obtained by rotating Shape _____

    _____

MAGIC SQUARES

Objective: Students will complete magic squares. Students should work individually to complete this activity.

Special Materials: none; *optional*—calculators

TEACHING NOTES

Magic squares are arrangements of numbers in the shape of a square. The numbers are placed in such a way that when they are added down each column, across each row, or along diagonals, the sums are equal. Magic squares provide a bridge between geometry and math puzzles.

1. Introduce this activity by explaining what a magic square is. You might also mention that the first example of a magic square has been found in an ancient Chinese document that was written around the year 2200 B.C. Apparently the ancient Chinese enjoyed math puzzles. Ask your students to name some modern games based on combinations of squares. Some examples include tic-tac-toe, Hollywood Squares, checkers, chess, and crossword puzzles.

2. Distribute Worksheet 2–12 and review the instructions with your students. Remind them of the attributes of a square: four right angles, four congruent sides, and two diagonals. Review the example on the worksheet and point out that all sums must be equal.

Answer Key

1.

10	3	8
5	7	9
6	11	4

2.

13	2	3	16
8	11	10	5
12	7	6	9
1	14	15	4

3.

17	24	1	8	15
23	5	7	14	16
4	6	13	20	22
10	12	19	21	3
11	18	25	2	9

Name _____ Date _____ Section _____

2–12 Magic Squares

A *magic square* is a special arrangement of numbers in the shape of a square. When the numbers of each column, row, or diagonal are added, their sums are equal. Note the magic square below.

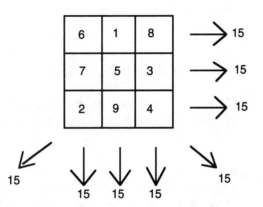

The sum of each column, row, and diagonal equals 15.

Magic squares may be of various sizes. If a magic square has three rows and three columns, it is called a 3 by 3 magic square. If it has four rows and four columns, it is called a 4 by 4 magic square. You may have 5 by 5 magic squares, 6 by 6 magic squares, and so on. The more columns and rows you have, the more numbers you must have and the more complicated the square becomes.

Every magic square has a *magic number*, which is the sum obtained when the numbers of a column, row, or diagonal are added. In the example above, the magic number is 15.

Directions: Complete each magic square below.

1.

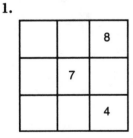

Use the numbers from 3 to 11. The magic number is 21.

2.

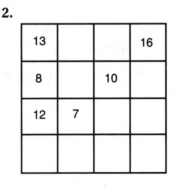

Use the numbers from 1 to 16. The magic number is 34.

3.

17		1	8	15
23			14	16
	6	13		22
	12	19		
		25		9

Use the numbers from 1 to 25. The magic number is 65.

TOOTHPICK PROBLEMS

Objective: Students will form squares and rectangles by removing or repositioning toothpicks. Students should work individually or in pairs to complete this activity.

Special Materials: 12 toothpicks per students, unlined paper to sketch their figures

TEACHING NOTES

Toothpicks are an inexpensive manipulative that lend themselves well to forming squares and rectangles. They are straight and the same length—perfect to represent line segments.

1. Introduce this activity by explaining that students will be asked to form squares and rectangles using toothpicks. If necessary, review the definitions of squares and rectangles. A square is a quadrilateral that has four congruent sides and four right angles. A rectangle is a quadrilateral that has four right angles. Note that a square is always a rectangle, but a rectangle is only sometimes a square. When a rectangle is mentioned on the worksheet, it refers to those rectangles that are not squares.

2. Distribute copies of Worksheet 2–13 and review the instructions with your students. Emphasize the difference between "remove" and "reposition." Removing a toothpick means to take the toothpick from its place and not to use it in the figure. Repositioning a toothpick means to remove a toothpick from its place and put it in another place to form the figure. Note that students must start each problem with the arrangement on the top of the worksheet. Remind them to sketch their figure upon completion of a problem.

Answer Key

Various arrangements are possible; one example of each is provided.

1.   2.   3.   4.

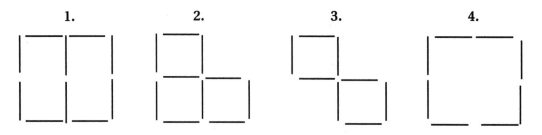

Activity 2–13   *(Cont'd)*

Answer Key *(Cont'd)*

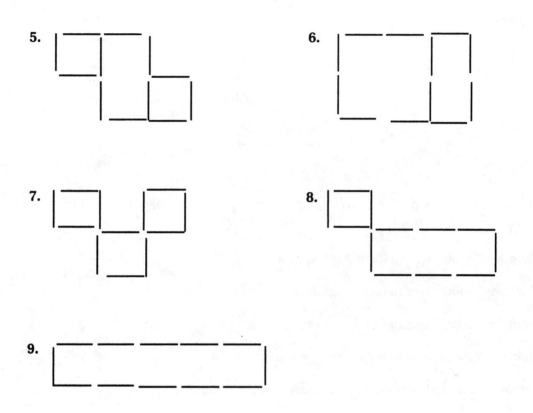

5.

6.

7.

8.

9.

10. Accept any reasonable problems.

2–13   Toothpick Problems

Constructing figures with toothpicks can be challenging. In this activity, you will create ten sketches for problems 1 to 10 below. Start each problem by arranging 12 toothpicks as pictured below.

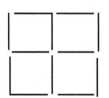

When you finish a problem, sketch your figure on unlined paper. Then form the original arrangement with your toothpicks and start the next problem.

1. Remove 2 toothpicks to form 2 rectangles.

2. Remove 2 toothpicks to form 3 squares.

3. Remove 4 toothpicks to form 2 squares.

4. Remove 4 toothpicks to form 1 square.

5. Reposition 3 toothpicks to form 2 squares and 1 rectangle.

6. Reposition 4 toothpicks to form 1 square and 1 rectangle.

7. Reposition 3 toothpicks to form 3 squares.

8. Reposition 5 toothpicks to form 1 square and 1 rectangle.

9. Reposition 7 toothpicks to form 1 rectangle.

10. Create a toothpick problem of your own. Supply an answer key.

Activity 2–14

THE CHURN DASH

Objective: Students will make an organized list to identify the numbers of squares, rectangles, and trapezoids in a figure. Students should work in groups of three or four to complete this activity.

Special Materials: none; *optional*—examples of quilts from reference books or electronic sources

TEACHING NOTES

The Churn Dash is one of the many possible block patterns of a quilt. Pictured on the student worksheet, it is simple and complex at the same time. It has only eight triangular pieces and nine squares, yet many sizes and shapes of geometric figures are formed.

Note that this activity can require some time. You might prefer to begin it in class, but have students complete it over a few class sessions or on their own.

1. Introduce this activity by explaining that quilting is the process of stitching together two layers of fabric filled with cotton or a similar substance. Quilted fabrics originally were used as clothing, and in time came to be used as bedcovers. Quilting originated in the ancient world and has enjoyed popularity through the ages. To make their quilts distinctive, many quilters design elaborate and intricate patterns. Quilts remain popular today, and it is likely that quilts may be found in the homes of many of your students.

2. Distribute copies of Worksheet 2–14 and review the instructions with your students. Explain that they should refer to the diagram of the Churn Dash block to answer the questions on the worksheet. It is best to do the first question as a class activity to be sure that students understand what is expected of them.

3. If necessary, remind students of the definitions of squares, rectangles, and trapezoids. Squares must have four right angles and four congruent sides. Rectangles must have four right angles. Emphasize that when they are asked to find rectangles in this activity, the rectangles are not squares. A trapezoid is a quadrilateral that has exactly one pair of parallel sides.

Answer Key

1. There are 18 squares. 9 are formed from one piece (the squares); 4 are formed from two pieces (the two triangles); 4 are formed from seven pieces (five squares and two triangles); 1 is formed from all pieces (the entire pattern)

2. There are 36 rectangles. 8 are formed from two pieces (two squares); 6 are formed from three pieces (three squares); 12 are formed from four pieces (of the 12 four are formed from four squares and eight are formed from two triangles and two squares); 2 are formed from five pieces (five squares); 4 are formed from six pieces (four triangles and two squares); 4 are formed from 11 pieces (four triangles and seven squares)

3. There are 20 trapezoids. 8 are formed from three pieces (a triangle and two squares); 4 are formed from four pieces (two triangles and two squares); 8 are formed from five pieces (three triangles and two squares)

111

2–14   The Churn Dash

The Churn Dash, pictured below, is a quilting design that represents the dasher on an old-fashioned butter churn. Made from nine small squares and eight triangles, a quilter cuts out the shapes and sews them together to form a large square. This process is repeated until the quilt is the desired size. The appeal of quilts often stems from the simplicity and complexity of geometric patterns.

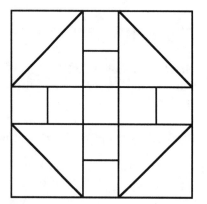

Answer the questions below about the Churn Dash. Use a separate sheet of paper for your work.

1. How many squares are formed?
   (*Hint:* Make a list of squares formed by 1 piece, 2 pieces, 7 pieces, and all pieces.)

2. How many rectangles (that are not squares) are formed?
   (*Hint:* Make a list of rectangles formed by 2 pieces, 3 pieces, 4 pieces, 5 pieces, 6 pieces, and 11 pieces.)

3. How many trapezoids are formed?
   (*Hint:* Make a list of trapezoids formed by 3 pieces, 4 pieces, and 5 pieces.)

SORTING QUADRILATERALS

Objective: Students will classify quadrilaterals. Students should work individually to complete this activity.

Special Materials: scissors, rulers, protractors

TEACHING NOTES

Students often think of quadrilaterals as fitting into "tight" categories. Their perceptions of specific types of quadrilaterals are limited, and they often fail to make a connection that some quadrilaterals may be a part of a larger group. This activity is designed for students to gain a better understanding of quadrilaterals. It is also a prerequisite for the next activity, 2–16, "Charts and Quadrilaterals." You may wish to have students save their work from this activity so that they may refer to it as they work on Activity 2–16.

Note that to complete this activity successfully, students should be able to identify:

▲ Concave and convex quadrilaterals

▲ Parallel lines

▲ Right angles

This activity contains two worksheets, 2–15A and 2–15B. The first worksheet contains a chart of 16 quadrilaterals. The second contains instructions for students to follow as they sort quadrilaterals and summarize their results.

1. Introduce this activity by discussing how students may sort things every day: sorting their clothes to wash (or for someone else to wash), books they use in the morning from books they'll need in the afternoon, or items they'll need for a camping trip are some examples. Sorting is a skill that is more important than many people realize.

2. Hand out copies of Worksheets 2–15A and 2–15B and review the instructions with your students. Explain that students are to cut out the figures on 2–15A and then sort them according to the instructions on 2–15B. Remind them to use rulers and protractors to verify the measures of segments and angles. The list that students are to compile will summarize their results.

Answer Key

1. 3 and 6;   **2.** 12,14;   **3.** 1, 7, 8, 11;   **4.** 2, 4, 5, 9, 10, 13, 15, 16;   **5.** 4, 5, 10, 15;
6. 5, 15;   **7.** 5, 9, 15, 16

2–15A   Sorting Quadrilaterals

Use the instructions on Worksheet 2–15B to cut and sort the following quadrilaterals.

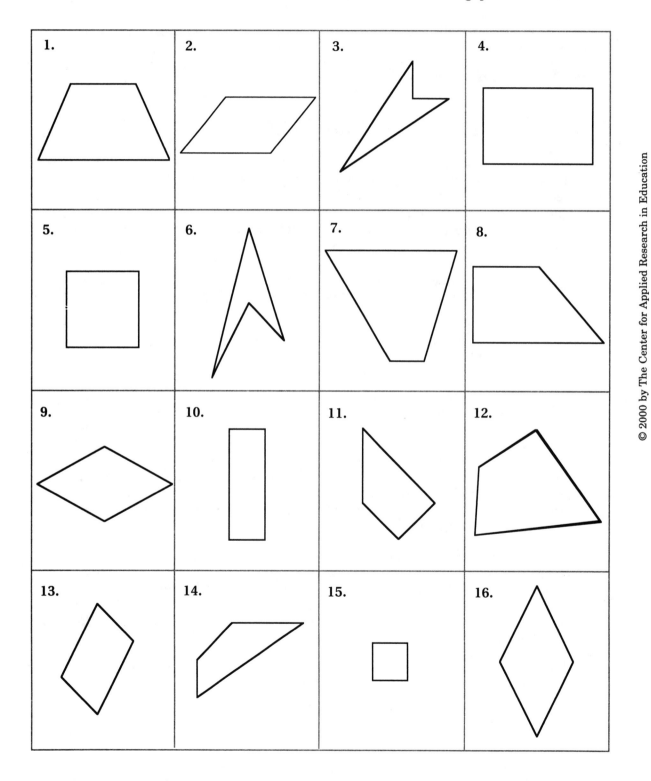

2–15B Sorting Quadrilaterals

In this activity you will sort quadrilaterals into different categories, depending upon certain characteristics. Follow the instructions below.

▲ Cut out the quadrilaterals on Worksheet 2–15A along the box lines. When you are done, you should have 16 separate quadrilaterals, each of which has its own number.

▲ Now sort the quadrilaterals, following the directions below. Be sure to fill in the spaces with answers based on your sorting.

1. Place the concave quadrilaterals in a pile. Which ones did you remove? (Write the numbers.) _____

2. The remaining quadrilaterals are convex. Place those that have no parallel sides in a pile. Which ones did you place in this pile? _____ These are *trapeziums*.

3. Of the remaining quadrilaterals, place those that have only one pair of parallel sides in a pile. Which ones did you place in this pile? _____ These are *trapezoids*.

4. Of the remaining quadrilaterals, place those that have two pairs of parallel sides in a pile. Which ones did place in this pile? _____ These are *parallelograms*.

5. Use the group of parallelograms and place those that have four right angles in a pile. Which ones did you place in this pile? _____ These are *rectangles*.

6. Use the group of rectangles and place those that have four congruent sides in a pile. Which ones did you place in this pile? _____ These are *squares*.

7. Resort the cards into the group of parallelograms and place those that have four congruent sides in a pile. Which ones did you place in this pile? _____ These are *rhombi*.

CHARTS AND QUADRILATERALS

Objective: Students will construct a chart to classify quadrilaterals. Students should work individually to complete this activity.

Special Materials: the quadrilaterals students cut out from Worksheet 2–15A; and Worksheet 2–15B (which students can use for reference)

TEACHING NOTES

This activity requires students to construct a chart, based on the quadrilaterals they worked with for Activity 2–15A. If your students do not have their sets of quadrilaterals, you may simply provide new copies of Worksheet 2–15A. Worksheet 2–15B will help students to recall the sorting process.

1. Introduce the activity by explaining that you are going to sort students in your school, much like your students sorted quadrilaterals in Activity 2–15. Using the board or an overhead projector, begin by dividing the students in your school into two groups, those in your class and those in the rest of the school. This is much like the concave and convex quadrilaterals of the previous activity. Now divide your class into those who are interested in sports and those who are not, much like the groups of trapeziums, trapezoids, and parallelograms. Take the group of students who like sports and group them according to their preference of basketball and baseball (or football, soccer, etc., depending upon the interests of your students). Note that this is much like classifying the rectangles and rhombi of the previous activity. The students who like both baseball and basketball would be part of both groups, like the squares are part of the rectangle and rhombus groups. Of course your diagram may be different, based upon the make-up of your class.

2. Distribute copies of Worksheet 2–16 and review the instructions with your students. Explain that they are to complete the chart.

Activity 2–16   *(Cont'd)*

Answer Key

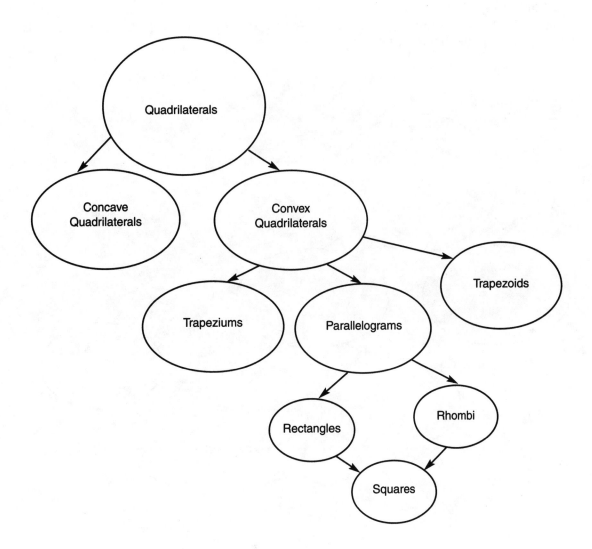

2–16   Charts and Quadrilaterals

Sometimes the relationships among groups of objects may be represented by a chart. In this activity you will use the quadrilaterals you cut out in Activity 2–15 to complete a chart.

In the chart below, the largest figure represents the largest group. Each branch shows another group that is part of the group above it. If a figure has two arrows pointing to it, then it is part of both groups.

Recall the quadrilaterals you sorted in Activity 2–15. You had 16 separate quadrilaterals. Use them to complete the chart below.

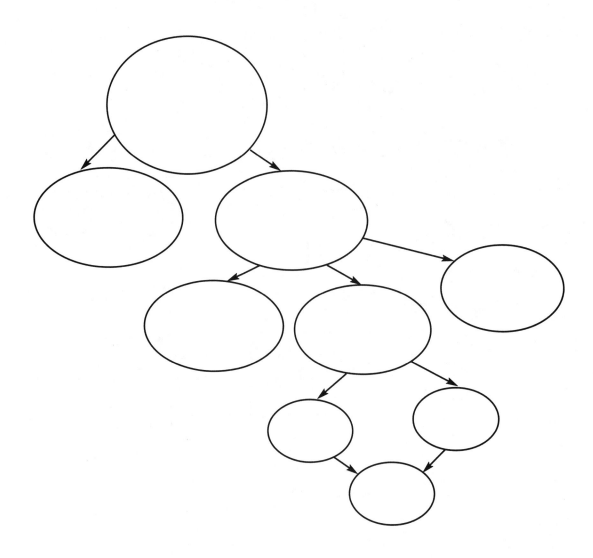

CREATING QUADRILATERALS BY CONNECTING MIDPOINTS

Objective: Students will connect the midpoints of quadrilaterals to form other quadrilaterals. They will also identify the quadrilaterals and the patterns that result. Students should work individually to complete this activity.

Special Materials: metric rulers, several pieces of unlined paper per student, colored pencils; *optional*—computers with software that has drawing capabilities, printers

TEACHING NOTES

In this activity students are asked to draw six quadrilaterals: a rectangle, square, rhombus, parallelogram, kite, and trapezoid. They will find that as they connect the midpoints of quadrilaterals, they will be creating new quadrilaterals.

1. Introduce this activity by asking students what would happen if they connected the midpoints of a quadrilateral. Would they expect the same type of quadrilateral to result? Explain that they will have a chance to find out in this activity.

2. Distribute Worksheet 2–17 and review the instructions with your students. Be sure that students understand the definition of a midpoint. Also make sure they can recognize rectangles, squares, rhombi, parallelograms, kites, and trapezoids. Caution them to follow the instructions precisely and use unlined paper for drawing the quadrilaterals. You may find it helpful to do the first problem together as a class.

3. If students have access to computers that have software with drawing or geometric capabilities, encourage them to complete this activity using the computers. Computers will enable them to easily draw quadrilaterals, manipulate their shapes, and correct mistakes. If they use computers, they should print out their results.

Answer Key

1. rectangle, rhombus, rectangle, rhombus...
2. square, square, square . . .
3. rhombus, rectangle, rhombus, rectangle . . .
4. parallelogram, parallelogram, parallelogram . . .
5. kite, rectangle, rhombus, rectangle, rhombus . . .
6. isosceles trapezoid, rhombus, rectangle, rhombus, rectangle . . .

Conclusions may vary but should note that for each problem, repetitive patterns result. Accept all reasonable conclusions.

2–17 Creating Quadrilaterals by Connecting Midpoints

Follow these instructions for numbers 1 to 6 below. Name the figures you draw and identify the pattern.

▲ Find the midpoints of each side and connect them to form a quadrilateral.

▲ Find the midpoints of each side of this quadrilateral and connect them to form a quadrilateral.

▲ Continue this process until you discover a pattern, or the sides of the quadrilaterals become too small to measure.

1. Draw a 6-cm by 8-cm rectangle. Follow the instructions above.

   What is the pattern? _____

   _____

2. Draw a 10-cm by 10-cm square. Follow the instructions above.

   What is the pattern? _____

   _____

3. Draw a 10-cm by 10-cm rhombus. Follow the instructions above.

   What is the pattern? _____

   _____

4. Draw a parallelogram with adjacent sides of lengths 6 cm and 8 cm. Follow the instructions above.

   What is the pattern? _____

   _____

5. Draw a kite with adjacent sides measuring 10 cm by 6 cm. Follow the instructions above.

   What is the pattern? _____

   _____

© 2000 by The Center for Applied Research in Education

6. Draw an isosceles trapezoid with bases of 12 cm and 10 cm and legs with a measure of 8 cm. Follow the instructions above.

What is the pattern? _____

_____

What can you conclude about any patterns you have noted? _____

_____

_____

_____

_____

_____

MAGIC HEXAGONS

Objective: Students will use hexagons to solve a "magic" hexagon puzzle. Students should work individually or in pairs to complete this activity.

Special Materials: none; *optional*—calculators

TEACHING NOTES

Most students enjoy puzzles. This one can provide a nice break from the routine of study, yet give students practice in important skills.

1. Introduce the activity by asking students what a hexagon is. They should define it as a six-sided polygon. In your discussion, provide some examples such as some floor tiles or the cells of a beehive. Explain that this activity focuses on a hexagonal puzzle.

2. Distribute copies of Worksheet 2–18 and review the instructions with your students. (You might wish to mention that depending on how the numbers are arranged on a magic hexagon, the relationship between the sums of numbers will vary.) Explain that although a hexagon has nine diagonals, this activity involves only the three that are drawn on the figure. Note that three numbers are provided on the puzzle.

Answer Key

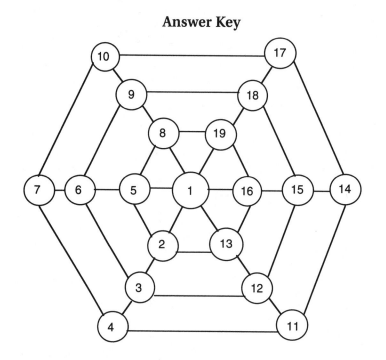

2–18 Magic Hexagons

A *magic hexagon* is a special arrangement of numbers in the shape of a hexagon. The numbers are placed in a manner so that the sums share unique relationships.

This activity involves three hexagons and three diagonals, as pictured below.

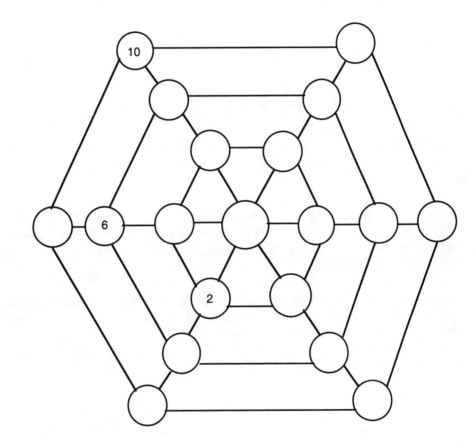

Three of the numbers are provided in the magic hexagon above. find the rest by following these clues.

1. The sum of the numbers along the diagonals, which are drawn on each hexagon, is the same.

2. The sum of the numbers on each diagonal of the smallest hexagon is 22.

3. The sum of the numbers on each diagonal of the largest hexagon equals 64.

4. The sum of the numbers on each diagonal of the other hexagon equals 43.

5. Each circle must be filled in with a number from 1 to 19 so that the sum of the numbers at the vertices of each hexagon equals 63. (Three numbers are filled in for you.)

COORDINATING POLYGONS

Objective: Students will graph points on the coordinate plane and connect them to form and identify polygons. Students should work individually to complete this activity.

Special Materials: rulers, graph paper

TEACHING NOTES

This activity centers around coordinate geometry. It combines the skill of plotting points on a coordinate plane to form polygons with the skill of identifying these polygons.

1. Introduce the activity by discussing coordinate geometry with your students. Explain that using coordinates is an important skill used in various subjects, including geometry, algebra and science. The ability to plot points accurately is the basis of all graphs.

2. Distribute copies of Worksheet 2–19 and review the instructions with your students. If necessary, review the procedure for plotting points on a coordinate plane. Emphasize that after they have plotted the points, students should select the "best" or "most" appropriate name for each polygon from the list of words at the bottom of the page.

Activity 2–19 *(Cont'd)*

Answer Key

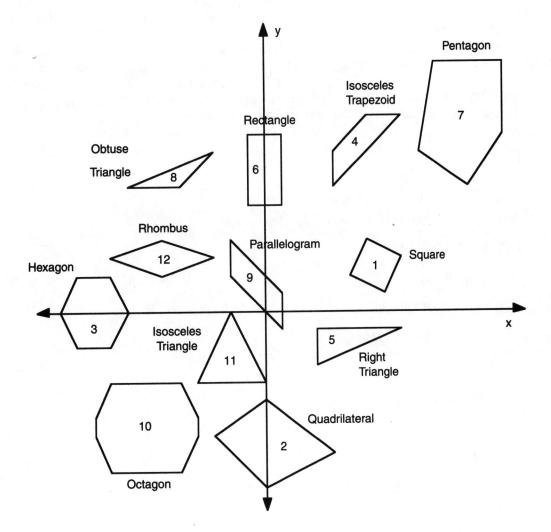

2–19 Coordinating Polygons

Coordinate geometry is the branch of mathematics that combines plotting points and using these points to form geometric figures.

To plot a point, look at the first number of an ordered pair and locate that number on the x-axis (the horizontal line). The second number is plotted on the y-axis (vertical line). If the second number is positive, move up the designated number of units. If it is negative, move down. If it is zero, don't move at all. Mark the point at the place on the graph where the numbers on the x- and y-axis cross.

Twelve sets of numbers follow. Each set will form a separate polygon. For each set, plot the points on your graph paper. Using your ruler, connect them in order from the first point to the last point, then back to the first point. After you have plotted all 12 sets, you should have formed 12 polygons on your graph paper. Select a word at the bottom of this page that best names each polygon and write the name of the polygon inside it.

1. (7, 1) (8, 3) (6, 4) (5, 2)

2. (0, –5) (4, –8) (0, –10) (–3, –7)

3. (–8, 0) (–9, 2) (–11, 2) (–12, 0) (–11, –2) (–9, –2)

4. (4, 7) (4, 9) (6, 11) (8, 11)

5. (3, –1) (3, –3) (8, –1)

6. (1, 6) (1, 10) (–1, 10) (–1, 6)

7. (9, 9) (10, 14) (14, 14) (14, 10) (12, 7)

8. (–3, 9) (–8, 7) (–5, 7)

9. (–2, 4) (1, 1) (1, –1) (–2, 2)

10. (–4, –6) (–4, –7) (–5, –9) (–9, –9) (–10, –7) (–10, –6) (–9, –4) (–5, –4)

11. (–2, 0) (0, –4) (–4, –4)

12. (–6, 2) (–9, 3) (–6, 4) (–3, 3)

hexagon	isosceles triangle	right triangle
obtuse triangle	square	octagon
parallelogram	pentagon	quadrilateral
rectangle	rhombus	isosceles trapezoid

© 2000 by The Center for Applied Research in Education

Part 3

POLYGONS— ADVANCED

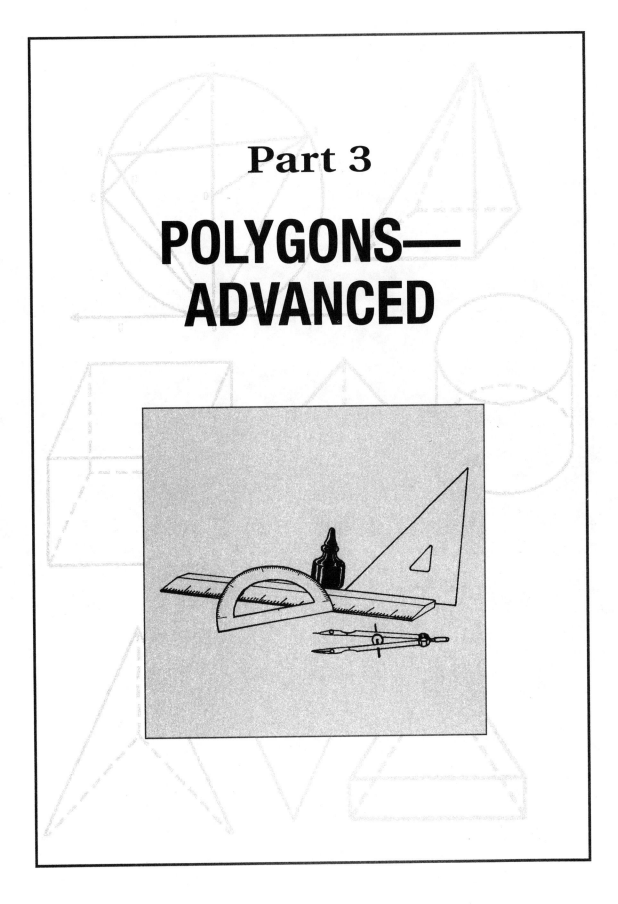

POLYGONS AND LINES OF SYMMETRY

Objective: Students will draw polygons that have a specific number of lines of symmetry. Students should work individually to complete this activity.

Special Materials: rulers, protractors, unlined paper

TEACHING NOTES

Because the sides and angles of many kinds of polygons are congruent, they can be used to illustrate symmetry. In this activity, as students draw polygons, they will also consider their lines of symmetry.

1. Introduce this activity by explaining that symmetry is a relationship in which opposite sides of an object or figure are mirror images of each other. Symmetry abounds in the natural and artificial world and is the foundation of much of the visually-perceived beauty around us. Human beings, for example, show symmetry with two eyes, two ears, two arms, and two legs. Most animals are symmetrical, as are many flowers. Many buildings are symmetrically designed because of the strength and balance symmetry provides.

2. Hand out copies of Worksheet 3–1 and review the instructions with your students. Note that some of the figures on the worksheet have just one line of symmetry, others have several, and some have none. Remind students to draw on the unlined paper and label the polygons.

Answer Key

1. scalene triangle; **2.** isosceles triangle; **3.** equilateral triangle; **4.** trapezoid, trapezium, or parallelogram; **5.** isosceles trapezoid or kite; **6.** rectangle; **7.** square; **8.** regular pentagon; **9.** regular hexagon; **10.** regular octagon

Regular polygons; explanations may vary.

3–1   Polygons and Lines of Symmetry

A *line of symmetry* is a line that can be drawn to divide an object into two congruent parts that are a reflection of each other. In the example below, a diagonal divides a square into two congruent triangles. This is why the diagonal is a line of symmetry.

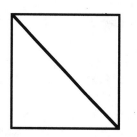

Draw and name each figure. Include the lines of symmetry.

1. a triangle with no lines of symmetry

2. a triangle with one line of symmetry

3. a triangle with three lines of symmetry

4. a quadrilateral with no lines of symmetry

5. a quadrilateral with one line of symmetry

6. a quadrilateral with two lines of symmetry

7. a quadrilateral with four lines of symmetry

8. a pentagon with five lines of symmetry

9. a hexagon with six lines of symmetry

10. an octagon with eight lines of symmetry

What type of polygons have the same number of lines of symmetry as the number of sides? Write an explanation on your paper.

FIGURATE NUMBERS

Objective: Students will use inductive reasoning to determine the nth number of various figurate numbers. Students should work in pairs to complete this activity.

Special Materials: unlined paper

TEACHING NOTES

The ancient Greeks believed that the world was based on mathematics, and thus could be explained through numbers. They were fascinated by mathematical patterns, believing that the understanding of these patterns led to truth. Among their many mathematical interests were figurate numbers.

    Note that this activity may require some time. You might have students begin it in class and finish it as a long-term assignment.

1. Introduce this activity by explaining that figurate numbers are whole numbers that can be represented by geometric figures. They are interesting mathematical curiosities based on polygons and can be subdivided into triangular numbers, square numbers, pentagonal numbers, etc.

2. Distribute copies of Worksheet 3–2 and review the instructions with your students. Discuss the various types of figurate numbers, and note that the possible representations are infinite for each type. Sketching arrays on unlined paper will help students determine the various figurate numbers.

3. To ensure that students understand what they are expected to do, you might complete triangular numbers as a class exercise. You may need to guide them through the reasoning and steps necessary to find the nth term.

Answer Key

triangular numbers:	$10, 15, \dfrac{n(n+1)}{2}$
square numbers:	$16, 25, n^2$
pentagonal numbers:	$22, 35, \dfrac{n(3n-1)}{2}$
hexagonal numbers:	$28, 45, n(2n-1)$
heptagonal numbers:	$34, 55, \dfrac{n(5n-3)}{2}$
octagonal numbers:	$40, 65, n(3n-2)$
nonagonal numbers:	$46, 75, \dfrac{n(7n-5)}{2}$

Name _____ Date _____ Section _____

3–2   Figurate Numbers

Figurate numbers are numbers that can be represented as geometric figures. They can be subdivided as noted below. (The first three figurate numbers of each group are illustrated.)

▲ *Triangular numbers:* Numbers that can be represented as a triangular array of points.

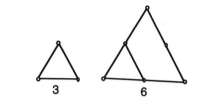

▲ *Square numbers:* Numbers that can be represented as a square array of points.

▲ *Pentagonal numbers:* Numbers that can be represented as a pentagonal array of points.

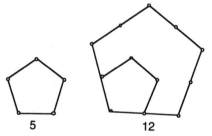

▲ *Hexagonal numbers:* Numbers that can be represented as a hexagonal array of points.

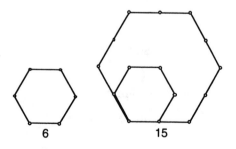

▲ *Heptagonal numbers:* Numbers that can be represented as a hectagonal array of points.

▲ *Octagonal numbers:* Numbers that can be represented as an octagonal array of points.

▲ *Nonagonal numbers:* Numbers that can be represented as a nonagonal array of points.

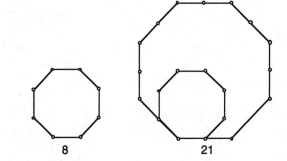

Use unlined paper to sketch the fourth and fifth figurate numbers of each shape. Record your findings on a separate sheet of paper. Then find the nth figurate number.

PASCAL'S TRIANGLE

Objective: Students will find the missing values of Pascal's Triangle and investigate some patterns associated with it. Students should work individually to complete this activity.

Special Materials: calculators

TEACHING NOTES

Blaise Pascal, a French mathematician who lived in the seventeenth century, made important contributions in many areas of mathematics. One of his most well known is the work he did with a special triangle, now called Pascal's Triangle, in which each number is the sum of the numbers to its immediate upper left and immediate upper right in the previous row.

1. Introduce this activity by providing background on Pascal's Triangle. You might mention that although mathematicians knew about this special triangle long before Pascal, it was Pascal who studied it and noted its properties. He related these properties to algebra and probability.

2. Hand out copies of Worksheet 3-3 and review the instructions with your students. Discuss the manner in which Pascal's Triangle is formed. Prior to having students work individually, you might wish to complete the triangle as a class exercise. (Students must complete the triangle correctly if they are to finish the rest of the activity successfully.) Emphasize that the rows of Pascal's Triangle can go on infinitely. Make sure your students understand that problems 1 through 4 are parts of Pascal's Triangle, for which they must find the missing numbers. Problems 6 through 10 refer to the triangle.

Answer Key

Row 4—1, 4, 6, 4, 1;   *Row 5*—1, 5, 10, 10, 5, 1;   *Row 6*—1, 6, 15, 20, 15, 6, 1;
Row 7—1, 7, 21, 35, 35, 21, 7, 1;   *Row 8*—1, 8, 28, 56, 70, 56, 28, 8, 1

1.   4   6   4   2.   70   56   28
       10   10   126   84
         20   210

3.   36   9   1   4.   120   210
       45   10   1   165   330   462
         55   11   1   495   792

5. palindrome;   6. a vertical line in the center;   7. 2^{15} or 32,768   8. the triangular numbers;   9. $2^{10} - 1$ or 1,023;   10. 1, 10, 45, 120, 210, 252, 210, 120, 45, 10, 1

Name _____ Date _____ Section _____

3–3   Pascal's Triangle

Pascal's Triangle, pictured below, is a triangular array of numbers. Each number is the sum of the numbers to its immediate upper left and immediate upper right. Some rows are completed for you. Complete rows 4 to 8. (Although only eight rows are shown in the example, Pascal's Triangle continues infinitely.)

```
                      1                          Row 0
                   1     1                       Row 1
                1     2     1                    Row 2
             1     3     3     1                 Row 3
          __   __   __   __   __                 Row 4
       __   __   __   __   __   __               Row 5
    __   __   __   __   __   __   __             Row 6
  __   __   __   __   __   __   __   __          Row 7
__   __   __   __   __   __   __   __   __       Row 8
```

Parts of Pascal's Triangle are found below. Fill in the blanks.

1. 4 __ 4
      10   10
         __

2. __   56   __
      126   84
         __

3. 36 __   1
      __   10   1
      __   __   1

4.   120   210
      __   __   __
         495   792

5. Each row is symmetric. It is read the same from left to right as right to left. What do you call a word, number, or phrase that has this property? _____

6. Describe the triangle's line of symmetry. _____

_____

7. The sum of the numbers in row n is 2^n. Find the sum of the numbers in the 15th row.

   _____

8. By looking at the second diagonal, 1, 2, 3, 4, 5, . . . , one finds the counting numbers. What type of numbers are found along the third diagonal?

   _____

9. The sum of all the numbers above row n is $2^n - 1$. Find the sum of all the numbers above row 10. _____

10. Each row represents the coefficient of $(x + y)^n$ where n represents the row of Pascal's Triangle. Find the respective coefficients in the expansion of $(x + y)^{10}$

    _____

SIDES, DIAGONALS, AND HANDSHAKES

Objective: Students will use geometric models to discover the number of diagonals of a polygon and to solve the "handshake problem." Students should work in pairs to complete this activity.

Special Materials: rulers, unlined paper

TEACHING NOTES

This activity requires students to find the number of diagonals of a polygon and the number of handshakes that are possible when a group of people meets. The worksheet is designed to guide students to the problem's solution by using the vertices of polygons to represent people and the line segments between them to represent the handshakes.

1. Introduce this activity by selecting four students to act out the scene of four people meeting. Have the students come up to the front of the room and stand in a square. Ask the class how many handshakes will be necessary for each of the students to shake the hand of the other three. Of course, you can simply watch the students shake hands and count how many hands are shook, but there is an easier way, especially when several people are involved.

2. Distribute copies of Worksheet 3-4 and review the instructions with your students. Direct the attention of your students to the example of the square and its diagonals which illustrates that six handshakes would be necessary for four people to shake each other's hand. *At this point don't tell students that the number of segments plus the number of diagonals equals the numbers of handshakes.* This is what they must discover through the exercises of the activity.

3. In completing the exercises of the worksheet, suggest that students draw polygons to help them determine the number of handshakes the various numbers of people will use. Encourage them to generalize the number of diagonals of a polygon that has *n* sides and the number of possible handshakes among *n* people.

Answer Key

three people:	3, 0, 3
four people:	4, 2, 6
five people:	5, 5, 10
six people:	6, 9, 15
seven people:	7, 14, 21
eight people:	8, 20, 28
n people:	n, $\dfrac{n(n-3)}{2}$, $\dfrac{n(n-1)}{2}$

Answers may vary. One example is the number of handshakes is the sum of the number of sides of a polygon and the number of diagonals.

3–4   Sides, Diagonals, and Handshakes

You can determine the number of possible handshakes among a group of people through the use of polygons. Consider four people, A, B, C, and D, who are represented by the vertices of the square below. The line segments and diagonals represent the ways people may shake hands: A-B, A-C, A-D, B-C, B-D, C-D. Assuming everyone shakes everyone else's hand, there would be six handshakes.

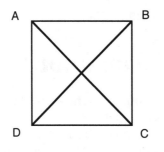

You can determine the number of handshakes among a group of people by using a representative polygon and its diagonals. Use unlined paper to draw polygons and diagonals. Then complete the chart below. (The case of four people meeting is done for you.)

Number of People	Number of Sides of the Polygon	Number of Diagonals	Number of Handshakes
3			
4	4	2	6
5			
6			
7			
8			
n			

What is the relationship between the number of sides, diagonals, and possible handshakes? (Write your answer on the back of this sheet.)

FINDING THE SUM OF THE INTERIOR ANGLES OF A POLYGON

Objective: Students will be able to determine two expressions to find the sum of the measures of the interior angles of a polygon. Students should work individually to complete this activity.

Special Materials: rulers, unlined paper

TEACHING NOTES

In this activity students will draw triangles in the interior of various types of polygons. The placement of the vertex of these triangles—in the interior or on the polygon—affects the number of triangles formed.

1. Introduce this activity by explaining that there are two different ways to find the sum of the measures of the angles in a polygon by using triangles. As they work through this activity, students will discover these ways.

2. Distribute copies of Worksheet 3-5 and review the instructions with your students. Make sure they understand that drawing the polygons in each chart is necessary to complete the charts. As an example, the second row in each chart is completed for them. Also, remind them that the sum of the measures of the angles in a triangle equals 180°.

Answer Key

CHART 1	CHART 2
triangle: 1, 180°	triangle: 3, 540°, 180°
quadrilateral: 2, 360°	quadrilateral: 4, 720°, 360°
pentagon: 3, 540°	pentagon: 5, 900°, 540°
hexagon: 4, 720°	hexagon: 6, 108°, 720°
heptagon: 5, 900°	heptagon, 7, 1260°, 900°
n–gon: n-2, (n–2)(180)°	n-gon: n, 180 n°, 180n–360°

Explanations may vary. One response may be $(n–2)(180) = 180n – 360$ by using the Distributive Property.

3–5   Finding the Sum of the Interior Angles of a Polygon

Follow the directions for each chart and find expressions that represent the sum of the interior angles of a polygon. The quadrilateral in each chart is done for you.

Chart 1: Draw each polygon included in the chart. For each, select one vertex and draw a diagonal to each nonadjacent vertex. Then complete the chart.

Name of Polygon	Number of Triangles Formed	Number of Degrees in a Triangle	Sum of the Interior Angles of a Polygon
Triangle		x 180° =	
Quadrilateral	2	x 180° =	
Pentagon		x 180° =	
Hexagon		x 180° =	
Heptagon		x 180° =	
n-gon		x 180° =	

Chart 2: Draw each polygon included in the chart. Select a point in the interior of each and draw a line segment from this point to each vertex of the polygon. Then complete the chart.

Name of Polygon	Number of Triangles Formed	Number of Degrees in a Triangle	Total Degrees	Number of Degrees in a Circle	Sum of the Interior Angles of the Polygon
Triangle		x 180° =		– 360°	
Quadrilateral	4	x 180° =	720°	– 360°	360°
Pentagon		x 180° =		– 360°	
Hexagon		x 180° =		– 360°	
Heptagon		x 180° =		– 360°	
n-gon		x 180° =		– 360°	

Show that the expression at the end of Chart 1 (last row and last column) is equivalent to the expression at the end of Chart 2 (last row and last column).

_____

_____

_____

_____

_____

_____

THE BIG TRIANGLE PROBLEM

Objective: Students will apply various theorems to find the missing measures of angles in triangles. Students should work in pairs to complete this activity.

Special Materials: none

TEACHING NOTES

The title of this activity is quite appropriate. Many "big" triangles may be found in the geometric figure contained on the worksheet. To successfully complete this activity students should know the following:

▲ The symbol for perpendicular is "⊥".
▲ Perpendicular lines form right angles.
▲ The measure of a right angle is 90°.
▲ The measure of a straight angle is 180°.
▲ Vertical angles are congruent.
▲ The sum of the measures of the angles in a triangle equals 180°.
▲ Each angle of an equilateral triangle equals 60°.
▲ The base angles of an isosceles triangle are congruent.
▲ The Angle Addition Postulate.

1. Introduce this activity by explaining that triangles are often made up of smaller triangles. This activity requires students to "see" several triangles and find the measures of other angles by applying the principles above.

2. Distribute copies of Worksheet 3–6 and review it with your students. Explain that they must record the given information accurately on the diagram, as this will help them to find the measures of the missing angles. Remind them that it is necessary for students working together to agree on measurements before recording them; they must work as a team.

3. After students have marked the given information on their diagrams, you might like to find the measure of one or two angles as a class. Be sure students understand how the measures were ascertained. If necessary, review the prerequisite skills noted above.

Answer Key

Each number in the answer key corresponds to the angle number. Thus, number 6 refers to the measure of angle 6.

6. 40; **7.** 30; **8.** 60; **9.** 6; **10.** 38; **11.** 16; **12.** 30; **13.** 60; **14.** 110; **15.** 90; **16.** 14; **17.** 86; **18.** 52; **19.** 120; **20.** 70

Name _____ **Date** _____ **Section** _____

3–6   The Big Triangle Problem

Below is a figure that contains several triangles. Record the given information on the figure. Using your knowledge of triangles and the measures of their angles, find the measures of the other angles on the figure. (You may not use a protractor. Use your reasoning skills and powers of deduction!) All of the missing measures can be found.

Record this information on the figure, and then find the missing measures.

▲ △ABC is isosceles with base $\overline{BC}$.

▲ $\overline{AE}$, $\overline{EG}$, $\overline{BF}$, and $\overline{CF}$ are line segments.

▲ m∠1 = 100, m∠2 = 56, m∠3 = 128, m∠4 = 36, m∠5 = 94.

▲ △DEF is equilateral.

▲ AE ⊥ EF, CG ⊥ EG.

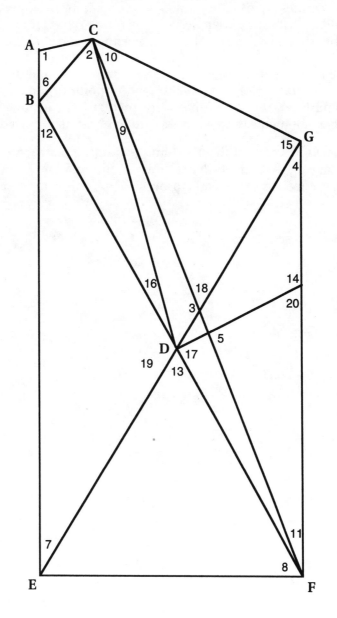

MEDIANS OF TRIANGLES

Objective: Students will use the Midpoint Formula to draw medians of triangles. Students should work individually to complete this activity.

Special Materials: rulers, graph paper

TEACHING NOTES

This activity integrates coordinate geometry and medians by applying the Midpoint Formula. Students will draw triangles with given vertices, find the midpoints of each side of the triangle using the Midpoint Formula, and then draw the medians.

1. Introduce this activity by reviewing the definition of a median of a triangle—a line segment drawn from a vertex to the midpoint of the opposite side. Offer some examples of the use of the word "median"; for instance, in statistics or the median of a highway. In all cases "median" refers to "middle."

2. Distribute copies of Worksheet 3–7 and review the instructions with your students. Make sure that students understand medians and the Midpoint Formula. If necessary, review the process of graphing ordered pairs.

Answer Key

The numbers refer to midpoints.

1. (4, 6.5), (10, 6.5), (7, 2)
2. (–10, 4.5), (–2.5, 9), (–2.5, 4.5)
3. (–.5, –4), (–6.5, –6), (–4, –3)
4. (9.5, –0.5), (7.5, –4.5), (5, –3)

3–7   Medians of Triangles

The *median of a triangle* is a segment drawn from a vertex of a triangle to the midpoint of a nonadjacent side. In this activity you will graph the vertices of a triangle and connect the vertices to form the triangle. Then you will use the Midpoint Formula to draw the medians.

The midpoint of a segment = $\left(\dfrac{x_1 + x_2}{2}, \dfrac{y_1 + y_2}{2}\right)$ where (x_1, y_1) and (x_2, y_2) are endpoints of a segment.

For example, if the endpoints of a segment are (8, 3) and (–2, 4), then the midpoint is $\left(\dfrac{8 + -2}{2}, \dfrac{4 + 3}{2}\right)$ or (3, 3.5).

For each of the four sets of points below, plot the points, label the coordinates, and connect the points to form a triangle. Select the endpoints of each segment and use the Midpoint Formula to find the coordinates of the midpoint of the segment. To draw the median, connect the midpoint to the opposite vertex. Record the midpoint of each segment on the graph.

1. (1, 2), (7, 11), (13, 2)

2. (–10, 0), (–10, 9), (5, 9)

3. (2, –1), (–3, –7), (–10, –5)

4. (7, 1), (12, –2), (3, –7)

TRIANGLES: THE POINTS, SEGMENTS, AND ANGLES

Objective: Students will review the symbols representing the line segments and angles of a triangle. Students should work individually to complete this activity.

Special Materials: none

TEACHING NOTES

Triangles, like most figures in geometry, have their own vocabulary. Some of the words of that vocabulary pertain only to triangles, while some apply to triangles and other figures.

1. Introduce this activity by explaining that the activity reviews the vocabulary associated with triangles. The activity centers around symbols and phrases that name or describe various points, segments, and angles.

2. Hand out copies of Worksheet 3-8 and review the instructions with your students. Explain that students must refer to the diagram in order to complete the matching. Note that only by matching symbols with their correct name or descriptive phrase will they be able to find the message.

Answer Key

Always tri your best.

3–8   Triangles: The Points, Segments, and Angles

Whenever you work with triangles, you use many different symbols. Study the diagram below. Write the letter of each phrase on the right in the blank before the symbol it matches on the left. When you are finished, read the letters down the column. If you matched the columns correctly, a message will be revealed.

_____ △ABG	Y. a right angle
_____ B	T. complementary angles
_____ ∠CGH	I. an altitude
_____ ∠GCD	Y. a perpendicular bisector
_____ ∠CFD	U. an angle bisector
_____ ∠CDE and ∠EDG	A. a right triangle
_____ ∠BAG and ∠AGB	R. a hypotenuse
_____ ∠CAB and ∠BAG	E. parallel segments
_____ $\overline{CF}$	S. perpendicular segments
_____ $\overline{AB}$	W. an exterior angle
_____ $\overline{CB}$	R. supplementary angles
_____ $\overline{DE}$	B. length of the altitude
_____ $\overline{AG}$	L. a midpoint
_____ CF	O. a median
_____ $\overline{CF}$ and $\overline{AB}$	A. a remote interior angle of ∠CGH
_____ $\overline{CF}$ and $\overline{DG}$	S. congruent angles
_____ $\overline{AB}$ and $\overline{BG}$	T. legs of a right triangle

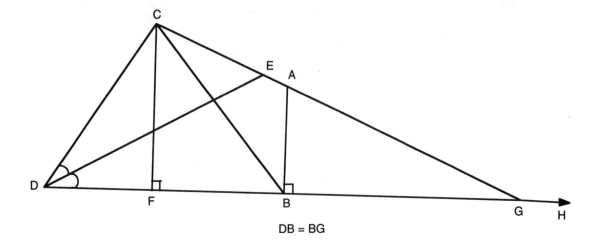

DB = BG

Activity 3–9

ATTRIBUTES OF TRIANGLES

Objective: Students will determine which attributes *must, may,* or *can't* apply to given triangles. Students should work in pairs or groups of three to complete this activity.

Special Materials: rulers, protractors, unlined paper

TEACHING NOTES

Students often memorize definitions in geometry and know facts in isolation, but they don't always synthesize the facts into real understanding. For example, most students of geometry know that a right triangle has one right angle, but they may not realize that right triangles have other attributes as well. This activity enables students to explore various attributes of triangles and expand their understanding.

Note that this activity contains two worksheets, 3–9A and 3–9B. The first, 3–9A, contains information about how triangles may be grouped. The second, 3–9B, contains a chart on which students are to identify specific characteristics of various triangles.

1. Introduce this activity by noting that triangles are classified according to the measures of their angles and the lengths of their sides. Make sure that students understand the characteristics of the various triangles that are presented. For example, they should know the definitions of the triangles presented on the worksheet and be able to draw acute, obtuse, and right angles. They should also understand congruency.

2. Distribute copies of Worksheets 3-9A and 3-9B. Review the guidelines for grouping triangles on Worksheet 3-9A. Note that the definitions do not include all facts about each triangle, but focus only on attributes related to grouping. For Worksheet 3-9B, students are to complete the chart.

3. Encourage students to draw the various triangles to ascertain their characteristics. Remind them to refer to the attributes of triangles listed on Worksheet 3-9A to help them draw accurate triangles.

Answer Key

Right: must, can't, must, can't, may, can't, may
Acute: can't, can't, must, must, may, may, may
Obtuse: can't, must, must, can't, may, can't, may
Scalene: may, may, must, may, can't, can't, can't
Isosceles: may, may, must, may, must, may, must
Equilateral: can't, can't, must, must, must, must, must
Right Isosceles: must, can't, must, can't, must, can't, must
Right Scalene: must, can't, must, can't, can't, can't, can't

148

3–9A   Attributes of Triangles

Triangles are most often classified according to their angles and the lengths of their sides.

TRIANGLES GROUPED ACCORDING TO THEIR ANGLES

▲ A *right triangle* has one right angle.

▲ An *obtuse triangle* has one obtuse angle.

▲ An *acute triangle* has three acute angles.

TRIANGLES GROUPED ACCORDING TO THEIR SIDES

▲ A *scalene triangle* has no congruent sides.

▲ An *isosceles triangle* has at least two congruent sides.

▲ An *equilateral triangle* has three congruent sides.

The above definitions are exact but often limiting. They state what attributes a particular type of triangle must have. For example, according to the definition, a right triangle must have a right angle. The definition does not mention the other angles or any of the sides of a right triangle. In this activity, you can explore the characteristics of triangles by completing the accompanying chart.

3–9B   Attributes of Triangles

Use your ruler, protractor, and unlined paper to draw the triangles listed at the left of the chart and find their attributes. Then complete the chart. Write "must" if a triangle must have the characteristic described below, "may" if a triangle may or may not have the characteristic, or "can't" if a triangle cannot have the characteristic.

CHARACTERISTICS OF TRIANGLES							
Types of Triangles	**1 right angle**	**1 obtuse angle**	**2 acute angles**	**3 acute angles**	**2 congruent angles**	**3 congruent angles**	**2 congruent sides**
Right							
Acute							
Obtuse							
Scalene							
Isosceles							
Equilateral							
Right Isosceles							
Right Scalene							

WHAT TYPE OF TRIANGLE?

Objective: Students will use the Triangle Inequality Theorem to determine if a triangle exists. They will find the length of the third side of a triangle given the length of two sides and the type of triangle to be formed. Students should work in pairs to complete this activity.

Special Materials: one yardstick for demonstration on the board; *optional*—calculators, rulers, protractors, unlined paper

TEACHING NOTES

While most students recognize triangles as polygons having three sides and three angles, many don't readily recognize the relationships between the lengths of the sides of various types of triangles. This activity gives them the opportunity to explore some of those relationships by using the Triangle Inequality Theorem and methods for classifying acute, right, and obtuse triangles based on the lengths of the sides.

1. Introduce this activity by drawing segments with the following lengths on the board: one foot, two feet, and three feet. Ask a volunteer to come to the board and use a yardstick to draw a triangle having these lengths as sides. Of course, it is impossible. Ask students to explain why this triangle cannot be drawn. Responses will likely include that the side three feet in length is too long, or that the side one foot in length is too short.

2. Distribute copies of Worksheet 3–10 and review the instructions with your students. Explain that the triangle used in the class example could not be drawn. The Triangle Inequality Theorem states that the sum of the lengths of any two sides of a triangle must be greater than the length of the third side. Since the sum of one and two equals three, the lengths of the three segments given could not form a triangle. Also review how to classify triangles by comparing the sum of the squares of the lengths of the two smaller sides with the square of the length of the longest side.

3. Explain that students are to complete each problem on the worksheet by finding the length of the third side of a triangle. Doing the first problem as a class exercise will help to ensure that students understand how they are to find the missing lengths. Note that several solutions are possible, but caution students to be certain that the length they provide will actually form a triangle. You may wish to provide students with rulers, protractors, and unlined paper so that they can verify their results.

Activity 3–10   *(Cont'd)*

Answer Key

Depending upon the level of your class, you might accept one answer obtained by guess and check or require solutions to the quadratic equations. Answers may vary; possible solutions are within the ranges below. (c represents the length of the longest side.)

1. $\sqrt{89} < c < 13$

2. $6 \leq c < \sqrt{61}$

3. $c = 13$

4. $2 \leq c < 2\sqrt{2}$

5. $c = 26$

6. $5 < c < 7$

7. $12 \leq c < 13$

8. $c = 25$

3–10 What Type of Triangle?

Suppose you wanted to see if it is possible for a triangle to have sides of specific lengths. You might use a ruler to draw the sides and try to form a triangle, or you may use the *Triangle Inequality Theorem:* The sum of the lengths of any two sides of a triangle is greater than the length of the third side.

Let's assume you want to see if it is possible for a triangle to have sides of lengths measuring 3, 7, and 8. Take the length of each side, add it to another side, and compare the sum to the third side. Do this for all sides.

$$3 + 7 > 8 \qquad 3 + 8 > 7 \qquad 7 + 8 > 3$$

Since the sums of any two sides are always greater than the third, it is possible to draw this triangle.

Now see if it is possible for a triangle to have sides of lengths measuring 1, 3, and 5. Follow the same procedure as above. However, since $1 + 3 < 5$, meaning that the sum of the lengths of two sides is less than the length of the third, the triangle cannot exist.

Another relationship relates the sum of the squares of the shorter sides of a triangle to the square of the length of the longer side. In each equation or inequality below, a and b represent the lengths of the two shorter sides of a triangle and c represents the length of the longest side.

If $a^2 + b^2 = c^2$ then the triangle is a right triangle.

If $a^2 + b^2 > c^2$ then the triangle is an acute triangle.

If $a^2 + b^2 < c^2$ then the triangle is an obtuse triangle.

The triangle in the first example—with sides measuring 3, 7, and 8—is an obtuse triangle because $3^2 + 7^2 < 8^2$

In the following problems, the lengths of two sides of a triangle are given. Find the length of the longest side to form the type of triangle named in each problem. Check your results by using the Triangle Inequality Theorem. (There can be more than one answer to some problems.)

1. Obtuse triangle: Lengths of sides, 5, 8, and _____

2. Acute triangle: Lengths of sides, 5, 6, and _____

3. Right triangle: Lengths of sides, 5, 12, and _____

4. Acute triangle: Lengths of sides, 2, 2, and _____

5. Right triangle: Lengths of sides 10, 24, and _____

6. Obtuse triangle: Lengths of sides 3, 4, and _____

7. Acute triangle: Lengths of sides, 5, 12, and _____

8. Right triangle: Lengths of sides, 7, 24, and _____

RIGHT TRIANGLES AND
SPECIAL RIGHT TRIANGLES

Objective: Students will use the Pythagorean Theorem or the properties of the 45°–45°–90° triangle and the 30°–60°–90° triangle to find the length of a leg or the length of a hypotenuse. Students should work individually to complete this activity.

Special Materials: none; *optional*—calculators

TEACHING NOTES

This activity presents students with two diagrams: a 45°–45°–90° triangle and a 30°–60°–90°triangle and a summary of the relationships among their sides. By examining the triangles and noting the relationships between the lengths of the legs to each other and the hypotenuse, students should be able to identify the type of triangle. To successfully complete this activity students should be able to multiply and simplify radicals and solve quadratic equations.

1. Introduce this activity by drawing a 45°–45°–90° triangle on the board or an overhead projector, using the letter a to represent the length of a leg. Ask students how the legs relate to each other. They are congruent, because the sides opposite congruent angles are congruent. Explain that to find the length of the hypotenuse, students may use $a^2 + a^2 = c^2$ and solve for c. $c = a\sqrt{2}$

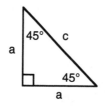

2. Then draw an equilateral triangle on the board or on an overhead projector with 2a representing the length of a side. Draw the altitude, to create two triangles as illustrated. Explain that to find the length of the altitude students may use $a^2 + b^2 = (2a)^2$ and solve for b. $b = a\sqrt{3}$

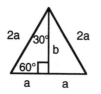

Activity 3–11   *(Cont'd)*

3. Hand out copies of Worksheet 3–11 and review the instructions and diagrams with your students. Be sure that students understand the relationships of the special right triangles, and encourage them to use this information in completing the problems of the activity. Emphasize that they may also use the Pythagorean Theorem because it applies to all right triangles. Instruct students to do their work on a separate sheet of paper, expressing their answers in simplified radical form. You may wish to do the first problem as a class exercise.

Answer Key

1. each leg = 5; 45°–45°–90° triangle

2. shorter leg = $2\sqrt{7}$; right triangle

3. hypotenuse = $3\sqrt{5}$; right triangle

4. longer leg = $12\sqrt{3}$; 30°–60°–90° triangle

5. shorter leg = 5; 30°–60°–90° triangle

6. each leg = $\dfrac{3\sqrt{2}}{2}$; 45°–45°–90° triangle

7. longer leg = 4; right triangle

8. hypotenuse = $3\sqrt{2}$; 45°–45°–90° triangle

9. shorter leg = $2\sqrt{3}$; 30°–60°–90° triangle

10. longer leg = $6\sqrt{3}$; 30°–60°–90° triangle

3–11   Right Triangles and Special Right Triangles

The Pythagorean Theorem, $a^2 + b^2 = c^2$, applies to all right triangles provided a and b represent the length of the legs of the triangle and c represents the length of the hypotenuse. There are two special types of right triangles: the 45°–45°–90° triangle and the 30°–60°–90° triangle, both of which are shown below.

45°–45°–90° triangle

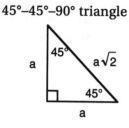

The two legs are congruent. The length of the hypotenuse is equal to the length of a leg times $\sqrt{2}$.

30°–60°–90° triangle

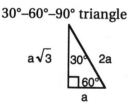

The length of the hypotenuse is twice the length of the shorter leg. The length of the longer leg is $\sqrt{3}$ times the length of the shorter leg.

If you wish to find the length of a leg or the hypotenuse, you may always use the Pythagorean Theorem. If it is a special right triangle, you may use the relationships listed above.

Using the following clues, find the missing lengths of the sides of each triangle. Then state if the triangle is a 45°–45°–90° triangle, a 30°–60°–90° triangle, or simply a right triangle.

1. The hypotenuse is $5\sqrt{2}$. Both legs are congruent. _____

_____

2. The longer leg is 6. The hypotenuse is 8. _____

_____

3. The shorter leg is 3. The longer leg is 6. _____

_____

4. The shorter leg is 12. The hypotenuse is 24. _____

_____

5. The longer leg is $5\sqrt{3}$. The hypotenuse is 10. _____

_____

6. The hypotenuse is 3. Both legs are congruent. _____

_____

7. The shorter leg is 3. The hypotenuse is 5. _____

_____

8. The legs are congruent. Each equals 3. _____

_____

9. The longer leg is 6. The hypotenuse is $4\sqrt{3}$. _____

_____

10. The shorter leg is 6. The hypotenuse is 12. _____

_____

EXPLAINING THE SINE, COSINE, AND TANGENT RATIOS

Objective: Students will be able to write explanations of the sine, cosine, and tangent ratios using the acute angles of a right triangle. Students should work in pairs to complete this activity.

Special Materials: none

TEACHING NOTES

This activity is designed to encourage students to reflect on the definitions of sine, cosine, and tangent ratios, and to explain why statements on the worksheet are true. To complete this activity, students should understand the relationship between the sides and angles of the 45°–45°–90° triangle and the 30°–60°–90° triangle.

1. Introduce this activity by stating that students *really* understand something when they can explain it. That is what students will be required to do in this activity.

2. Distribute copies of Worksheet 3–12 and review the instructions with your students. Note that the ratios and special right triangles are included for their reference.

Answer Key

Explanations may vary. The essentials are noted as follows.

1. The ratios are defined for the acute angles of a right triangle.

2. $\sin 30° = \dfrac{a}{2a} = \dfrac{1}{2}$

3. $\cos 60° = \dfrac{a}{2a} = \dfrac{1}{2}$

4. $\tan 60° = \dfrac{a\sqrt{3}}{a} = \sqrt{3}$

5. $\tan 45° = \dfrac{a}{a} = 1$

6. The length of the opposite leg and the adjacent leg are the same.

7. The two acute angles of a right triangle are complementary.

8. The length of any side of a right triangle is less than the length of the hypotenuse.

9. The length of the leg opposite an acute angle larger than 45° is greater than the length of the other leg.

10. The length of the leg opposite the "small" angle is very short in relation to the hypotenuse. Therefore the sine ratio is small. The length of the leg opposite the angle is also short in relation to the leg adjacent to it. Therefore the tangent ratio is small.

3–12 Explaining the Sine, Cosine, and Tangent Ratios

Write an explanation of why each of the statements below is true. Use a separate sheet of paper for your explanations.

Reflecting upon the trigonometric ratios for the acute angles of a right triangle will help you to write your explanations. a is an acute angle of a right triangle.

$$\tan a = \frac{\text{length of the leg opposite the angle}}{\text{length of the leg adjacent to the angle}}$$

$$\sin a = \frac{\text{length of the leg opposite the angle}}{\text{length of the hypotenuse}}$$

$$\cos a = \frac{\text{length of the leg adjacent to the angle}}{\text{length of the hypotenuse}}$$

Also remember the relationship of the sides of the special right triangles below.

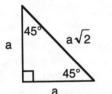

Explain why . . .

1. The tangent of 90° is undefined.

2. The sine of 30° is 0.5.

3. The cosine of 60° is 0.5.

4. The tangent of 60° = $\sqrt{3}$.

5. The tangent of 45° = 1.

6. The sine of 45° and the cosine 45° are the same ratios.

7. The sine of the measure of an angle is equal to the cosine of 90° minus the measure of the angle.

8. The sine of the measure of any acute angle in a right triangle is less than 1.

9. The tangent of the measure of any acute angle larger than 45° is greater than 1.

10. A "small" angle has sine and tangent ratios that are both very small.

IDENTIFYING WHAT IS NEEDED TO PROVE TRIANGLES ARE CONGRUENT

Objective: Students will be able to identify what additional information must be given to prove that two triangles are congruent by using the methods of SSS, ASA, SAS, AAS, or HL. Students should work in pairs to complete this activity.

Special Materials: none

TEACHING NOTES

Proving that two triangles are congruent by using various postulates and theorems is a worthwhile exercise in deductive reasoning. In this activity students are not asked to write a proof, but instead are asked to identify what information is needed in order to use a specific postulate or theorem.

To complete this activity successfully, students should be able to apply the SSS, ASA, SAS, AAS, and HL theorems or postulates.

1. Introduce this activity by asking students to share their experiences about getting "stuck" on a problem because they could not get to the next step. Explain that in this activity everyone will get stuck, because not enough information is provided to complete the proofs. Students must identify the information that is needed.

2. Hand out copies of Worksheet 3–13 and review the instructions with your students. Emphasize that there may be more than one answer for some questions, and that students should supply all of the information that is needed.

Answer Key

1. $\overline{AC} \cong \overline{DC}$

2. $\overline{AD} \cong \overline{CB}$

3. $\angle ABD \cong \angle CBD$

4. $\angle A \cong \angle D$

5. $\overline{AD} \cong \overline{CF}$ or $\overline{ED} \cong \overline{EF}$

6. $\angle B$ and $\angle E$ are right angles

7. $\overline{EA} \cong \overline{BC}$ or $\overline{ED} \cong \overline{BD}$ or $\overline{AD} \cong \overline{CD}$

8. $\overline{CA} \cong \overline{EB}$

9. $\overline{AD} \cong \overline{CB}$

10. $\overline{AB} \cong \overline{CD}$ or $\overline{BC} \cong \overline{DA}$

Name _____ Date _____ Section _____

3–13 Identifying What Is Needed to Prove Triangles Are Congruent

There are five methods by which to prove that triangles are congruent: SSS, ASA, SAS, AAS, and HL (for right triangles).

  Study the diagrams and the information that is provided. Some information is missing. Determine what information is needed to prove that the triangles are congruent using the given theorem or postulate. There may be more than one correct answer for each. Remember to supply all the missing information that is needed.

1. C is the midpoint of $\overline{BE}$.
   Prove $\triangle ABC \cong \triangle DEC$ by HL.

   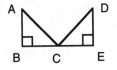

   Missing Information

   _____

   _____

2. Prove $\triangle ABD \cong \triangle CDB$ by SAS.

   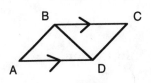

   Missing Information

   _____

   _____

3. $\triangle ABC$ is isosceles. $\angle A$ and $\angle C$ are base angles. Prove $\triangle ABD \cong \triangle CBD$ by ASA.

   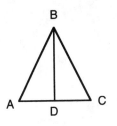

   Missing Information

   _____

   _____

4. C is the midpoint of $\overline{AD}$.
   Prove that $\triangle ABC \cong \triangle DEC$ by ASA.

   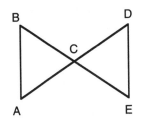

   Missing Information

   _____

   _____

5. ∠A ≅ ∠C. Prove △ADE ≅ △CFE by AAS.

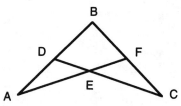

Missing Information

_____

_____

6. Prove △ABC ≅ △DEF by HL.

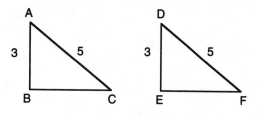

Missing Information

_____

_____

7. Prove △ADE ≅ △CDB by ASA.

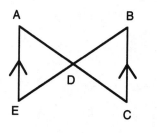

Missing Information

_____

_____

8. Prove △EAB ≅ △CBA by SSS.

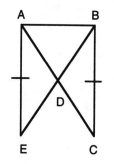

Missing Information

_____

_____

9. Prove △ABD ≅ △CDB by SAS.

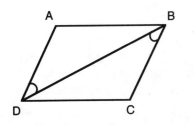

Missing Information

_____

_____

10. Prove △ABC ≅ △CDA by HL.

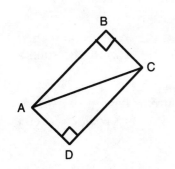

Missing Information

_____

_____

PROVING TRIANGLES SIMILAR

Objective: Students will create problems regarding similar triangles that other students will solve. Students should work individually and then in pairs to complete this activity.

Special Materials: rulers, unlined paper; *optional*—calculators

TEACHING NOTES

This activity reinforces the study of similar triangles. It requires that students have had practice working with similar triangles and understand the methods such as AA, SSS, and SAS to prove triangles are similar.

1. Introduce the activity by reviewing the concept of similar triangles. If necessary, also review the theorems and postulates noted above, as well as the concept of scale factor and a similarity statement.

2. Distribute copies of Worksheet 3–14 and review the instructions with your students. Note the list of methods used to prove that two triangles are similar. An example of a problem which students may create is included. Students may use this as a model, but they are not limited to this type of problem. They may choose to write a problem that uses the scale factor to determine the length of a side.

3. Explain that students will work individually at first and create three problems. They must also provide an answer key on a separate sheet of paper. They are to then exchange the problems with another student. After each student works on the other's problems, they should confer and correct each other's work, referring to the answer keys as necessary.

4. Accept all reasonable problems.

3–14   Proving Triangles Similar

Similar triangles have the same shape but are not necessarily the same size. Corresponding angles are congruent. Corresponding sides are in proportion. This proportion is called the *scale factor*.

You can prove that two triangles are similar by using any of the three methods below:

▲ *Angle–Angle* (AA)—If two angles of one triangle are congruent to two angles of another triangle, then the triangles are similar.

▲ *Side–Side-Side* (SSS)—If the corresponding sides of one triangle are in proportion to the corresponding sides of another triangle, then the triangles are similar.

▲ *Side–Angle-Side* (SAS)—If an angle of one triangle is congruent to an angle of another triangle and the sides that include these angles are in proportion, then the triangles are similar.

For this activity, you are to create three separate problems involving similar triangles. Provide an answer key on a separate sheet of paper. You will then exchange your problems with another student, but keep your answer key. You and your partner should try to solve each other's problems. When you are finished, correct each other's work, using the answer keys. If something is incorrect, agree on how to correct it. If the problem is unclear, edit the problem.

Here is a sample problem:

Use the information listed below to prove that the two triangles are similar. State which method you used and write a similarity statement. Then find the measure $\overline{AB}$.

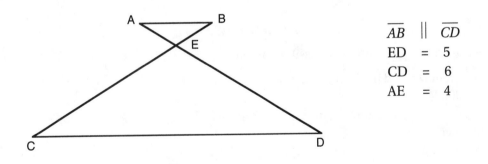

$$\overline{AB} \parallel \overline{CD}$$
$$ED = 5$$
$$CD = 6$$
$$AE = 4$$

Solution: $\triangle ABE \sim \triangle DCE$ by AA because $\angle AEB \cong \angle DEC$ (vertical angles are congruent) and $\angle ABE \cong \angle DCE$ (alternate interior angles are congruent). $\dfrac{5}{6} = \dfrac{4}{x}$ because corresponding sides are in proportion, AB = 4.8.

Now create three problems of your own on a separate sheet of paper.

IDENTIFYING ATTRIBUTES OF TRIANGLES

Objective: Students will apply the concepts relating to triangles by identifying which items do not belong to the group. They must then change the items so that all members of a group belong. Students should work in pairs to complete this activity.

Special Materials: none

TEACHING NOTES

In this activity students must examine several rows of four items related in some way to triangles and identify the attributes common to most of the items in each row. Of the four items, one does not belong. Students must identify this item and change it so that it belongs with the other three.

1. Introduce this activity by explaining that triangles often have much in common. In this activity, students will have a chance to identify items that are related in some way.

2. Distribute copies of Worksheet 3-15 and review the instructions with your students. To ensure that everyone understands what to do, consider doing the first problem as a class exercise.

Answer Key

Answers may vary; examples of possible correct responses follow.

1. All except D could be the measures of angles in a triangle. "D" should be changed to 10°, 80°, 90°.

2. All except A are measures of the angles of an isosceles triangle. "A" should be changed to 70°, 70°, 40°.

3. All except A are the sides of similar triangles. "A" should be changed to 8, $9\frac{1}{3}$, $13\frac{1}{3}$

4. All except C are triangles. "C" should be changed to 4, 5, 7.

5. All except A are ways to prove that triangles are congruent. "A" could be changed to ASA.

6. All except B are related to right triangles. "B" should be changed to right angle.

7. All except D are sides of a right triangle. "D" should be changed to 13, 84, 85.

8. All except A are sides of an acute triangle. "A" should be changed to 8, 9, 10.

3–15   Identifying Attributes of Triangles

In each row below, of the four items, three share a common characteristic. State the common characteristic, find the item that doesn't belong with the other three, and change the item so that it does belong. All items relate to triangles and there may be more than one answer. Use another sheet of paper for your work.

Item:	A	B	C	D
1.	43°, 47°, 90°	30°, 60°, 90°	100°, 50°, 30°	15°, 80°, 90°
2.	80°, 70°, 30°	50°, 65°, 65°	50°, 80°, 50°	80°, 20°, 80°
3.	8, 9, 12	6, 7, 10	18, 21, 30	12, 14, 20
4.	2, 3, 4	8, 10, 10	3, 4, 7	7, 9, 10
5.	AAA	SAS	SSS	AAS
6.	legs	obtuse angle	hypotenuse	Pythagorean Theorem
7.	3, 4, 5	5, 12, 13	7, 24, 25	12, 84, 85
8.	5, 8, 10	5, 6, 7	6, 7, 8	8, 10, 11

Activity 3–16

FIBONACCI RECTANGLES

Objective: Students will generate the Fibonacci Rectangles and discover the relationships among these rectangles, Fibonacci numbers, ϕ, and the Golden Spiral. Students should work individually to complete this activity.

Special Materials: rulers, graph paper

TEACHING NOTES

Leonardo of Pisa (1170-1250), known as Fibonacci, was one of Italy's greatest mathematicians. Although he pursued many subjects in math, he is best known for his work with the special rectangle and number sequence that bear his name.

1. Introduce this activity by writing the sequence 1, 1, 2, 3, 5, 8, . . . on the board or an overhead projector. Ask students to find the next three numbers. They should answer 13, 21, and 34. Explain that these numbers are a part of the Fibonacci Sequence, a special sequence of numbers in which each number is the sum of the previous two numbers. The numbers in this sequence are called Fibonacci Numbers. The numbers appear in some rectangles, which are referred to as Fibonacci Rectangles or Golden Rectangles. In a Golden Rectangle, the ratio of the longest side to the shortest side is 1.61803, correct to five decimal places. The ratio, called phi (symbol ϕ), results in a visually-appealing rectangle, which artists and architects often use in their work. Note that the sequence is also common in nature. The leaves of many plants, scales of pine cones, and nautilus snail shells, for example, include the ratio of the Golden Rectangle.

2. Distribute copies of Worksheet 3–16 and review the instructions with your students. Explain that students will create a series of Fibonacci Rectangles, after which they will complete a chart and answer questions.

Answer Key

1	1
2	1
3	2
5	3
8	5
13	8
21	13
34	21
55	34
89	55

1. These are Fibonacci Numbers.

2. The ratios and decimals are as follows: **a.** 1 to 1 or 1.0; **b.** 2 to 1 or 2.0; **c.** 3 to 2 or 1.5; **d.** 5 to 3 or 1.$\bar{6}$; **e.** 8 to 5 or 1.6; **f.** 13 to 8 or 1.625; **g.** 21 to 13 or 1.61538 . . . ; **h.** 34 to 21 or 1.61904 . . . ; **i.** 55 to 34 or 1.61764 . . . ; **j.** 89 to 55 or 1.61818 . . . ; All of these ratios approach phi

3.

168

3–16   Fibonacci Rectangles

Fibonacci Rectangles are rectangles whose length and width are Fibonacci Numbers. A *Fibonacci Number* is a number in the sequence 1, 1, 2, 3, 5, 8, ... The sequence starts with two 1's, the sum of which is 2, the third term in the sequence. Each subsequent number is found by adding the two numbers before it. The sequence is infinite.

Follow the instructions below to create Fibonacci Rectangles. Look for patterns in the rectangles and then complete the accompanying chart. After you have completed the chart, answer the questions.

1. Draw a 1 × 1 square near the center of your graph paper like the example at the right. Label it 1 for reference. Record the length of its sides on the chart.

2. Draw a square to the left of the first square. Record the length and width of this rectangle on the chart.

3. Draw a square below the rectangle you have drawn in the previous step. Record the length and width of the rectangle on the chart.

4. Draw a square to the right of the rectangle you have drawn in the previous step. Record the length and width of the rectangle.

5. Continue in this manner, drawing squares above, to the left, below, and to the right until you fill your graph paper. Look for a pattern and complete the chart.

Longer Side	Shorter Side
1	1
2	1

Now answer these questions.

1. What do the numbers on the chart represent? _____

_____

2. Write the ratio of the longer side to the shorter side of the first 10 Fibonnaci Rectangles you have drawn. Then express each ratio as a decimal.

      Ratio   **Decimal**

a. _____   _____

b. _____   _____

c. _____   _____

d. _____   _____

e. _____   _____

f. _____   _____

	Ratio	Decimal
g.	_____	_____
h.	_____	_____
i.	_____	_____
j.	_____	_____

Describe the relationship between these ratios and phi. _____

_____

3. Starting at the right-hand corner of the 1×1 square you drew in Step 2 earlier, draw a curve or arc to the opposite vertex. Continue drawing a curve or arc to join the opposite vertices of each new square you have added in the previous steps. The beginning of this process is illustrated at the right. If you followed the directions, you created a portion of the Golden Spiral, a spiral formed from the squares in the Golden Rectangle.

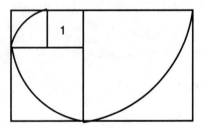

Activity 3–17

ATTRIBUTES OF QUADRILATERALS

Objective: Students will determine which attributes apply to quadrilaterals. Students should work individually to complete this activity.

Special Materials: rulers, protractors, unlined paper

TEACHING NOTES

Students often memorize definitions in geometry and can repeat facts, but they don't always internalize the facts into real understanding. For example, most students know that a square has four right angles and four congruent sides, but they may not realize that it has other attributes such as two pairs of parallel sides. This activity enables students to explore various attributes of quadrilaterals and expand their understanding.

Note that this activity contains two worksheets, 3–17A and 3–17B. The first worksheet contains information explaining how quadrilaterals are grouped according to the number of parallel sides. The second worksheet contains a chart on which students are to identify specific characteristics of quadrilaterals.

1. Introduce this activity by noting that quadrilaterals are often classified according to the number of parallel sides. Review the basic characteristics of quadrilaterals. Also review concave and convex polygons, and the meanings of congruent and parallel.

2. Hand out copies of Worksheets 3–17A and 3–17B. Direct the attention of your students to Worksheet 3–17A. Note the characteristics presented, and point out that these attributes are limited to grouping quadrilaterals. The various quadrilaterals have other characteristics as well. Review the instructions for Worksheet 3–17B, and remind students to refer to the information from the first worksheet to complete the chart on the second. Encourage students to draw the various quadrilaterals to verify the attributes of each.

Answer Key

Trapezium: can't, may, can't, may, can't, can't
Kite: can't, must, can't, must, can't, can't
Deltoid: can't, must, can't, must, can't, can't
Trapezoid: can't, may, can't, may, can't, may
Isosceles Trapezoid: can't, must, can't, must, can't, must
Parallelogram: may, must, may, must, must, may
Rectangle: must, must, may, must, must, must
Rhombus: may, must, must, must, must, may
Square: must, must, must, must, must, must

3–17A   Attributes of Quadrilaterals

Quadrilaterals are often classified according to their number of parallel sides. The definitions of each type of quadrilateral are given below. Note that each quadrilateral may have other attributes not listed here.

▲ *Trapezium*—a quadrilateral with *no pairs of parallel sides*. There are two special types of trapeziums:

> *Kite*—a convex trapezium that has two congruent pairs of adjacent sides.

> *Deltoid*—a concave trapezium that has two congruent pairs of adjacent sides.

▲ *Trapezoid*—a quadrilateral that has only *one pair of parallel sides*.

> *Isosceles Trapezoid*—a special type of trapezoid. Its legs are congruent but they are *not* parallel.

▲ *Parallelogram*—a quadrilateral whose *opposite sides are parallel*. Special types of parallelograms include:

> *Rectangle*—a parallelogram that has four right angles.

> *Rhombus*—a parallelogram that has four congruent sides.

> *Square*—a parallelogram that has four congruent sides and four right angles.

3–17B   Attributes of Quadrilaterals

Use your ruler and protractor to draw the quadrilaterals listed on the chart. Determine their attributes and complete the chart by writing "must" if a quadrilateral must have the characteristic, "may" if it may or may not have the characteristic, or "can't" if it cannot have the characteristic.

Types of Quadrilaterals	Four Congruent Angles	Two Congruent Angles	Four Congruent Sides	Two Congruent Sides	Both Pairs of Opposite Angles Congruent	Two Pairs of Adjacent Angles Congruent
Trapezium						
Kite						
Deltoid						
Trapezoid						
Isosceles Trapezoid						
Parallelogram						
Rectangle						
Rhombus						
Square						

CLASSIFYING QUADRILATERALS

Objective: Students will interpret a diagram and use it to draw specific quadrilaterals. Students should work individually to complete this activity.

Special Materials: rulers, protractors, unlined paper; *optional*—Worksheet 3–17A for reference

TEACHING NOTES

Classifying is an important skill that we use every day. We classify books according to subject; we classify tasks as "do now," "do later," or "do whenever"; and we classify students when we place them in specific academic tracks. It is little wonder that we also classify geometric figures according to their attributes.

1. Introduce this activity by writing the following classification chart of animals on the board or an overhead projector.

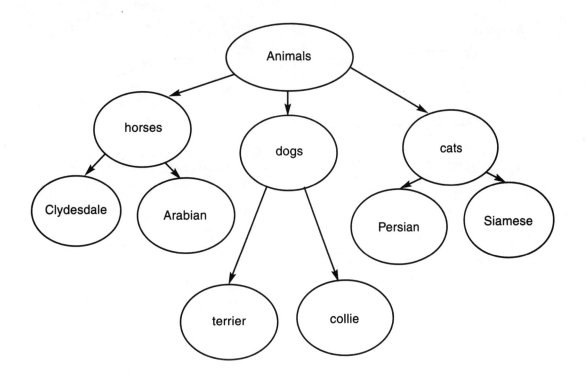

Activity 3–18 *(Cont'd)*

2. Explain that this is a simplified chart showing animals divided into three groups: horses, dogs, and cats. Each group is then further divided. Note that as one reads the chart from bottom to top, the word "all" should be used. "All" horses are animals, for example. As one reads the chart from top to bottom, the word "some" should be used. "Some" animals are dogs.

3. Distribute copies of Worksheet 3–18 and review the instructions with your students. Note that the diagram on the worksheet is similar to the example you presented in class. Explain that students should study the diagram, then fill in the appropriate blanks in the sentences with "all" or "some" to make the statement true. For those sentences they complete with "some," they must provide a sketch to provide a counter-example. Depending on your class, you may find that it is helpful to complete problems 1 and 2 as a class exercise.

4. If you feel that students will benefit from the reference information Worksheet 3–17 provides, distribute copies and review the attributes of quadrilaterals.

Answer Key

Sketches, where required, may vary.

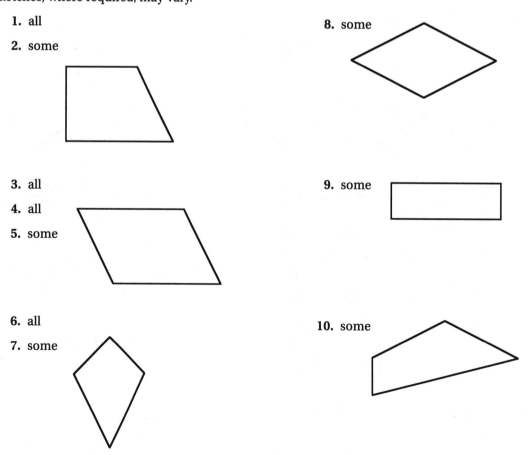

1. all

2. some

3. all

4. all

5. some

6. all

7. some

8. some

9. some

10. some

3–18 Classifying Quadrilaterals

The diagram below classifies quadrilaterals. When you read the diagram from top to bottom, use the word "some." For example, some quadrilaterals are trapeziums. When you read the diagram from bottom to top, use the word "all." For example, all trapeziums are quadrilaterals.

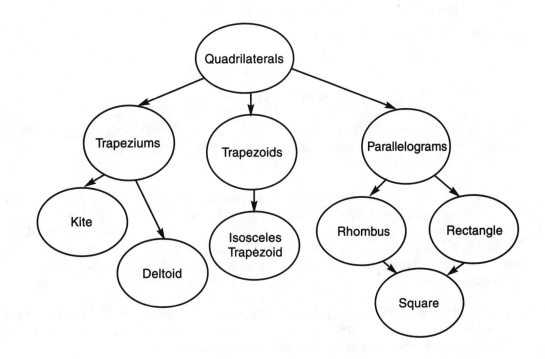

Study the diagram and fill in the beginning of the sentences that follow. Use the words "some" or "all." For the sentences you complete with "some," provide a sketch (on other paper) to justify your answer.

1. _____ squares are rhombi.

2. _____ trapezoids are isosceles.

3. _____ trapeziums are quadrilaterals.

4. _____ rhombi are parallelograms.

5. _____ parallelograms are rectangles.

6. _____ deltoids are trapeziums.

7. _____ quadrilaterals are parallelograms.

8. _____ rhombi are squares.

9. _____ rectangles are squares.

10. _____ trapeziums are kites.

Activity 3-19

DIAGONALS OF QUADRILATERALS

Objective: Students will identify which properties of diagonals apply to a parallelogram, square, rhombus, rectangle, trapezoid, isosceles trapezoid, and a kite. Students should work individually or in pairs to complete this activity.

Special Materials: rulers, protractors

TEACHING NOTES

The focus of this lesson is for students to discover the properties of the diagonals of quadrilaterals and record their findings on a chart. Students are given seven quadrilaterals to identify. They are to draw diagonals and determine if a property listed on a chart applies to each quadrilateral.

To complete the activity successfully, students should be able to identify quadrilaterals, and also be able to prove that two triangles are congruent.

Note that this activity contains two worksheets, 3-19A and 3-19B. Worksheet 3-19A contains seven quadrilaterals that students must name and for which they must draw the diagonals. They will use this worksheet to complete the chart on Worksheet 3-19B.

1. Introduce this activity by briefly reviewing quadrilaterals and their attributes with your students. Remind them that although quadrilaterals have much in common, each type has its own distinctive qualities.

2. Distribute copies of Worksheet 3-19A and review the instructions with your students. Also hand out copies of Worksheet 3-19B and review the instructions. Emphasize that students will use 3-19A as a reference to complete the chart on 3-19B. Depending upon the abilities of your students, you may wish to review the methods for proving that triangles are congruent (SSS, SAS, ASA, AAS, and HL). You may also wish to complete the first problem as a class exercise to ensure that students understand what to do.

Activity 3–19   *(Cont'd)*

Answer Key

Worksheet 3–19A—**1.** parallelogram;   **2.** square;   **3.** rhombus;   **4.** rectangle;
5. trapezoid;   **6.** isoceles trapezoid;   **7.** kite

Worksheet 3–19B—Note that supporting statements, where required, are in parentheses. Statements may vary; accept any correct statements.

Parallelogram—no, yes ($\triangle$ABE $\cong$ $\triangle$CDE by ASA), no, no

Square—yes ($\triangle$ABD $\cong$ $\triangle$BAC by SAS), yes ($\triangle$ABE $\cong$ $\triangle$CDE by ASA), yes ($\triangle$ABE $\cong$ $\triangle$BCE $\cong$ $\triangle$CDE $\cong$ $\triangle$DAE by AAS), yes ($\triangle$ABE $\cong$ $\triangle$BCE $\cong$ $\triangle$CDE $\cong$ $\triangle$DAE by AAS)

Rhombus—no, yes ($\triangle$ABE $\cong$ $\triangle$CDE by ASA), yes ($\triangle$ABE $\cong$ $\triangle$BCE $\cong$ $\triangle$CDE $\cong$ $\triangle$DAE by AAS), yes ($\triangle$ABE $\cong$ $\triangle$BCE $\cong$ $\triangle$CDE $\cong$ $\triangle$DAE by AAS)

Rectangle—yes ($\triangle$ABD $\cong$ $\triangle$BAC by SAS), yes ($\triangle$ABE $\cong$ $\triangle$CDE by ASA), no, no

Trapezoid—no, no, no, no

Isosceles trapezoid—yes ($\triangle$ABD $\cong$ $\triangle$BAC by SAS), no, no, no

Kite—no, no, yes ($\triangle$ABC $\cong$ $\triangle$ADC by SSS, then $\triangle$ABE $\cong$ $\triangle$ADE by SAS), no

Name _____ **Date** _____ **Section** _____

3–19A   Diagonals of Quadrilaterals

Write the name of each quadrilateral below. Then, using a ruler, draw the diagonals of each quadrilateral. Label the intersections of the diagonals point E.

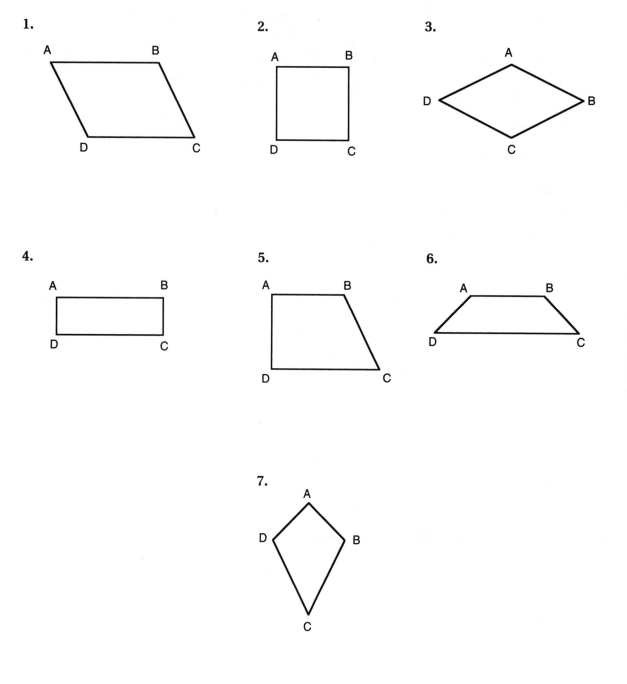

1.

2.

3.

4.

5.

6.

7.

3–19B   Diagonals of Quadrilaterals

Use the diagrams you finished on Worksheet 3–19A to help you complete the chart. The questions appear at the top of each column. Answer "yes" or "no" and place your answer on the chart. Justify any "yes" answers by writing a supporting statement at the bottom of the page.

Quadrilateral	Are the diagonals congruent?	Do the diagonals bisect each other?	Are the diagonals perpendicular?	Does each diagonal bisect two angles of the quadrilateral?
Parallelogram				
Square				
Rhombus				
Rectangle				
Trapezoid				
Isosceles Trapezoid				
Kite				

_____

_____

_____

_____

_____

_____

THE BIG QUADRILATERAL PUZZLE

Objective: Students will be able to find the measures of angles in quadrilaterals. Students should work in pairs to complete this activity.

Special Materials: none

TEACHING NOTES

In this activity students are given a big quadrilateral that contains other quadrilaterals and triangles. Although some facts and the measures of some angles are given, the measures of most angles are missing. It is up to your students to find the missing measures.

To complete this activity successfully, students should know:

▲ The sum of the interior angles in a triangle equals 180°.

▲ The sum of the interior angles of a quadrilateral equals 360°.

▲ Two perpendicular lines form a right angle.

▲ The measure of a right angle is 90°.

▲ The measure of a straight angle is 180°.

▲ Vertical angles are congruent.

▲ The Angle Addition Postulate.

1. Introduce this activity by explaining that the analysis of a large geometric diagram can often be simplified by looking for the relationships among the smaller figures that make it up. Studying the parts can often make a big, or seemingly impossible, problem manageable.

2. Distribute copies of Worksheet 3–20 and review the instructions with your students. Emphasize that they are to find the measures of all the missing angles. Tell them to write the given information on the diagram and use this information, plus their knowledge of quadrilaterals and triangles, to deduce the measures of the missing angles. Caution them to place a measurement on the diagram only if they are sure the measurement is correct. Depending on the abilities of your students, you may find it necessary to review the prerequisite facts listed above. Have some extra copies of the worksheet available for students who make errors.

Answer Key

Each number refers to the angle number on the diagram. **8.** 18;   **9.** 115;   **10.** 50;   **11.** 82;   **12.** 100;   **13.** 97;   **14.** 93;   **15.** 75;   **16.** 35;   **17.** 17;   **18.** 32;   **19.** 14

3–20   The Big Quadrilateral Puzzle

Study the big quadrilateral below and record the given information on the diagram. Use the facts and your knowledge of quadrilaterals and triangles to find the measures of the missing angles. Write the measures in their proper place on the diagram, being sure that any measures you record on the diagram are correct. Incorrect answers may lead to more incorrect answers. You may not use protractors or rulers. (*Hint:* Record every measure you know, even if it is not an angle you are asked to find. It may help you find a missing measure.)

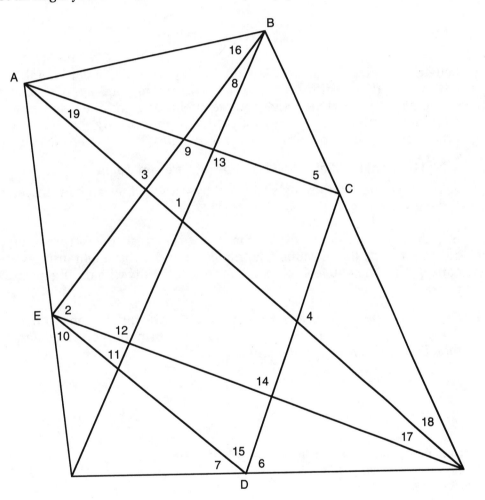

Given:		**Find:**	
m∠EAB = 95	m∠ABC = 104	m∠8	m∠9
m∠BED = 80	$\overline{AC} \perp \overline{CD}$	m∠10	m∠11
m∠1 = 83	m∠2 = 62	m∠12	m∠13
m∠3 =101	m∠4 = 104	m∠14	m∠15
m∠5 = 46	m∠6 = 70	m∠16	m∠17
m∠7 = 35		m∠18	m∠19

THE BIGGER QUADRILATERAL PUZZLE

Objectives: Students will be able to find the measures of angles in a quadrilateral. Students should work in pairs to complete this activity.

Special Materials: none

TEACHING NOTES

This activity is similar to the previous one, 3–20, "The Big Quadrilateral Puzzle," only it is somewhat more difficult and requires more skills. Because of this, students should complete the previous activity before attempting this one.

To complete this activity successfully students must have a sound understanding of the relationships of quadrilaterals and triangles. They should also know:

▲ The base angles of an isosceles trapezoid are congruent.

▲ The alternate interior angles formed by parallel lines and a transversal are congruent.

1. Introduce this activity by explaining that it is similar to, but somewhat more advanced than, the previous quadrilateral puzzle. You might also review any concepts or skills you feel your students had difficulty with during the previous puzzle.

2. Distribute copies of Worksheet 3–21 and review the instructions with your students. Remind students to record the given information on the diagram and then find the measures of the indicated angles.

Answer Key

Each number refers to the angle number on the diagram. **1.** 50;　**2.** 22;　**3.** 108; **4.** 50;　**5.** 65;　**6.** 50;　**7.** 43;　**8.** 65;　**9.** 75;　**10.** 18;　**11.** 25;　**12.** 40;　**13.** 115; **14.** 65;　**15.** 115

Name _____ Date _____ Section _____

3–21 The Bigger Quadrilateral Puzzle

Study the diagram of the isosceles trapezoid below and note that it contains several other quadrilaterals and triangles. Record the given information on the diagram. Then use this information and your understanding of quadrilaterals and triangles to find the measures of the missing angles. Write the measures in their proper place on the diagram, being sure that any measures you record on the diagram are correct. Incorrect measures may lead to more incorrect measures. You may not use rulers or protractors. (*Hint:* Record every measure you know even if it is not a measure you are asked to find. It may help you to find missing measures.)

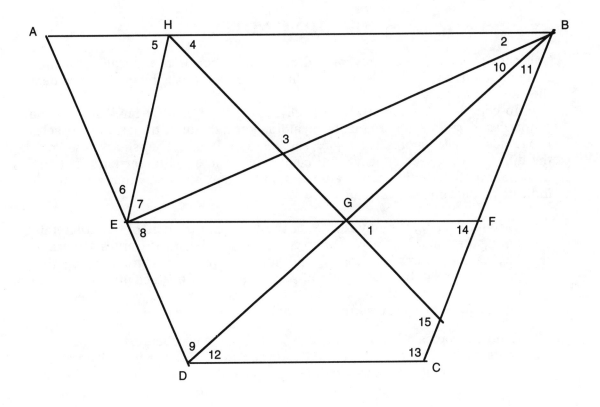

Given:

Quadrilateral ABCD is an isosceles
  trapezoid with base $\overline{DC}$

$\overline{AB} \parallel \overline{EF} \parallel \overline{DC}$

$\overline{AE} \cong \overline{EH}$

$\angle AHE \cong \angle EHG$

$\angle BGH$ is a right angle

$m\angle BGF = 40$

$m\angle BEF = 22$

Find:

m∠1	m∠2
m∠3	m∠4
m∠5	m∠6
m∠7	m∠8
m∠9	m∠10
m∠11	m∠12
m∠13	m∠14
m∠15	

IDENTIFYING ATTRIBUTES OF QUADRILATERALS

Objective: Students will determine which quadrilateral of a group does not share similar attributes with the others. Students should work individually to complete this activity.

Special Materials: none

TEACHING NOTES

This activity can be used to review and/or reinforce concepts and skills presented in a unit about quadrilaterals. The best time to present this activity would be near the end of the unit.

To complete this activity successfully, students should be familiar with the properties of various quadrilaterals, including kites, deltoids, trapezoids, isosceles trapezoids, parallelograms, rectangles, squares, and rhombi. They should also know the difference between concave and convex quadrilaterals, understand that tick marks are used to denote congruent sides and angles, and know that arrowheads indicate parallel lines and segments.

1. Introduce this activity by reviewing the various attributes of quadrilaterals, noting that quadrilaterals are often grouped according to attributes. For example, parallelograms, rectangles, and squares are usually grouped together because they all have two pairs of parallel sides. In this activity, rather than placing quadrilaterals in groups, students are asked to determine which quadrilateral of a given group does not belong with the others.

2. Hand out copies of Worksheet 3–22 and review the instructions with your students. Make sure they understand that they are to find the quadrilateral that does not belong with the others in its group, and state why it does not belong.

Answer Key

1. All are parallelograms except D.
2. All are rhombi except B.
3. All base angles in each figure are congruent except A.
4. All are convex quadrilaterals except C.
5. All are trapezoids except D.
6. All are irregular quadrilaterals except A.
7. All are rectangles except D.
8. All measures of the angles are correct except B.
9. All sides are correctly marked except A.
10. All diagonals are congruent except A.

3–22   Identifying Attributes of Quadrilaterals

Examine the quadrilaterals in each row and determine which one does not belong with the other three. On a separate sheet of paper write the letter of the quadrilateral that doesn't belong with the others in its row. Provide a reason for your choice.

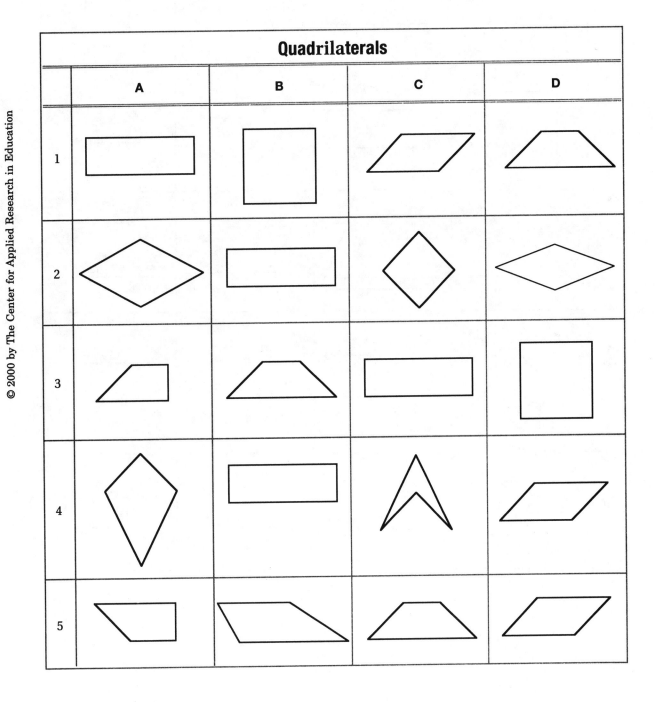

Quadrilaterals

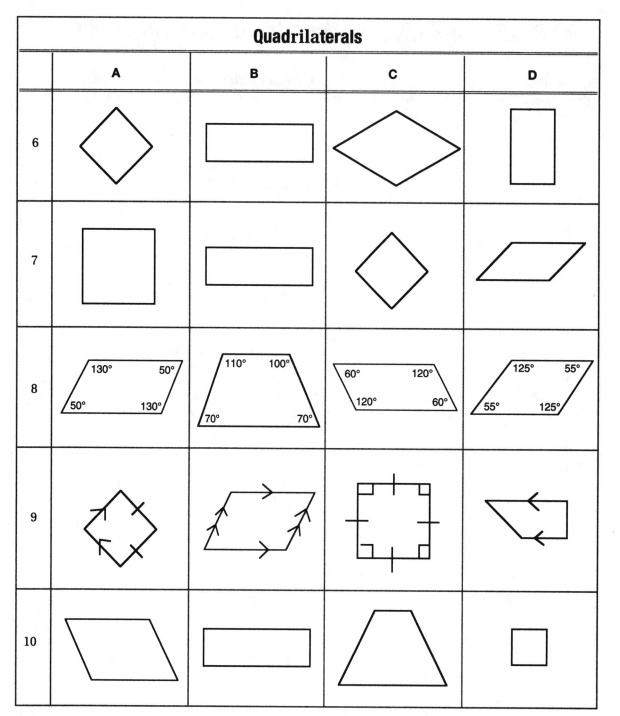

THE BASICS OF TRANSFORMATIONS

Objective: Students will be able to reflect, rotate, and translate a polygon. Students should work individually to complete this activity.

Special Materials: none; *optional*—scissors, graph paper

TEACHING NOTES

Transformations help students to sharpen their visual perceptions of geometric figures. While some students are able to master transformations easily, others may have some trouble. However, most become proficient with a little practice.

Note that this activity contains two worksheets, 3–23A and 3–23B. The first one provides basic information about reflections (flips), rotations (turns), and translations (glides). Students will find it helpful in completing the problems presented on Worksheet 3–23B. If your students understand reflections, rotations, and translations, Worksheet 3–23A is probably unnecessary.

1. Introduce this activity by explaining that understanding transformations helps people to recognize images from different perspectives. Understanding transformations can enhance an individual's spatial perception and enable him or her to see relationships between figures.

2. Hand out copies of Worksheet 3–23A and review the information with your students. Be sure that your students understand the concepts of a reflection (which requires a line to flip the image over), a rotation (which requires a point and a direction), and a translation (which requires a number of spaces and a direction). Students should also understand congruency.

3. Distribute copies of Worksheet 3–23B and review the instructions with your students. Note that they must use the figures on the grid to complete the exercises. While many students will be able to do the transformations simply by referring to the grid, some may have trouble visualizing the movements. For these students, you may wish to distribute scissors and graph paper so that they may create and physically move models of the rectangle.

Answer Key

1. 5;   **2.** 3;   **3.** 5;   **4.** 7;   **5.** 1;   **6.** 2;   **7.** 1;   **8.** 4

3–23A   The Basics of Transformations

The position of a figure can be transformed by reflecting it, rotating it, and/or translating it. Although a transformed figure may at first appear to have a different shape, close examination will show it to be the same. Following are three basic transformations.

▲ *Reflection*—an object is reflected over a line. This is also called a *flip*. The image is congruent to the original figure.

If Triangle A is reflected over the y-axis, the image is Triangle 1.

If Triangle A is reflected over the line y = –1, the image is Triangle 2.

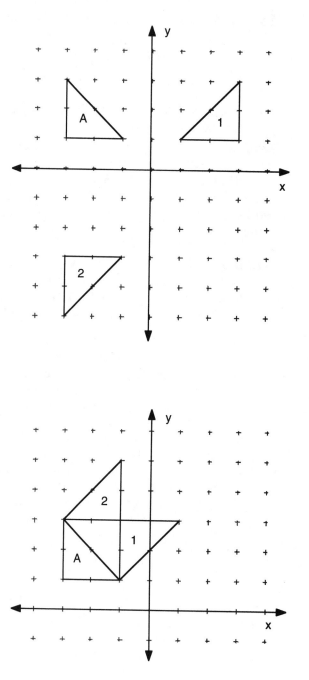

▲ *Rotation*—an object is rotated, or turned, around a point. The rotation may also be called a *turn*. It may be clockwise (the way the hands of a clock move) or counterclockwise (the opposite direction of the movements of the hands of a clock). The degree of the rotation must also be defined. The image is congruent to the original figure.

If Triangle A is rotated 90° clockwise around (–1,1), the image is Triangle 1.

If Triangle A is rotated 90° counterclockwise around (–3,3), the image is Triangle 2.

▲ *Translation*—an object is moved to the right, left, up, or down a fixed distance. This is also called a *glide*. The image is congruent to the original figure.

If Triangle A is translated four units to the right, the image is Triangle 1.

If Triangle A is translated three units down, the image is Triangle 2.

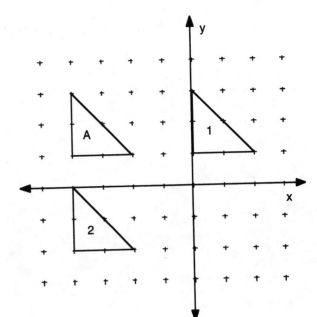

3–23B   The Basics of Transformations

All rectangles are congruent in the grid below. Follow the instructions and then write the number of the rectangle that matches the figure you moved.

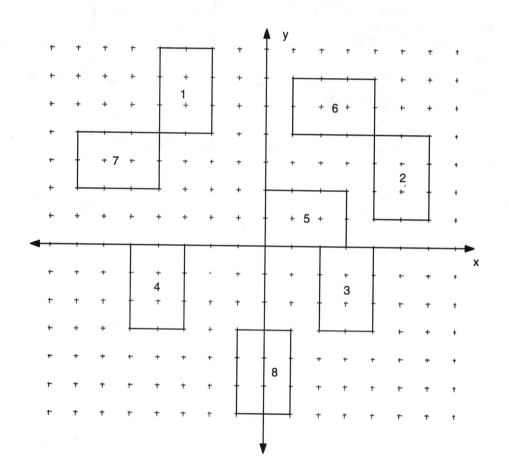

1. Reflect Figure 1 over the y-axis. Translate it three units down and rotate it 90° counter-clockwise around (3, 1).

   Which figure does Figure 1 now match? _____

2. Translate Figure 2 one unit down. Reflect it over the x-axis and reflect it over the line x = 4.

   Which figure does Figure 2 now match? _____

3. Reflect Figure 3 over the y-axis. Rotate it 90° clockwise around (–2, 0) and glide it five units to the right.

   Which figure does Figure 3 now match? _____

4. Rotate Figure 4 90° clockwise around (–3, 0). Reflect it over the line y = 2 and translate it one unit to the left.

    Which figures does Figure 4 now match? _____

5. Translate Figure 5 five units to the left. Rotate it 90° clockwise around (–2, 2) and glide it up two spaces.

    Which figure does Figure 5 now match? _____

6. Rotate Figure 6 90° clockwise around point (4, 4) and translate it down three units.

    Which figure does Figure 6 now match? _____

7. Rotate Figure 7 90° clockwise around point (–4, 4) and reflect it over the line x = –4.

    Which figure does Figure 7 now match? _____

8. Reflect Figure 8 over the x-axis. Translate it four units to the left and reflect it over the line y = 1.5.

    Which figure does Figure 8 now match? _____

Activity 3–24

WRITING DIRECTIONS FOR TRANSFORMATIONS

Objective: Students will be able to write a set of directions and follow a series of transformations. Students should work individually first and then with a partner to complete this activity.

Special Materials: two to three sheets of graph paper per student; *optional—* copies of Worksheet 3–23A for reference

TEACHING NOTES

Because this activity requires students to write a set of transformations, it is a good follow-up to Activity 3–23. It can stand alone, however, provided your students understand reflections, rotations, and translations.

1. Introduce the activity by reviewing transformations. If necessary, distribute copies of Worksheet 3–23A, which provides reference information.

2. Hand out copies of Worksheet 3–24 and review the instructions with your students. Explain that students are to write a set of directions for transforming each figure and should include at least one reflection, rotation, and translation for each. Suggest that they use graph paper to plan, or map out, the movements of their transformations. Note that the directions they write should be clear and suggest they use a step-by-step format. Depending on your students, you might find it helpful to do the first problem as a class exercise.

3. When students are done with the activity, let them exchange their directions with a classmate and try to follow each other's directions for drawing transformations. Students should then work together to clarify any directions that they found to be confusing.

4. Accept any reasonable directions.

3–24   Writing Directions for Transformations

Write a set of directions to reflect, rotate, and translate each figure below. Make an answer key on graph paper showing where the image of the transformed figure will be. When you are done, exchange your sets of directions with those of another student. Using graph paper, follow each other's directions for transforming the figures. Rewrite any directions that prove to be unclear or confusing.

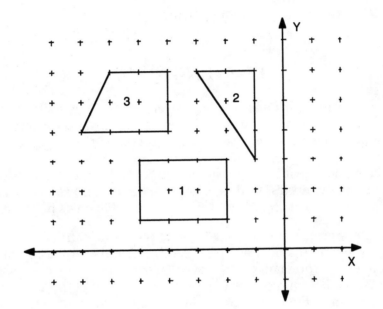

Directions for transforming Figure 1: _____

_____

_____

Directions for transforming Figure 2: _____

_____

_____

Directions for transforming Figure 3: _____

_____

_____

POLYGONS AND FORMULAS

Objective: Students will evaluate formulas to find the measures of angles and the number of diagonals of polygons. Students should work individually to complete this activity.

Special Materials: none; *optional*—calculators

TEACHING NOTES

Focusing on both polygons and regular polygons, this activity is designed to be a culminating exercise in the study of angles and line segments associated with polygons. It requires students to work with formulas related to polygons.

1. Introduce this activity by explaining that formulas are relationships between two or more quantities. In this activity students will use various formulas to find the measures of angles and the number of diagonals of polygons.

2. Distribute copies of Worksheet 3–25 and review the instructions with your students. Explain that students are to use the formulas at the top of the page to evaluate each expression that follows. They are to then write the letter, or, in one case, symbol, that comes before the expression above the correct answer at the bottom of the page. Correct answers will reveal a message. Depending on the abilities of your students, it may be helpful to review the formulas thoroughly before proceeding with this activity.

Answer Key

EQUAL SIDES & ANGLES

3–25   Polygons and Formulas

The formulas below can help you calculate the measures of angles and the numbers of diagonals of various types of polygons. In each formula, n stands for the number of sides of the polygon.

▲ The measure of each interior angle of a regular polygon is $\dfrac{180° \ (n{-}2)}{n}$.

▲ The measure of each exterior angle of a regular polygon is $\dfrac{360°}{n}$.

▲ The sum of the interior angles of any polygon equals (n-2)(180°).

▲ The number of diagonals of any polygon is $\dfrac{n^2 - 3n}{2}$.

Use the formulas to evaluate the following expressions and match them with their correct answer below. Write the letter or symbol before the phrase on the space above the correct number. If your answers are correct, you will find what every regular polygon has.

A. The measure of each exterior angle of a regular pentagon

S. The measure of each exterior angle of a regular triangle

I. The sum of the interior angles of an octagon

A. The number of diagonals of a triangle

E. The measure of each interior angle of a regular triangle

N. The measure of each exterior angle of an octagon

D. The sum of the interior angles of a pentagon

G. The number of diagonals of a hexagon

Q. The sum of the measures of the interior angles of any quadrilateral

L. The sum of the interior angles of a triangle

U. The measure of each interior angle of a regular octagon

&. The sum of the interior angles of a hexagon

S. The number of diagonals of a pentagon

L. The number of diagonals of an octagon

S. The number of diagonals of a quadrilateral

E. The measure of each interior angle of a regular quadrilateral

E. The measure of each interior angle of a regular pentagon

| ―― | ―― | ―― | ―― | ―― | ―― | ―― | ―― | ―― | ―― | ―― |
| 60 | 360 | 135 | 72 | 20 | 120 | 1080 | 540 | 90 | 5 | 720 |

| ―― | ―― | ―― | ―― | ―― | ―― |
| 0 | 45 | 9 | 180 | 108 | 2 |

Part 4

CIRCLES

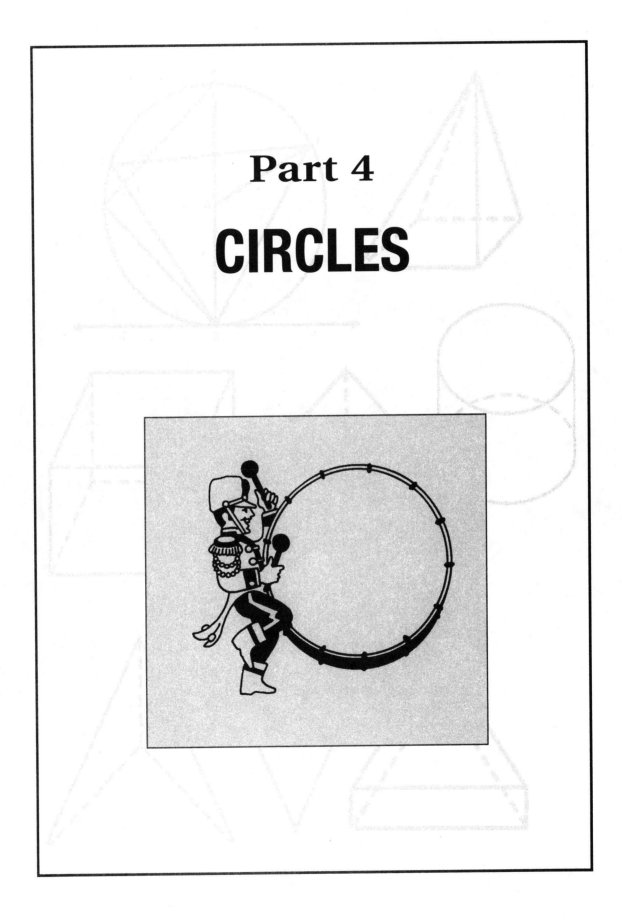

A CROSSWORD PUZZLE OF CIRCLE VOCABULARY

Objective: Students will create a crossword puzzle using a list of terms that apply to circles. Students may work individually or in pairs to complete this activity.

Special Materials: rulers, graph paper; *optional*—computers and software capable of generating crossword puzzles, printers

TEACHING NOTES

Understanding fundamental terms is essential for the beginning of any unit of study. This activity, which requires students to focus on the vocabulary associated with circles, works well as an introduction to circles or may be used as a review.

Prior to the activity, collect crossword puzzles from newspapers and magazines, which you may hand out to your students as examples. If students have already done the crossword puzzle activities presented earlier in this book, they may not require examples.

1. Introduce the activity by explaining that students are to create a crossword puzzle using words associated with circles. You might also share some examples of crossword puzzles.

2. Distribute copies of Worksheet 4–1 and review the guidelines with your students. Note that students are to use the words included on the worksheet for the answers to their puzzles. Hand out at least two sheets of graph paper per student, and suggest that students use one copy to plan their puzzle and another for the final copy.

3. If students have access to computers with software that enables them to create crossword puzzles, you may encourage them to produce their puzzles using their computers. While most of these kinds of programs will generate the form of the puzzle, students still must enter the answers and clues.

4. Accept any reasonable puzzle. At the end of the activity, make copies of the puzzles and allow students to exchange and try to solve them.

4–1   A Crossword Puzzle of Circle Vocabulary

Create a crossword puzzle using the terms below, all of which apply to circles. The following guidelines will help you to design your puzzle.

1. Use the terms below for the answers to your puzzle. You may add other terms that apply to circles if you wish. Arrange the answers in the boxes on your paper so that one letter appears per box. Be sure to place the answers down and across, trying to have about the same number of down and across answers.

2. Write lightly in pencil so that it is easier to erase any mistakes you might make. Keep revising the design of your puzzle until you find a form you like.

3. Make sure that you spell all words correctly.

4. After you are satisfied with the appearance of your puzzle, write a small number in the first box of each answer. Number the answers consecutively, one set of numbers for the down answers and another set for the across answers.

5. On a separate sheet of paper, write clues for your answers. Be sure that your facts are correct. If necessary, consult the glossary of your math text or a dictionary.

6. Double-check your work, and create a final copy of your puzzle on a new piece of paper. Draw heavy lines on the boxes of your answers to make your answers stand out. Write the clues below the puzzle or on a separate sheet of paper.

Use the following words for the answers in your puzzle:

radius	diameter
center	central angle
circumference	pi
inscribed angle	chord
secant line	semicircle
tangent line	annulus
concentric circles	arc

Add other "circle" words and phrases, such as on-deck circle, circular saw, circle graph, etc.

MAGIC CIRCLES

Objective: Students will complete a magic circle. Students should work individually to complete this activity.

Special Materials: none; *optional*—calculators

TEACHING NOTES

This activity involves two magic circles in which students must arrange numbers along the diameters so that the sum of the numbers of each diameter is the same. The activity provides practice using problem-solving strategies with circles.

1. Introduce this activity by explaining that magic circles are a circular array of numbers arranged so that the sums of the numbers added along the diameters are equal. Reinforce the vocabulary associated with circles such as center, diameter, radius, and, in the second magic circle, concentric circles.

2. Distribute copies of Worksheet 4–2 and review the instructions with your students. Make sure they understand that the sums of the numbers along the diameters must be the same. Note that some numbers have been filled in for them.

Answer Key

Answers may vary; one possible solution for each is shown below.

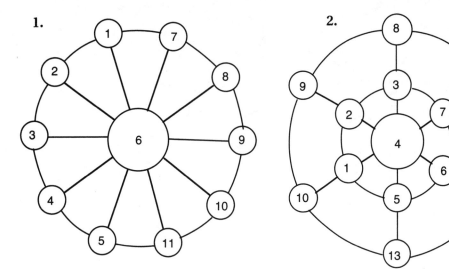

4–2   Magic Circles

A *magic circle* is a circular array of numbers arranged in a special manner. When the numbers along each diameter are added, their sums are equal.

1. Use the numbers from 1 to 11 to complete the magic circle below so that the sum of the numbers along each diameter is 18. Each number must be used only once. (Some numbers are filled in for you.)

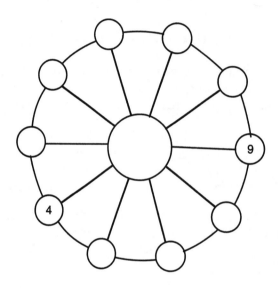

2. Use the numbers from 1 to 13 to complete the magic circles below so that the sum of the numbers along each diameter of the smaller circle is 12, and the sum of the numbers along each diameter of the larger circle is 33. Each number must be used only once. (Some numbers are filled in for you.)

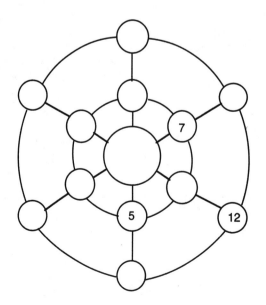

© 2000 by The Center for Applied Research in Education

DRAWING CIRCLES

Objective: Students will use a compass (or geometric software) to draw circles of various sizes. Students should work individually to complete this activity.

Special Materials: compasses, rulers, protractors, two unlined sheets of paper per student; *optional*—computers with software capable of drawing circles with a specific radius and diameter, printers

TEACHING NOTES

Although many of your students are no doubt bright kids, handing them a compass and telling them to draw a circle with a radius of two inches may result in class-wide confusion. This activity focuses on the practical skills necessary for drawing circles. If your students have access to computers with geometric software that is capable of drawing circles of specific sizes, you may want students to work with the software. However, we suggest that you first have them use compasses to draw their circles. The hands-on experience is valuable for virtually all students.

1. Introduce this activity by showing students a compass. If possible, show them one of the old "wooden" models used for drawing circles on the board and demonstrate its use. (If you don't have one of these, simply walk around the classroom and show them a smaller model.) Depending on your students, you may need to show some of them individually how to work with a compass.

2. Hand out copies of Worksheet 4–3 and review the instructions with your students. Make sure they understand the definitions on the worksheet and remind them to follow the directions carefully. Depending on your students, you may want to do the first problem as a class activity.

Answer Key

1. check students' drawings;   **2.** circles have same size and shape;   **3.** an infinite number;   **4.** yes;   **5.** yes, if the circles have the same center; no, if the circles have different centers;   **6.** yes or no, depending upon how the circles are drawn

4–3   Drawing Circles

A *circle* is a set of all points in a plane that are equidistant from a center point. Following are some important terms that apply to circles.

▲ *center*—the point from which every point on the circle is equidistant.

▲ *radius*—a line segment drawn from the center point to the circle.

▲ *diameter*—a line segment whose endpoints are on the circle and contain the center point.

▲ *concentric circles*—two or more circles in the same plane that have the same center.

▲ *tangent circles*—two or more circles in the same plane that have one common point.

Draw the following circles on unlined paper and answer the questions.

1. Draw a circle with a 2-inch radius.

2. Draw a circle with a 4-inch diameter. How are the circles you drew in numbers 1 and 2 related? _____

3. Draw two concentric circles. How many more circles can be drawn that are concentric to these two? _____

4. Draw a 3-inch square. Draw one circle inside the square so that the circle "touches" each side of the square. Draw another circle around the outside of the square so that it touches each vertex of the square. Are these circles concentric? _____

5. Draw another 3-inch square. Draw a circle anywhere inside the square, and draw a circle around the outside of the square. Are these circles concentric? _____

   Explain your answer. _____

   _____

   _____

6. Draw a 2- by 4-inch rectangle. Draw three circles inside the rectangle. Are these circles concentric? _____ Explain your answer. _____

   _____

   _____

   _____

Activity 4–4

CIRCLES AND SYMMETRY

Objective: Students will shade sectors of a circle to produce designs that have lines of symmetry and rotational symmetry. Students should work in pairs to complete this activity.

Special Materials: colored pencils (4 for each pair of students), compasses, rulers, protractors, scissors, unlined paper

TEACHING NOTES

Circles can be used to demonstrate examples of symmetry. Each diameter, for example, is a line of symmetry. Many common circular objects are symmetric, including Ferris wheels, wheels of chance, hubcaps, bicycle tires, and the steering wheels of many cars.

1. Introduce this activity by drawing a circle with its diameter extending from the top of the circle to the bottom on the board or on an overhead projector. Explain that the diameter is a vertical line of symmetry because both parts of the circle are mirror images of each other. Now draw another circle with the diameter drawn horizontally. Explain that this is also a line of symmetry because both parts of the circle are mirror images of each other.

2. Draw the well-known peace sign on the board. Ask your students if it has a vertical or horizontal line of symmetry. (It has only a vertical line of symmetry.) Explain that it also has rotational symmetry, because after a rotation every point coincides with the original shape. Since three rotations result in the original position, the peace sign has rotational symmetry of order 3. Emphasize that a figure has rotational symmetry if, after a rotation, every point coincides with the original shape. The number of possible rotations that result in the original position is called the order of rotational symmetry.

3. Distribute copies of Worksheet 4–4 and review the instructions with your students. Note that the circle is divided into eight parts, each of which is called a sector. Students are to color the number of sectors so that the figure has the type of symmetry described in each problem. Point out that they should record their answers to problems 1 through 10 on the circles that accompany the problems. Remind students that the figures must be the same color if they are symmetric. Compasses, rulers, protractors, and scissors should be used if students need to make circles and manipulate them to verify their answers.

Answer Key

Answers may vary. An example of a correct solution for each problem follows. (The numbers represent the numbered parts of the shaded circle.)

1. 2 and 5;   **2.** 1 and 2;   **3.** 1 and 5;   **4.** 2, 3, 4, and 5;   **5.** 8, 1, 2, and 3;   **6.** 1, 2, 5, and 6;
7. 1, 8, 4, and 5;   **8.** 1, 8, 4, and 5;   **9.** 1, 2, 5, and 6;   **10.** 1, 3, 5, and 7

4–4 Circles and Symmetry

Circles can be used to demonstrate symmetry. The circle below is divided into eight parts, or *sectors*, labeled 1 to 8.

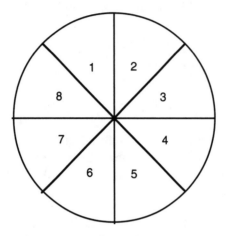

  If you shade sectors 1, 2, 3, 4, 7, and 8 the same color, the circle will have a vertical line of symmetry. That is the line drawn from the top of the circle to the bottom. Each side of the circle will be a reflection of the other.

  If you shade sectors 1, 2, 3, 4, 5, and 6 the same color, the circle will have a horizontal line of symmetry. This is the line drawn from the left side of the circle to the right, dividing it into two identical halves.

  If you shade sectors 8, 1, 4, and 5 the same color, the resulting figure will have rotational symmetry of order 2. Two rotations of those colored sectors result in the original position of the circle.

  Follow the directions below to show circles and symmetry.

COLOR TWO SECTORS SO THAT THE CIRCLE HAS:

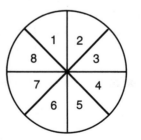

1. One horizontal line of symmetry

2. One vertical line of symmetry

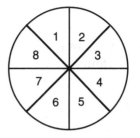

3. A rotational symmetry of degree 2

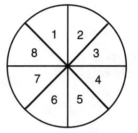

COLOR FOUR SECTORS SO THAT THE CIRCLE HAS:

4. One horizontal line of symmetry and
no vertical line of symmetry

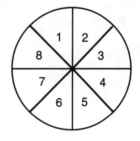

5. One vertical line of symmetry and
no horizontal line of symmetry

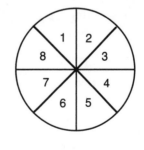

6. One horizontal line of symmetry and
one vertical line of symmetry

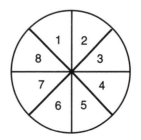

7. Two lines of symmetry, but no horizontal or vertical lines of symmetry

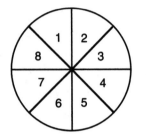

8. Rotational symmetry of degree 2

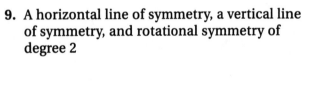

9. A horizontal line of symmetry, a vertical line of symmetry, and rotational symmetry of degree 2

10. Rotational symmetry of degree 4

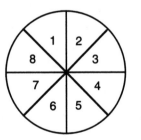

INSCRIBED POLYGONS

Objective: Students will form inscribed polygons and make a conjecture about the sides and angles of regular polygons. Students should work individually to complete this activity.

Special Materials: scissors, compasses, rulers, protractors, two sheets of unlined paper per student

TEACHING NOTES

In this activity students will use paper folding to inscribe polygons in a circle. By measuring the lengths of the sides and degrees of the interior angles, students will discover that the sides and angles of regular polygons are congruent.

1. Introduce this activity by explaining that paper folding is an effective way to visualize geometric concepts. Explain that the students will form inscribed polygons by folding a circle and connecting certain points.

2. Distribute copies of Worksheet 4–5 and review the instructions with your students. Emphasize that students should follow the directions closely to ensure that the inscribed polygons are regular polygons. At the end of the activity, point out that the inscribed polygons students created are regular polygons, meaning that their sides are congruent and their angles are congruent.

Answer Key

1. Figure 1, triangle; Fig. 2, hexagon; Fig. 3 square; Fig. 4, 12-sided figure or dodecagon

2. Figure 1, about 7 in., 60°; Fig. 2, about 4 in., 120°; Fig. 3, about $5\frac{3}{4}$ in., 90°; Fig. 4, about $2\frac{1}{8}$ in., 150°

3. Accept any reasonable conjecture. One acceptable conjecture is that the sides of each inscribed polygon they created are congruent and the angles of each inscribed polygon are congruent. These inscribed polygons are regular polygons.

4–5   Inscribed Polygons

An *inscribed polygon* is a polygon with each of its vertices on the circle. The sides of the polygon are inside the circle. Follow the instructions to create four different inscribed polygons and then write a conjecture about the inscribed polygons you formed.

1. Use a compass and two sheets of unlined paper to draw two circles, each with a radius of 4 inches. Cut out each circle.

2. Fold one circle in half so that the fold extends from top to bottom. Fold it again so that the fold is horizontal. Now open the circle. It should look like the circle to the right. (The broken lines represent the folds.)

3. Hold the circle so that a fold runs from top to bottom. Fold the left side of the circle so that it meets the center fold. Fold the right side so that it meets the center fold. Unfold the circle. It should look like the one at the right.

4. Hold the circle so that only one fold runs horizontally. Fold the top so that it meets the center fold. Fold the bottom so that it meets the center fold. Unfold the circle, which should look like the one to the right.

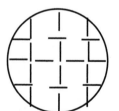

5. Starting at the top, label each point where the fold is on the circle, starting with the letter A and ending with L. Label the back of the circle in the same manner.

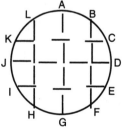

6. Take the second circle you cut out and follow steps 2 through 5. After following the steps, you should have two identical circles, labeled A through L on both sides.

© 2000 by The Center for Applied Research in Education

7. Now that the circles are folded and labeled, form each inscribed polygon according to the instructions below. Form Figure 1 on one side of a circle, Figure 2 on the other side, and Figures 3 and 4 on either side of the second circle.

   Figure 1—Connect points A, E, I, and A.
   Figure 2—Connect points A, C, E, G, I, K, and A.
   Figure 3—Connect points A, D, G, J, and A.
   Figure 4—Connect points A, B, C, D, E, F, G, H, I, J, K, L, and A.

   Now complete the following on a separate sheet of paper for each figure.

1. Identify the polygon.

2. Record the length of each line segment and measure of each interior angle of the figure.

3. Make a conjecture about the figure formed and the relationship of the angles and sides.

TANGENTS: CIRCLES AND LINES

Objective: Students will draw tangent circles and tangent lines. Students should work in pairs to complete this activity.

Special Materials: compasses, rulers, unlined paper

TEACHING NOTES

In this activity students will explore circles and tangent lines according to specific criteria. The emphasis of the activity is on their drawings.

1. Introduce this activity by telling students that the activity they are about to do requires them to "go off on a tangent." Explain that the expression means to expound on a topic that is only remotely related to the topic that is central to a discussion. This "tangent" is much like a tangent line that intersects a circle at only one point and then continues infinitely.

2. Hand out copies of Worksheet 4–6 and review the instructions with your students. Be sure they understand the concept of tangent lines and tangent circles. Caution students that they must follow the instructions carefully and make their drawings as accurate as possible. Note that although they may draw circles of any size, they should not make them so large that they fill the page. Also, remind them to number their drawings.

Answer Key

Drawings may vary; the following are examples of correct solutions.

Activity 4–6   *(Cont'd)*

Answer Key   *(Cont'd)*

3.

4.

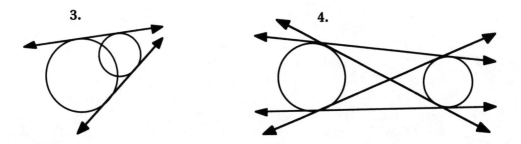

5.

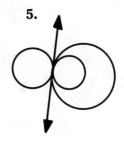

6.

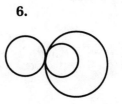

7.

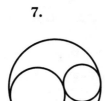

8.

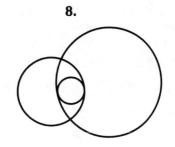

4–6   Tangents: Circles and Lines

A *tangent* to a circle lies in the plane of the circle and intersects the circle at one point. A line that is tangent to two or more circles is a *common tangent*. Circles may have common tangents and circles may be tangent to each other.

▲ Line AB is a common tangent of the two circles.

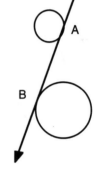

▲ Line CD is a common tangent to the two circles, which are also tangent to each other.

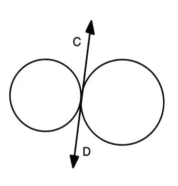

Draw circles and tangents on unlined paper according to the instructions below. Be sure to number your circles.

1. Draw two circles that have no common tangents.

2. Draw two circles that have one common tangent.

3. Draw two circles that have two common tangents.

4. Draw two circles that have four common tangents.

5. Draw three circles that have one common tangent.

6. Draw three tangent circles.

7. Draw three circles, each of which is tangent to the other two.

8. Draw three circles, two of which intersect and one being tangent to the other two.

CIRCLES: SYMBOLS OF SEGMENTS AND ANGLES

Objective: Students will review the symbols representing the line segments and angles of circles. Students should work individually to complete this activity.

Special Materials: none

TEACHING NOTES

Like most figures in geometry, circles have their own vocabulary. Some of the words of that vocabulary pertain only to circles, while some apply to other geometric figures as well.

To successfully complete this activity, students should have a basic understanding of circles. In addition, they should know that an angle inscribed in a semicircle is a right angle, and that a tangent line forms a right angle with the radius at the point of tangency.

1. Introduce this activity by explaining that the activity reviews the vocabulary associated with circles, focusing on symbols that name or describe segments and angles. Students will be required to identify parts of a circle and match the symbols with their word counterparts.

2. Hand out copies of Worksheet 4–7 and review the instructions with your students. Explain that they must refer to the diagram in order to complete this activity. Note that only by matching symbols with their correct name or descriptive phrase will they be able to find the value of pi, correct to 13 decimal places. At the end of the activity be sure to point out that pi is an irrational number and is represented by a nonterminating, nonrepeating decimal.

Answer Key

Pi is approximately equal to 3.1415926535897 . . .

4–7   Circles: Symbols of Segments and Angles

Use the diagram below and write the number of the word or phrase on the right in the blank before the symbol it matches on the left. Some words or phrases are used more than once. When you are finished, write each number in the blank space below as you read the numbers down the column. If you are correct, you will discover the next 13 decimal places of π, which is the ratio of the circumference to the diameter in a circle.

Pi is approximately equal to 3. ____ ____ ____ ____ ____ ____ ____ ____ ____

____ ____ ____ ____ . . .

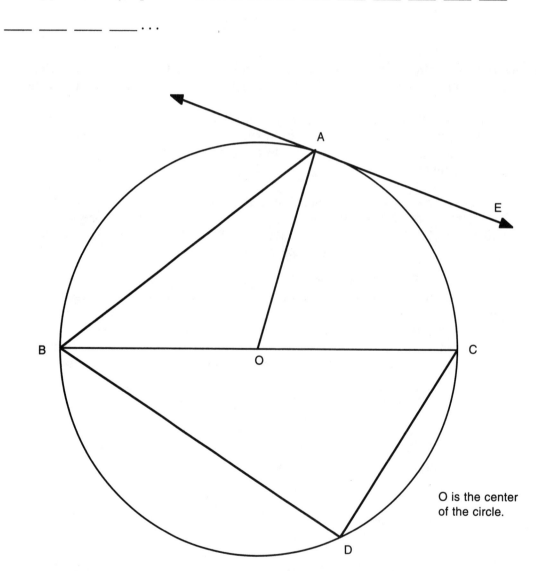

O is the center
of the circle.

_____∠BDC

_____$\overline{BA}$

_____∠OAE

_____∠ABD

_____$\overline{OA}$

_____$\overleftrightarrow{AE}$

_____$\overset{\frown}{AC}$

_____∠BCD

_____$\overset{\frown}{BC}$

_____∠CBD

_____$\overline{BC}$

_____$\overline{OC}$

_____∠AOC

1. right angle

2. tangent line

3. semicircle

4. chord (not the diameter)

5. inscribed angle

6. minor arc

7. central angle

8. diameter

9. radius

THE BIG CIRCLE PUZZLE

Objective: Students will apply various theorems to find the measures of angles, line segments, and arcs in a diagram of a circle. Students should work individually or in pairs to complete this activity.

Special Materials: none

TEACHING NOTES

In this activity students will apply their understanding of various theorems. Although the activity focuses around skills associated with circles, it serves as an excellent review for a wide range of skills.

To complete this activity successfully, students should know the following:

▲ The length of a diameter is twice the length of the radius.

▲ All radii of the same circle are congruent.

▲ The measure of each angle in an equilateral triangle is 60°.

▲ The measure of a straight angle is 180°.

▲ The measure of a central angle equals the measure of its intercepted arc.

▲ The measure of a semicircle is 180°.

▲ The measure of a circle is 360°.

▲ Vertical angles are congruent.

▲ The Angle Addition Postulate.

▲ The Arc Addition Postulate.

▲ The Pythagorean Theorem.

▲ The AAS Postulate, or HL Theorem for proving that triangles are congruent.

1. Introduce this activity by mentioning to your students that they will have the opportunity to apply theorems relating to circles. Depending on your class, you might review the prerequisite skills noted above.

2. Distribute copies of Worksheet 4–8 and review the instructions with your students. Explain that they should write the given information on the diagram and continue recording measures as they find them. Caution them to work carefully and accurately because one incorrect answer can lead to others. Suggest that they use the appropriate tick marks to help them identify congruent angles, arcs, and segments. Encourage students to skip any problem they are having trouble with and move on to another. Hard-to-find answers may become obvious after the students have identified more measures.

Answer Key

1. 20; **2.** 10; **3.** 10; **4.** 60; **5.** 60; **6.** 60; **7.** 120; **8.** 300; **9.** 6; **10.** 12; **11.** 8;
12. 2; **13.** 120; **14.** 60; **15.** 90; **16.** 300; **17.** 60; **18.** 120

4–8   The Big Circle Puzzle

You are given the following information:

$\overline{DF}$ and $\overline{CA}$ are diameters of Circle O.

m$\overline{AB}$ = 10	m$\overline{HI}$ = 6
m∠HIO = 90	m$\overline{OF}$ = 10
∠DOA ≅ ∠BOF	

Find the measure of each segment, arc, and angle in the diagram below. Use tick marks to show congruent segments, arcs, and angles. Write the measure of each segment, arc, and angle as you find it. Check your work as you proceed. Do not make any assumptions. Record your answers below.

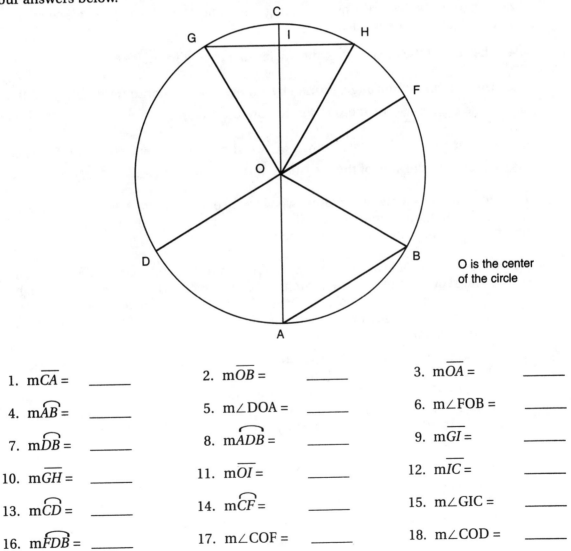

O is the center
of the circle

1. m$\overline{CA}$ = _____	2. m$\overline{OB}$ = _____	3. m$\overline{OA}$ = _____
4. m$\overparen{AB}$ = _____	5. m∠DOA = _____	6. m∠FOB = _____
7. m$\overparen{DB}$ = _____	8. m$\overparen{ADB}$ = _____	9. m$\overline{GI}$ = _____
10. m$\overline{GH}$ = _____	11. m$\overline{OI}$ = _____	12. m$\overline{IC}$ = _____
13. m$\overparen{CD}$ = _____	14. m$\overparen{CF}$ = _____	15. m∠GIC = _____
16. m$\overparen{FDB}$ = _____	17. m∠COF = _____	18. m∠COD = _____

THE BIGGER CIRCLE PUZZLE

Objective: Students will use various theorems to find the measures of angles and arcs. Students should work in pairs to complete this activity.

Special Materials: none

TEACHING NOTES

This activity is designed to follow Activity 4-8, "The Big Circle Puzzle." Most of the theorems required for the previous activity also apply to this activity. In addition, be sure your students know the following:

▲ Congruent sides are opposite congruent angles and congruent angles are opposite congruent sides.

▲ The sum of the measures of the angles in a triangle equals 180°.

▲ The measure of the angle formed by a tangent and a chord intersecting on the circle equals $\frac{1}{2}$ the measure of the intercepted arc.

▲ The measure of the angle formed by two chords that intersect within the circle equals $\frac{1}{2}$ the sum of the measures of the intercepted arcs.

Note that this activity contains two worksheets, 4–9A and 4–9B. The first contains the given information and the list of angles and arcs for which students must find the measures. The second contains the diagram of the "bigger" circle.

1. Introduce this activity by telling students that it is similar to the last, except that it requires them to use more theorems associated with circles. You might also mention that it is more involved. If necessary, review the theorems listed above, as well as any of the theorems listed in Activity 4-8 that you feel need reinforcement or clarification.

2. Distribute copies of Worksheets 4–9A and 4–9B and review the instructions with your students. Remind them that they should be sure a measurement is correct before placing it on the diagram because an incorrect measurement can lead to wrong answers. Encourage students to write all the measures they find on the diagram and use the appropriate tick marks.

Answer Key

1. 61; 2. 122; 3. 29; 4. 29; 5. 90; 6. 90; 7. 10; 8. 45; 9. 70; 10. 58; 11. 35;
12. 61; 13. 55; 14. 58; 15. 90; 16. 45; 17. 141; 18. 80; 19. 100; 20. 39;
21. 39; 22. 96; 23. 96; 24. 84; 25. 26

4–9A   The Bigger Circle Puzzle

You are given the following information:

$\overleftrightarrow{GF}$ is tangent to Circle O at D.

$m\overset{\frown}{DE} = 122$ $m\overset{\frown}{AC} = 20$ $m\overset{\frown}{DC} = 90$

   Label the circle on the accompanying worksheet with the given information, then find the measure of each angle and arc below. Write the measure of each angle and arc as you find it on the circle, and use tick marks to designate congruent angles. Check your work as you proceed. Do not make any assumptions. Record your answers below.

1. $m\angle EDF =$ _____

2. $m\angle DOE =$ _____

3. $m\angle OED =$ _____

4. $m\angle ODE =$ _____

5. $m\angle BDG =$ _____

6. $m\angle BCD =$ _____

7. $m\angle ADC =$ _____

8. $m\angle CDG =$ _____

9. $m\overset{\frown}{AB} =$ _____

10. $m\overset{\frown}{BE} =$ _____

11. $m\angle ADB =$ _____

12. $m\angle DAE =$ _____

13. $m\angle AED =$ _____

14. $m\angle BOE =$ _____

15. $m\angle BDF =$ _____

16. $m\angle CDB =$ _____

17. $m\angle AIB =$ _____

18. $m\angle CHD =$ _____

19. $m\angle DHB =$ _____

20. $m\angle AIC =$ _____

21. $m\angle BIJ =$ _____

22. $m\angle AJB =$ _____

23. $m\angle EJD =$ _____

24. $m\angle AJD =$ _____

25. $m\angle JEO =$ _____

© 2000 by The Center for Applied Research in Education

4–9B   The Bigger Circle Puzzle

Using the given information and your knowledge of circles, record the measures of the angles and arcs on the circle below.

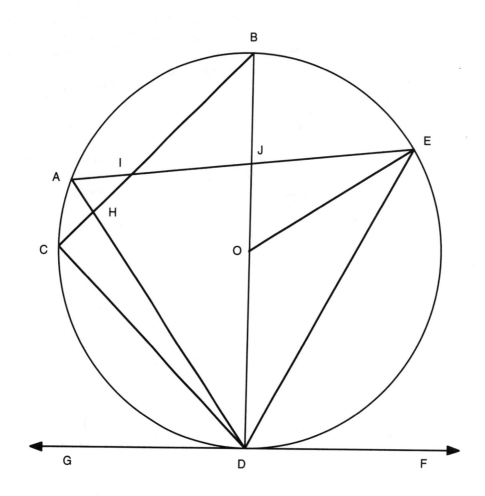

THE BIGGEST CIRCLE PUZZLE

Objective: Students will find the measures of angles, arcs, and segments associated with a circle. Students should work in pairs to complete this activity.

Special Materials: none; *optional*—calculators

TEACHING NOTES

This activity requires students to understand the skills and concepts necessary to successfully complete the two previous activities on circles, 4–8, "The Big Circle Puzzle," and 4–9, "The Bigger Circle Puzzle." To complete this final circle puzzle, they should also know the following:

▲ If two chords intersect inside a circle, then the product of the lengths of the segments of one chord is equal to the product of the lengths of the segments of the other chords.

▲ The Secant–Secant Segment Theorem.

▲ The Secant–Secant Theorem.

▲ The Tangent–Tangent Theorem.

Note that this activity contains two worksheets, 4–10A and 4–10B. The first contains the given information and the angles, arcs, and segments for which students must find the measures. The second sheet contains the circle with which they will work.

1. Introduce this activity by explaining that the activity requires students to apply the principles of finding the measures of arcs, as well as finding the lengths of segments and angles formed in the exterior of the circle. Note that they must draw upon their overall knowledge of circles if they are to complete the activity.

2. Distribute copies of Worksheet 4–10A and 4–10B, and review the instructions with your students. If they have worked on either or both of the two previous circle puzzles (Activities 4–8 and 4–9), explain that this activity is similar but more challenging. Remind students to place the given information on the diagram and record all the new information they find. Caution them to be sure their measures are correct because an incorrect answer can lead to more mistakes. Note that students are to round answers, when necessary, to the nearest whole number.

Answer Key

1. 150;   **2.** 43;   **3.** 124;   **4.** 50;   **5.** 24;   **6.** 31;   **7.** 12;   **8.** 82;   **9.** 119;   **10.** 50;
11. 80;   **12.** 16;   **13.** 100;   **14.** 8;   **15.** 78

4–10A   The Biggest Circle Puzzle

You are given the following information:

O is the center of the circle.

$\overline{AB}$, $\overline{CD}$, and $\overline{EF}$ are diameters.

m$\overset{\frown}{GB}$ = 26	m∠AOC = 30
m∠OAH = 50	m∠AHF = 65
m∠IGA = 24	IF = 10.5
PI = 4.5	PC = 3.4
CM = 10	HM = 7.5

     Label the circle on the accompanying worksheet with the given information, then find the measure of each angle, arc, and segment below. Write the measure of each angle, arc, and segment as you find it on the diagram and use tick marks to designate congruent angles. Check your work as you proceed. Do not make any assumptions. Record your answers below. (Round to the nearest whole number where necessary.)

1. m$\overset{\frown}{CB}$ = _____

2. m∠AJC = _____

3. m$\overset{\frown}{CG}$ = _____

4. m∠FOB = _____

5. m$\overset{\frown}{FG}$ = _____

6. m∠FPC = _____

7. m∠FIG = _____

8. m$\overset{\frown}{FI}$ = _____

9. m∠IKF = _____

10. m$\overset{\frown}{AE}$ = _____

11. m∠ELD = _____

12. m$\overline{CD}$ ≈ _____

13. m∠COF = _____

14. m$\overline{FM}$ ≈ _____

15. m∠FNB = _____

4–10B   The Biggest Circle Puzzle

Using the information you were given and your knowledge of circles, fill in the measures of the angles, arcs, and segments on the diagram below.

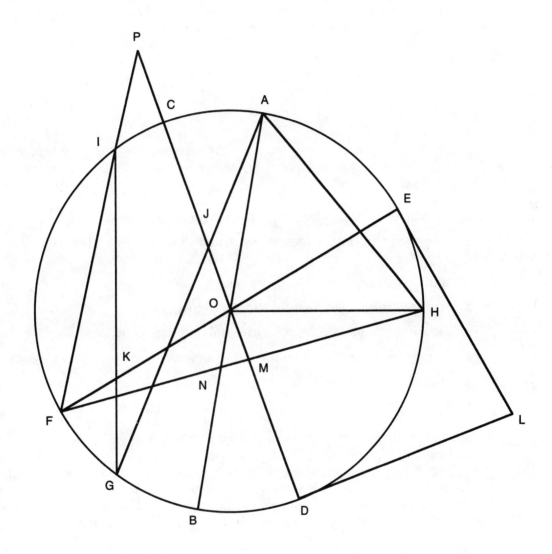

$\overline{LD}$ and $\overline{LE}$ are tangent to the circle.

EXPLAIN THE REASON—CIRCLES

Objective: Students will write an explanation of concepts relating to circles. Students should work individually or in pairs to complete this activity.

Special Materials: none

TEACHING NOTES

In this activity, students must understand why certain facts about circles are true, and then explain why the statements are true. The activity requires that students know the following:

▲ The diameter of a circle is twice the length of the radius.

▲ Congruent circles have the same size and similar circles have only the same shape.

▲ Radii of the same circle are congruent.

▲ An angle inscribed in a semicircle is a right angle.

▲ Two tangent segments from an external point are congruent.

▲ A tangent segment is perpendicular to a radius at the point of tangency.

▲ A right triangle has one right angle.

▲ The SSS method is a way to prove that two triangles are congruent.

1. Introduce this activity by explaining that to say something is true without understanding *why* it is true always presents a weak argument. Young children will often justify the question "Why is that true?" by saying, "Because it is." That may be okay for young children, but not for geometry students. Emphasize that your students must understand and be able to explain why something in geometry is true. That is the focus of this activity.

2. Distribute copies of Worksheet 4–11 and review the instructions with your students. If necessary, review any of the prerequisite skills noted above. Emphasize that students must write a clear and concise explanation of each fact.

Activity 4–11   *(Cont'd)*

Answer Key

Explanations may vary; following are sample answers.

1. A diameter is twice the radius, therefore the circles have the same size.

2. The length of the diameter is twice the length of the radius, and the radius is the distance from the center to the circle. Therefore the diameter is the longest chord.

3. All circles have the same shape and are therefore similar.

4. $\overline{OA}$ and $\overline{OB}$ are radii and are therefore congruent.

5. $\angle C$ is a right angle because it is inscribed in a semicircle.

6. $\overline{FG}$ and $\overline{GH}$ are tangent segments from the same external point and are therefore congruent.

7. $\angle OIJ$ is a right angle because the radius and tangent segment form a right angle at the point of tangency.

8. The radii are congruent. Tangent segments are congruent. $\overline{OJ}$ is congruent to itself, therefore the triangles are congruent by SSS.

4–11 Explain the Reason—Circles

Eight facts about circles are listed below. For each one, write an explanation of why the fact is true. Use a separate sheet of paper for your explanations.

1. A circle with a radius of 5 inches is congruent to a circle with a diameter of 10 inches.
2. The diameter of a circle is the longest chord.
3. All circles are similar.

   In problems 4 through 8, O is the center of each circle.

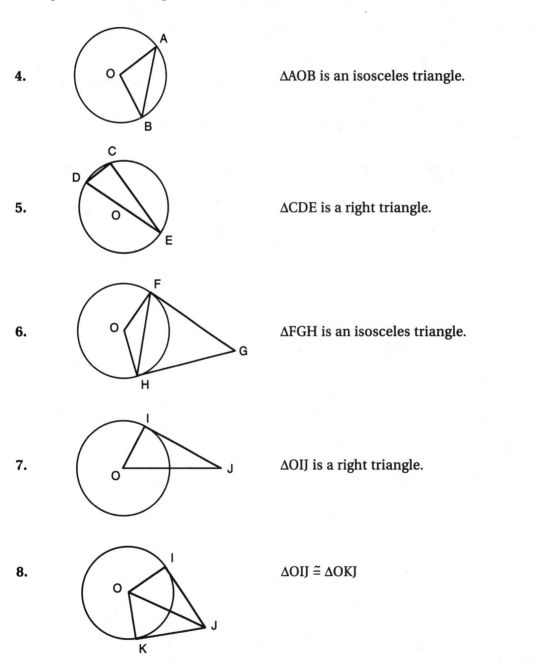

4. ΔAOB is an isosceles triangle.

5. ΔCDE is a right triangle.

6. ΔFGH is an isosceles triangle.

7. ΔOIJ is a right triangle.

8. ΔOIJ ≅ ΔOKJ

CIRCLES AND COORDINATE GEOMETRY

Objective: Students will graph circles on the coordinate plane. Students should work individually to complete this activity.

Special Materials: compasses, graph paper; *optional*—large compass for drawing circles on the board or a compass for use on the overhead projector

TEACHING NOTES

In this activity students are given information from which they must determine either the center and a point on a circle or two points on the circle. Once they have determined the points, they may use a compass to draw the circle. To complete this activity successfully, students should know the following:

▲ All points on a circle are equidistant from the center.

▲ The diameter of a circle is twice the length of the radius.

▲ Tangent lines "touch" the circle at only one point.

▲ Congruent circles have the same size.

▲ The coordinate plane is divided into quadrants by the x-axis and the y-axis. Students should also know how to graph ordered pairs and equations of lines.

1. Introduce this activity by asking students what information is needed to draw a circle. Answers should include a center point and a radius or diameter, or the center and at least one point on the circle. Without such information, a specific circle cannot be drawn. Illustrate some examples on the board or on an overhead projector.

2. Hand out copies of Worksheet 4–12 and review the instructions with your students. If necessary, review the prerequisite skills stated above and remind students to be accurate when they graph the circles.

Activity 4–12   *(Cont'd)*

Answer Key

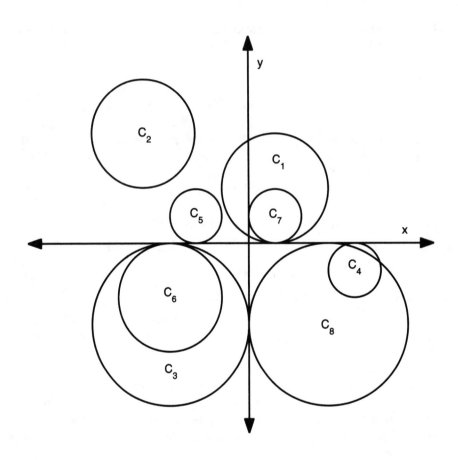

4–12 Circles and Coordinate Geometry

Use your compass to graph each circle according to the information given below.

1. The center is (1, 2) and the radius is 2. Label the circle C_1.

2. (–4, 4) is the center and (–2, 4) is a point on the circle. Label this circle C_2.

3. (0, –3) and (–6, –3) are the endpoints of the diameter. Label this circle C_3.

4. The center is (4, –1) and the circle is tangent to x = 3. Label this circle C_4.

5. The center is (–2, 1) and the circle is congruent to C_4. Label this circle C_5.

6. The center is (–3, –2) and the circle is tangent to the x-axis. Label this circle C_6.

7. The circle is in the interior of C_1 and is tangent to the x-axis. The radius is half of the radius of C_1. Label this circle C_7.

8. The radius is 3 and the circle is tangent to C_3 and the y-axis. Label this circle C_8.

THE CIRCULAR DEFINITION OF AN ANGLE

Objective: Students will draw angles in standard position. Students should work individually to complete this activity.

Special Materials: protractors, rulers, graph paper; *optional*—yardstick for demonstrating on board; drinking straw for demonstrating on overhead projector

TEACHING NOTES

This activity introduces the concept of angles defined by rotating a ray around a point. It extends students' concepts of angles to include those whose measures are larger than 180°.

1. Introduce this activity by drawing a ray on the board or on an overhead projector as illustrated.

2. If you are using the board, place a yardstick on top of the ray so that the endpoint of the ray and the yardstick align. (If you are using an overhead projector, a drinking straw can be used instead of the yardstick.) Move the yardstick counterclockwise around the endpoint, forming a circle. Emphasize to your students that the measure of the angle becomes larger and larger as the yardstick is rotated.

3. Distribute copies of Worksheet 4–13 and review the instructions with your students. Discuss the vocabulary and concept of rotating. Suggest to your students that they use the same coordinate plane for drawing all of the angles.

Activity 4–13   *(Cont'd)*

Answer Key

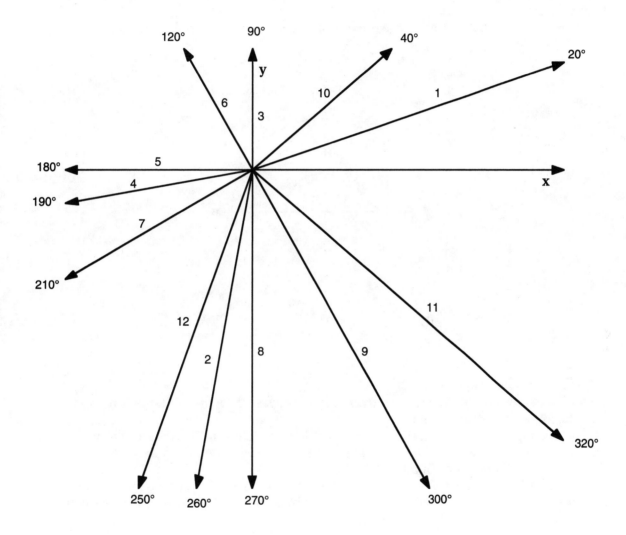

4–13 The Circular Definition of an Angle

Angles can be defined by their rotation around a point. Consider a ray positioned along the right-hand side of the x-axis with its endpoint at the origin. The other side of the angle coincides with this ray, but it is rotated counterclockwise around the origin.

The original ray is the *initial side* of the angle. The vertex is the origin. The *terminal side* is the ray that is rotated. An angle positioned in this manner is in *standard form* and is illustrated below.

Quadrants are numbered with Roman numerals. As the terminal side is rotated coun-

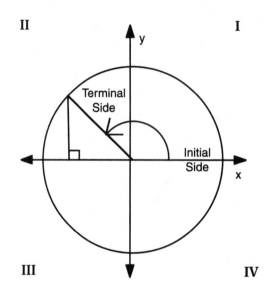

terclockwise around the origin, the terminal side "moves" through each quadrant and the angle becomes larger and larger.

For example, the terminal side of a 170° angle is in Quadrant II, the terminal side of a 200° angle is in Quadrant III, the terminal side of a 270° angle is on the y-axis, and the terminal side of a 310° angle is in Quadrant IV.

Use graph paper to draw each angle below. Remember, the initial side must be on the x-axis and the origin is the vertex. Label each angle by writing the angle number by the terminal side of the angle.

1. 20°   **2.** 260°   **3.** 90°   **4.** 190°   **5.** 180°   **6.** 120°

7. 210°   **8.** 270°   **9.** 300°   **10.** 40°   **11.** 320°   **12.** 250°

THE ARCHIMEDEAN SPIRAL—A CURVE FROM CONCENTRIC CIRCLES

Objective: Students will draw concentric circles and angles to create an Archimedean Spiral. Students should work individually to complete this activity.

Special Materials: compasses, protractors, rulers, unlined paper; *optional—* computers with software that has the capability to draw geometric figures, printers

TEACHING NOTES

The Archimedean Spiral, named appropriately enough after Archimedes—one of the finest of the ancient Greek mathematicians—is the most basic spiral formed from the intersection of angles and concentric circles.

To complete this activity successfully students should be familiar with the initial and terminal sides of an angle in standard position. They should also be able to draw angles larger than 180°.

1. Introduce this activity by explaining that examples of the Archimedean Spiral are common in our modern world. The tape in a VCR, a coil of adhesive tape, and some types of decorative ornaments are examples of Archimedean Spirals. Students will draw the spiral in this activity.

2. Distribute copies of Worksheet 4–14 and review the instructions with your students. Be sure that students understand the vocabulary and caution them to follow the directions precisely. Note that each time students draw an angle, they should use the original radius.

3. If your students have access to computers with software that is capable of drawing concentric circles and angles, consider having them complete this activity on their computers. Drawing spirals provides a unique experience with graphics software.

Activity 4–14   *(Cont'd)*

Answer Key

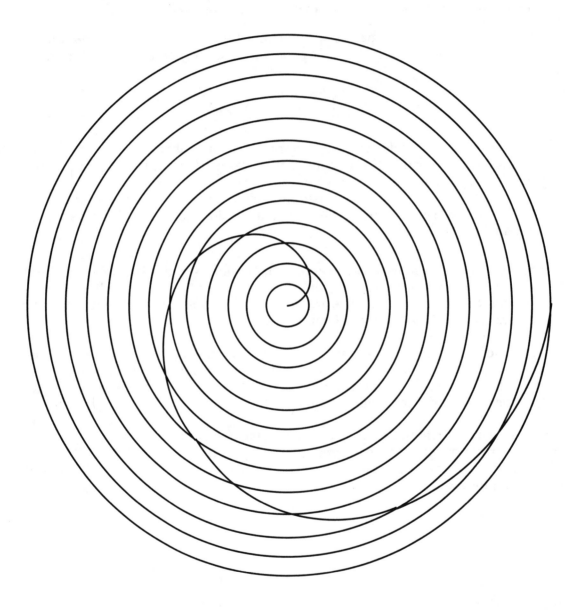

4–14   The Archimedean Spiral— a Curve from Concentric Circles

A *spiral* is a plane curve formed by a point that moves around a fixed center, continually increasing or decreasing its distance from the center. Imagine a curve winding about like a turning screw thread.

There are many kinds of spirals. One of the most simple spirals is the *Archimedean Spiral*, which is a curve that originates from the center of concentric circles. As it moves outward, the spiral turns around itself and fills space uniformly.

Follow the instructions to draw an Archimedean Spiral.

1. Find the center of your paper. This will be the center of all the concentric circles that will form your spiral.

2. Draw 12 concentric circles. The innermost circle should have a radius of $\frac{1}{4}$ inch, the next circle should have a radius of $\frac{1}{2}$ inch, the third circle should have a radius of $\frac{3}{4}$ inch, with each new circle increasing a quarter inch so that the radius on the twelfth circle is 3 inches.

3. Draw a radius so that it corresponds to the initial side of an angle in standard position.

4. Draw a 30° angle, using the radius drawn in Step 3 as the initial side of the angle.

5. Continue drawing angles, increasing the measure of each by 30° until you draw an angle of 330°. The radius drawn in Step 3 must be the initial side of each angle.

6. Draw a point in the center of the circles. Draw a point where the first circle intersects the terminal side of the 30° angle. Draw a point where the second circle intersects the terminal side of the 60° angle and so on.

7. To draw the spiral, draw an arc connecting the center of the circle (which is called the pole of the spiral) to the point marked on the first circle, then to the point marked on the second circle and so on.

Assuming you have followed the instructions correctly, you have created an Archimedean Spiral.

THE CIRCULAR DEFINITIONS
OF THE TRIGONOMETRIC FUNCTIONS

Objective: Students will determine the sign and/or value of the sine, cosine, and tangent ratios. Students should work individually to complete this activity.

Special Materials: none

TEACHING NOTES

This activity introduces the circular definition of the sine, cosine, and tangent ratios. The worksheet explains the process of defining, as well as the definitions of these functions.

1. Introduce this activity by reviewing the sine, cosine, and tangent ratios as defined by using the right triangle. "a" represents an acute angle.

$$\sin a = \frac{\text{length of the leg opposite the angle}}{\text{length of the hypotenuse}}$$

$$\cos a = \frac{\text{length of the leg adjacent to the angle}}{\text{length of the hypotenuse}}$$

$$\tan a = \frac{\text{length of the leg opposite the angle}}{\text{length of the leg adjacent to the angle}}$$

2. Hand out copies of Worksheet 4–15 and review the instructions with your students. Make sure that students understand the information presented on the worksheet. Note that the trigonometric ratios are extended to include all angles, not just the acute angles of a right triangle. Also explain that the rotations may create a 0° angle, an angle in the first quadrant, a 90° angle, an angle in the second quadrant, a 180° angle, and so on. Remind students that the concept of division by 0 is undefined and some of the ratios are undefined because the denominator equals 0.

3. Carefully discuss problem 1 as a class exercise. Although the problem is done on the student worksheet, reviewing it together will help students understand how the worksheet is to be completed. You might also like to provide the explanations for the answers. (x is positive because x is greater than 0 on that part of the number line. y = 0 because it is on the x-axis. $\sin \theta = 0$ because 0 divided by any number is equal to 0. $\cos \theta = 1$ because the value of x and the radius are the same. $\tan \theta = 0$ because 0 divided by any number is equal to 0.)

Activity 4–15 *(Cont'd)*

Answer Key

2. All values are positive.

3. $x = 0$, y is positive, $\sin \theta = 1$, $\cos \theta = 0$, $\tan \theta$ = undefined

4. x is negative, y is positive, $\sin \theta$ is positive, $\cos \theta$ is negative, $\tan \theta$ is negative

5. x is negative, $y = 0$, $\sin \theta = 0$, $\cos \theta = -1$, $\tan \theta = 0$

6. x is negative, y is negative, $\sin \theta$ is negative, $\cos \theta$ is negative, $\tan \theta$ is positive

7. $x = 0$, y is negative, $\sin \theta = -1$, $\cos \theta = 0$, $\tan \theta$ = undefined

8. x is positive, y is negative, $\sin \theta$ is negative, $\cos \theta$ is positive, $\tan \theta$ is negative

4–15 The Circular Definitions of the Trigonometric Functions

Circles can be used to define trigonometric functions. This method starts with an angle in standard position. One side, the terminal side, is rotated around the origin. The direction that indicates the rotation from the initial side of the angle is shown by the arrow. (x,y) is a point on the terminal ray of the angle.

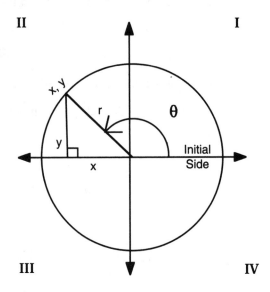

By applying the Pythagorean Theorem, the radius, r, of the circle equals $\sqrt{x^2 + y^2}$.

The trigonometric functions can be defined as follows: θ represents any angle in standard position.

$$\sin\ \theta = \frac{y}{r} \qquad \cos\ \theta = \frac{x}{r} \qquad \tan\ \theta = \frac{y}{x}$$

For each case below, state whether x, y, sin θ, cos θ, and tan θ are positive, negative, 1, 0, –1, or undefined. The first problem is done for you.

1. $\theta = 0°$:   x is positive, y = 0, sin θ = 0, cos θ = 1, tan θ = 0.

2. θ is in Quadrant I: _____

   _____

3. $\theta = 90°$: _____

   _____

4. θ is in Quadrant II: _____

   _____

5. $\theta = 180°$: _____

_____

6. θ is in Quadrant III: _____

_____

7. $\theta = 270°$: _____

_____

8. θ is in Quadrant IV: _____

_____

Part 5

3–D FIGURES

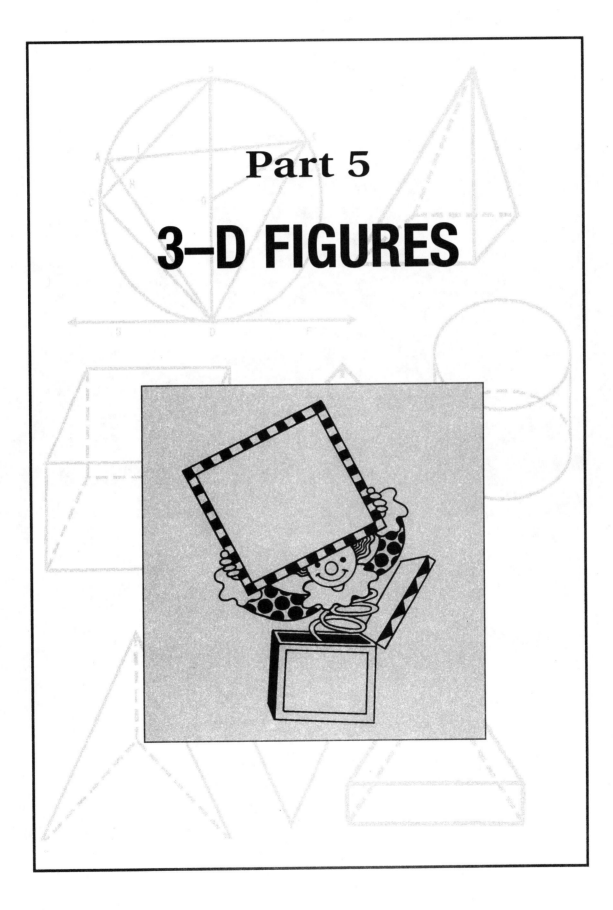

VISUALIZING WITH PENTOMINOES

Objective: Students will determine which pentomino nets will fold into an open box. Students should work in pairs to complete this activity.

Special Materials: scissors, rulers, graph paper

TEACHING NOTES

The ability to visualize is a vital part of imagination. Visualizing pentominoes can sharpen students' spatial perception and their skills in recognizing the properties of three-dimensional figures.

1. Introduce this activity by asking students to imagine a cube-shaped cardboard box without a lid. Now ask them to visualize the parts of this box lying flat and unfolded. Students should visualize two pairs of opposite sides and a bottom, all of which are congruent squares. Explain that in this activity students will use their visualization skills to decide if pentomino nets can be folded into the shape of an open box.

2. Distribute copies of Worksheet 5–1 and review the instructions with your students. Note that the worksheet contains 12 nets. Students are to determine which of these nets will fold into an open box. Emphasize that students are to first try to visualize each net, and then copy the arrangements on graph paper, cut them out, and fold them to see if they were correct.

Answer Key

All arrangements can form an open box except numbers 4, 6, 9, and 10.

5–1 Visualizing with Pentominoes

Pentominoes are figures formed by joining five congruent squares along the sides so that the sides are adjacent. There are only 12 pentominoes. They are pictured below. Eight of them can be folded to form an open box. Use your imagination to identify these arrangements. Then draw each pentomino on graph paper, cut it out, and try to assemble it to see if you were correct.

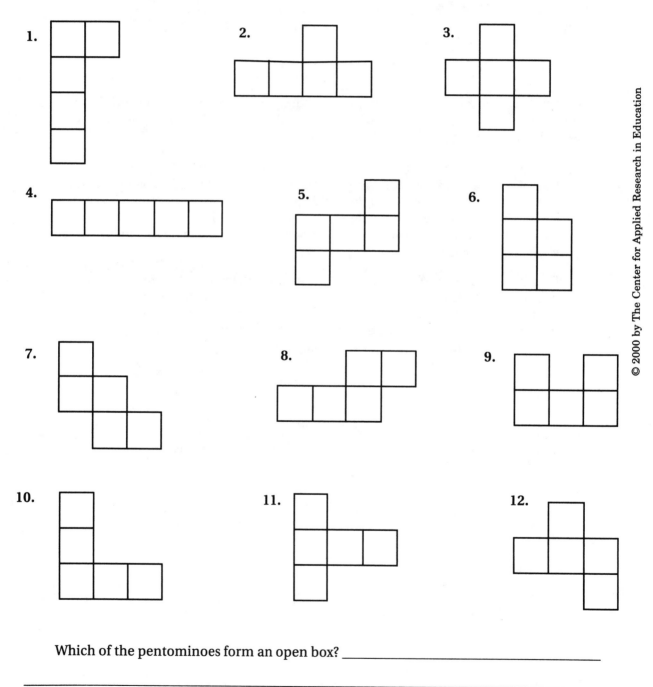

Which of the pentominoes form an open box? _____

OPPOSITE FACES OF A CUBE

Objective: Students will identify which faces of a cube are parallel. Students should work in pairs to complete this activity.

Special Materials: scissors, rulers, graph paper

TEACHING NOTES

This activity requires students not only to visualize a cube from a net, but to identify which faces are parallel. Unless your students have had experience working with nets, you should assign the prior activity, 5–1, "Visualizing with Pentominoes," first.

1. Introduce this activity by asking students to identify opposite sides within the classroom. Obvious examples include the floor and the ceiling, the front and back covers of a closed textbook, or the front of the room and the back of the room. Emphasize that each of these figures is a polygon and each is parallel to its opposite.

2. Distribute copies of Worksheet 5–2 and review the instructions with your students. Note that three of the six faces of each cube are represented by upper-case letters. Students are to identify which faces are on opposite sides of the cube. They are to write the letter on the square that is opposite the square labeled with the same letter. Suggest that students use graph paper to make a model of the cube to help them label the faces correctly.

Activity 5–2 *(Cont'd)*

Answer Key

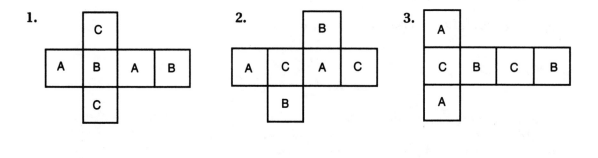

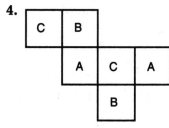

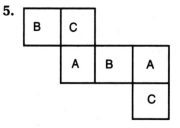

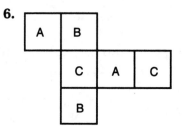

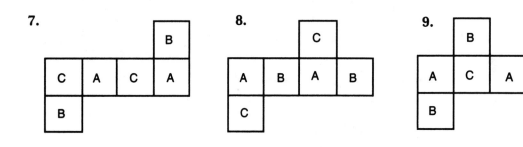

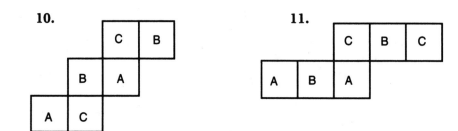

5–2   Opposite Faces of a Cube

A *cube* is a three-dimensional object that has six congruent faces, each of which is a square. The opposite faces are parallel: the top and bottom faces are parallel, the front and back faces are parallel, and the two sides are parallel.

    The eleven nets below may each be folded to form a cube. On each one, the face labeled A is not parallel to the face labeled B, which is not parallel to the face labeled C. Visualize each net as a cube and determine which squares are opposite each other. Use an "A" to label the square opposite the square marked "A"; use a "B" to label the square opposite the square marked "B"; and use a "C" to label the square opposite the square marked "C".

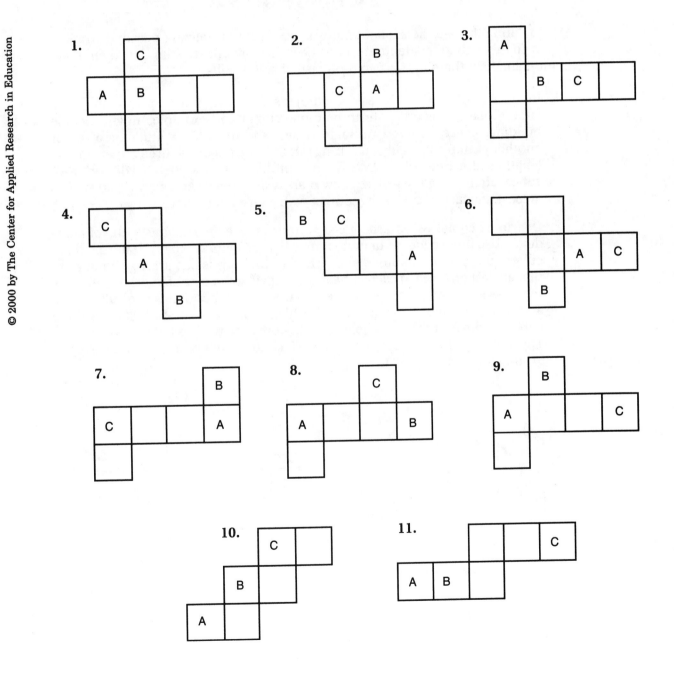

Activity 5–3

STACKING CUBES

Objective: Students will determine the number of possible arrangements of cubes. Students should work in pairs to complete this activity.

Special Materials: four dice or cubes per pair of students

TEACHING NOTES

Manipulating three-dimensional figures is useful for visualizing possible arrangements. In this activity, students are able to use dice or cubes to stimulate their imagination and help them to sharpen their visualization skills.

1. Introduce this activity by asking students to define and offer examples of a cube. Cubes, of course, are three-dimensional and examples might include building blocks, square cardboard boxes, and dice. Show students a die or another example of a cube, pointing out that the cube has three dimensions— length, width, and height. Explain that for this activity students will work with cubes, attempting to visualize how many ways cubes can be arranged so that at least one face of each is in contact with a face of another.

2. Distribute copies of Worksheet 5–3 and review the instructions with your students. Use three cubes to demonstrate what students are to do. Stack the three cubes on top of one another, and point out that this is one arrangement. Note that at least one face of each cube is flush against the face of another cube. Ask the class to consider an arrangement of the three cubes that is two cubes high, and arrangements that are one cube high. Suggest that students use three cubes (of the four they were given) to demonstrate the possible arrangements. These arrangements are shown below. Make sure students understand how the arrangements are formed.

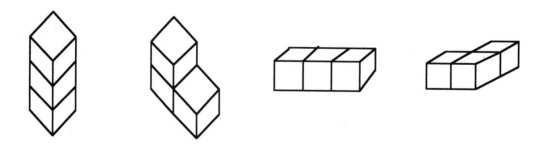

Activity 5–3   *(Cont'd)*

3. Now explain that students are to find the total number of ways four cubes can be arranged, provided that at least one face of each cube is flush against the face of another cube. Depending on your class, you may wish to give them a hint—there are 12 possible arrangements.

Answer Key

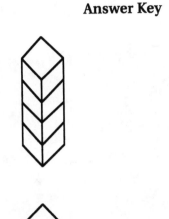

1. 1 arrangement

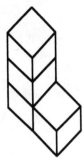

2. 1 arrangement

3. 5 arrangements

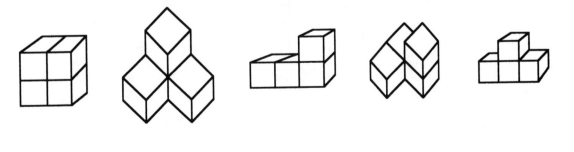

4. 5 arrangements

5–3   Stacking Cubes

Find how many ways four cubes can be arranged, so that at least one face of each cube is in contact with at least one face of one other cube.

1. Take four cubes and stack them four cubes high.

   How many different arrangements are possible? _____

2. Take four cubes and stack them three cubes high.

   How many different arrangements are possible? _____

3. Take four cubes and stack them two cubes high.

   How many different arrangements are possible? _____

4. Take four cubes and stack them one cube high.

   How many different arrangements are possible? _____

CREATING PRISMS FROM NETS

Objective: Students will create prisms from nets and verify Euler's Formula. Students should work in pairs to complete this activity.

Special Materials: scissors, glue or glue sticks, tape; *optional*—a small cardboard box that you can undo to reveal the net from which it is formed

TEACHING NOTES

Leonhard Euler (1707–1783) was a Swiss mathematician whose major focus was on pure mathematics. Today Euler is best known for Euler's Formula, $V - E + F = 2$, which relates the vertices, edges, and faces of polyhedra. This activity encourages students to use nets to explore Euler's Formula.

Note that this activity contains two worksheets, 5–4A and 5–4B. Worksheet 5–4A contains a net and instructions to create a triangular prism, while Worksheet 5–4B provides definitions associated with prisms and exercises students are to complete.

1. Introduce this activity by stating that a net is a pattern used to form a three-dimensional figure. Explain that each net forms a prism. You can easily demonstrate a net and prism with a small cardboard box. Hold the box up and show students its three dimensions. Now take the box apart, revealing the pattern of the net.

2. Distribute copies of Worksheets 5–4A and 5–4B and review the instructions with your students. Explain that students must first create their prisms, using Worksheet 5–4A. Caution them to follow the instructions carefully. After they have formed their prisms, they are to work with a partner and create new prisms according to the instructions on Worksheet 5–4B. They are to then list the number of bases, number of lateral faces, total number of faces, number of edges, and number of vertices for each prism. They are also to verify Euler's Formula. Encourage them to use the definitions provided to complete the worksheet.

Answer Key

1.		2.		3.		4.	
a.	2	a.	2	a.	2	a.	2
b.	4	b.	3	b.	3	b.	4
c.	6	c.	5	c.	5	c.	6
d.	12	d.	9	d.	9	d.	12
e.	8	e.	6	e.	6	e.	8
f.	$8 - 12 + 6 = 2$	f.	$6 - 9 + 5 = 2$	f.	$6 - 9 + 5 = 2$	f.	$8 - 12 + 6 = 2$

5–4A   Creating Prisms from Nets

A *net* is a pattern from which a three-dimensional figure can be formed. A triangular prism may be formed from the net below. Follow these steps to create the triangular prism.

1. Cut along the solid lines.

2. Fold the net along the dotted lines.

3. Fold the flaps inward (toward the side without numbers).

4. Glue the prism together.

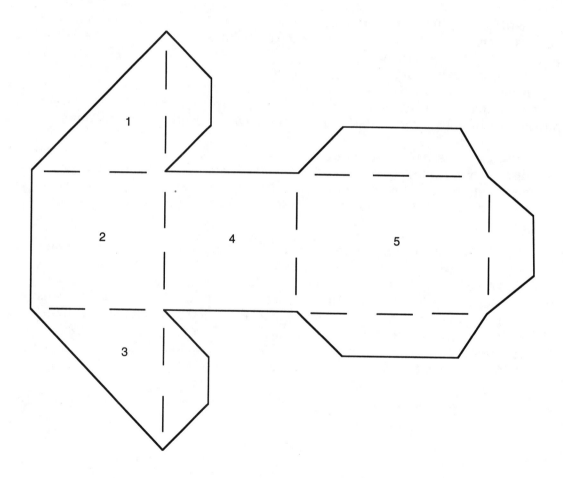

Note that the bases are triangles labeled 1 and 3.

5–4B   Creating Prisms from Nets

A *prism* is a special type of 3-dimensional figure. It has two congruent parallel bases, which may be any type of polygon. The sides of the prism are quadrilaterals.

Prisms are named by the shape of their bases. The prism you created is called a *triangular prism*, because the bases (labeled 1 and 3) are triangles. The sides of the prism are labeled 2, 4, and 5.

The *faces*, or sides and bases, of the prism are polygons. The number of faces is represented by the letter F. The sides of the prism are also sometimes called *lateral faces*. The prism you created has a total of five faces. (Faces 1 and 3 are bases and faces 2, 4, and 5 are the sides or lateral faces.)

The *edge* of a prism is the line segment where two faces intersect. The number of edges is represented by the letter E. The prism you created has nine edges where the following faces meet: 1 and 2; 1 and 4; 1 and 5; 3 and 2; 3 and 4; 3 and 5; 2 and 4; 2 and 5; and 4 and 5.

The *vertex* is a point where the edges of a solid meet. The number of vertices is represented by the letter V. The prism you created has six vertices. Each vertex of the prism is a vertex of the bases.

Euler's Formula states that $V - E + F = 2$, and applies to all prisms. You can use the prism you created to verify Euler's Formula by substituting numbers for V, E, and F: $6 - 9 + 5 = 2$.

Work with a partner to create new prisms by placing faces together according to the instructions below. Then list the (a) number of bases, (b) number of lateral faces, (c) total number of faces, (d) number of edges, (e) number of vertices, and (f) verify Euler's Formula by substituting the appropriate values into the formula for each prism you and your partner created.

1. Place Face 2 of your prism next to Face 2 of your partner's prism so that the base is a parallelogram.

   a. _____   b. _____   c. _____

   d. _____   e. _____   f. _____

2. Place Face 1 of your prism next to Face 1 of your partner's prism so that the base is a triangle.

   a. _____   b. _____   c. _____

   d. _____   e. _____   f. _____

3. Place Face 2 of your prism next to Face 2 of your partner's prism so that the base is a triangle.

   a. _____   b. _____   c. _____

   d. _____   e. _____   f. _____

4. Place Face 5 of your prism next to Face 5 of your partner's prism so that the base is a square.

   a. _____   b. _____   c. _____

   d. _____   e. _____   f. _____

CONSTRUCTING NETS AND REGULAR PYRAMIDS

Objectives: Students will construct a net to create a regular pyramid and verify Euler's Formula. Students should work individually to complete this activity.

Special Materials: rulers, protractors, scissors, tape, drawing paper; *optional—*computers with software that has the capability to draw geometric figures; models of pyramids that students have previously made or are commercially produced

TEACHING NOTES

This activity is a fine follow-up to Activity 5–4, in which students created prisms from nets to verify Euler's Formula. However, it can also stand alone. To complete this activity successfully, students should be able to identify faces, vertices, and edges of pyramids.

1. Introduce this activity by explaining that students will create their own nets to form a regular pyramid. If you have models of pyramids, you may wish to share them with your students, pointing out faces, vertices, and edges.

2. Hand out copies of Worksheet 5–5 and review the instructions with your students. Be sure that students understand what a net is and emphasize the importance of following the directions on the worksheet. If students have access to computers with software capable of constructing geometric figures, you may wish to have them use the software to form the net.

Answer Key

Answers may vary; the height is less than the slant height. Euler's Formula applies to regular prisms.

Name _____ Date _____ Section _____

5–5   Constructing Nets and Regular Pyramids

A *pyramid* is a polyhedron that has only one base. The lateral faces are triangles.

A *regular pyramid* is a special type of pyramid. Its base is a regular polygon and the sides are isosceles triangles.

Follow the steps below to make a net to form a regular pyramid. Label the slant height and prism height.

1. Draw a regular polygon.

2. Draw congruent isosceles triangles so that the bases of the triangles are also sides of the polygon. (Every side of the polygon should be a base of the triangle.)

3. Measure and record the height of the triangle. This is the *slant height* of the pyramid. Record the slant height.

    slant height of your pyramid = _____

4. Cut your net along the sides of the triangles.

5. Fold the triangles along the bases.

6. Position the vertex angles of the triangles so that they form a point.

7. Tape the adjacent sides of triangles together.

8. Place the prism on its base. Measure the distance from the highest point to the base. This is the *height* of the prism. Record the height.

    height of your prism = _____

9. Compare the slant height to the height of the pyramid.

    _____

    _____

10. Using your pyramid, count the number of vertices, number of faces, and the number of edges. Substitute these values in Euler's Formula, $V - E + F = 2$, to verify it.

    _____

Activity 5–6

PLATONIC SOLIDS

Objective: Students will research Platonic Solids to answer questions and complete a table. Students should work individually to complete this activity.

Special Materials: encyclopedias, math reference books, on-line references

TEACHING NOTES

This activity centers around research of regular polyhedra, which are also called Platonic Solids. There are five such solids, all of which are solid figures bounded by regular polygons so that the same number of faces meets at each vertex. To successfully complete this activity, students should be familiar with faces, edges, and vertices of a solid.

Since students will likely conduct at least some of their research in your school library, you may find it helpful to inform your librarian about this activity. This will enable the staff to provide the references and materials students will need.

1. Introduce this activity by explaining that students are to use the library, their own resources, or the internet to gather information relating to regular polyhedra. Suggest that students consult various references for their research.

2. Distribute copies of Worksheet 5–6 and review the instructions with your students. Note that after conducting their research, they are to complete the chart on the worksheet and answer the accompanying questions. Be sure to set a reasonable deadline, based upon the abilities of your students.

Answer Key

1. Regular Tetrahedron: 4; 6; 4; equilateral triangles

2. Regular Hexahedron or Cube: 6; 12; 8; squares

3. Regular Octahedron; 8; 12; 6; equilateral triangles

4. Regular Dodecahedron; 12; 30; 20; regular pentagons

5. Regular Icosahedron; 20; 30; 12; equilateral triangles

6. Plato, 428 B.C.–347 B.C., Greek

7. Tetrahedron—fire; hexahedron—earth; octahedron—air; dodecahedron—universe; icosahedron—water

8. He was a Swiss mathematician. He developed Euler's Formula, $V - E + F = 2$, which applies to the Platonic Solids.

5–6   Platonic Solids

Regular polyhedra are solid figures bounded by *regular polygons* in such a manner that the same number of faces meets at each vertex. There are only five regular polyhedra, which are also called *Platonic Solids*.

Using the resources in your library, math references found on the Internet, or other materials, complete the chart below and answer the questions that follow.

Name	Number of Faces	Number of Edges	Number of Vertices	Type of Faces
1. Regular Tetrahedron				
2. Regular Hexahedron or Cube				
3. Regular Octahedron				
4. Regular Dodecahedron				
5. Regular Icosahedron				

Answer the following questions on another sheet of paper.

6. For whom were the Platonic Solids named? Include this person's name, life span, and nationality.

7. The Greeks believed that each Platonic Solid was connected to nature. List each solid and identify the part of nature it represented.

8. Who is Leonhard Euler and how is his work related to the Platonic Solids?

SOLIDS BY THE NUMBER

Objective: Students will apply the definitions of prism, pyramid, regular polyhedra, and Euler's Formula. Students should work in pairs to complete this activity.

Special Materials: none; *optional*—models of prisms, pyramids, and regular polyhedra

TEACHING NOTES

This activity is a good culmination of the study of prisms, pyramids, and regular polyhedra. To successfully complete this activity, students should be:

▲ Familiar with the definitions of pyramids and prisms.

▲ Able to identify the five regular polyhedra.

▲ Able to identify the faces, edges, and vertices of a solid figure.

▲ Able to apply Euler's Formula, $V - E + F = 2$.

1. Introduce this activity by explaining that "by the numbers" is a phrase commonly used as a "hook" in a broad range of articles. For example, sports articles may be organized according to the numbers: the number of people who watched a game, the score, the averages of the players, a list of special statistics, etc. Articles about movies may list the top ten in a particular category and then provide reasons for the rankings. Even articles about food may be arranged "by the numbers," noting calories, carbohydrates, fat content, and the amount of vitamins a specific food contains. This activity examines solid figures "by the numbers."

2. Hand out copies of Worksheet 5–7 and review the instructions with your students. Depending on the abilities of your students, you may find it helpful to review the prerequisite skills. If necessary, encourage them to use their texts to review and clarify concepts and facts.

Answer Key

1. 8; **2.** 3; **3.** 9; **4.** 5; **5.** 2; **6.** 1; **7.** 6; **8.** 11; **9.** 4; **10.** 12; **11.** 10; **12.** 7

5–7   Solids by the Numbers

Fill in the blanks with the appropriate numbers. Consult your text if necessary.

1. The number of vertices of a cube is _____.

2. The number of lateral faces of a triangular prism is _____.

3. The sum of the faces and base of an octagonal pyramid is _____.

4. The total number of regular polyhedra (also called Platonic Solids) is _____.

5. In Euler's Formula V – E + F is equal to _____.

6. The number of bases in a pyramid is _____.

7. The number of faces of a cube is _____.

8. One less than the number of edges of a regular octahedron is _____. (A regular octahedron has 8 faces and 6 vertices.)

9. The number of faces of a regular tetrahedron is _____. (A regular tetrahedron has 6 edges and 4 vertices.)

10. The number of vertices of a regular icosahedron is _____. (A regular icosahedron has 20 faces and 30 edges.)

11. Half of the number of vertices of a regular dodecahedron is _____. (A dodecahedron has 12 faces and 30 edges.)

12. The total number of faces and bases of a pentagonal prism is _____.

CREATING THREE-DIMENSIONAL MODELS

Objective: Students will use pipe cleaners to create three-dimensional models. Students should work individually or in pairs to complete this activity.

Special Materials: 27 12-inch pipe cleaners per individual or pair of students, protractors; *optional*—models of three-dimensional figures

TEACHING NOTES

Models of three-dimensional figures can help students recognize length, width, and height. When students actually create three-dimensional figures, their understanding of these figures is enhanced.

1. Introduce this activity by showing students a model of a three-dimensional figure. If you don't have a model, you can use a cardboard box or even a desk. Point out the three dimensions of length, width, and height.

2. Distribute copies of Worksheet 5–8 and review the instructions with your students. Emphasize that students must make a model of a cube, a pyramid, and a triangular prism. Suggest that students attach the pipe cleaners simply by hooking and twisting the ends together.

3. Accept any reasonably formed models. You might also wish to display some of your students' creations.

5–8 Creating Three-dimensional Models

We live in a three-dimensional world of length, width, and height. In this activity you will create models of the following three-dimensional figures: a cube, pyramid, and triangular prism. Directions for creating a model of the cube are below. For the pyramid and triangular prism, create your model based on the diagrams.

Use 12 pipe cleaners to create a cube.

1. Start with four pipe cleaners. Attach them at right angles to make a square.

2. Position the square so that one side is flat on your desk. (Two sides should extend upward, and the top should be parallel to the bottom.) Attach a pipe cleaner to one of the bottom vertices so that it forms a right angle with the bottom segment. Attach another pipe cleaner to the other bottom vertex in a similar manner, so that it forms a right angle with the bottom segment and is parallel to the previous pipe cleaner you attached.

3. Repeat Step 2 using the vertices on the top of the square.

4. Place the original square you made down on your desk so all four original segments are flat. You should have four parallel pipe cleaners rising upward from the vertices of the square.

5. Using four new pipe cleaners, make another square as in Step 1.

6. Attach the square formed in Step 5 to the four upward-pointing pipe cleaners.

7. Examine your work. You should have a cube.

Use 6 pipe cleaners to create a pyramid with a triangular base and three faces.

Use 9 pipe cleaners to create a triangular prism.

Activity 5–9

DRAWING THREE-DIMENSIONAL FIGURES

Objectives: Students will draw three-dimensional figures on graph paper. Students should work individually to complete this activity.

Special Materials: graph paper, rulers, models of three-dimensional figures

TEACHING NOTES

Drawing three-dimensional figures is an enjoyable activity that can help students to more easily recognize the properties of prisms, cylinders, pyramids, and cones. Most students are eager to participate.

1. Introduce this activity by showing students models of three-dimensional figures. (If you don't have a model, a cardboard box will do.) Hold the models up and show them from different perspectives. Point out that as you move them and view them from different angles, the models will appear to shift.

2. Distribute copies of Worksheet 5–9 and review the instructions with your students. Note that the first part of the worksheet provides guidelines and illustrations to help students draw their figures. Students should study the directions for the examples and note how to draw them. Emphasize that it is not necessary for them to redraw or copy the sample illustrations. For the second part of the worksheet, students are to draw three-dimensional figures on graph paper. Caution them to follow the directions carefully.

Answer Key

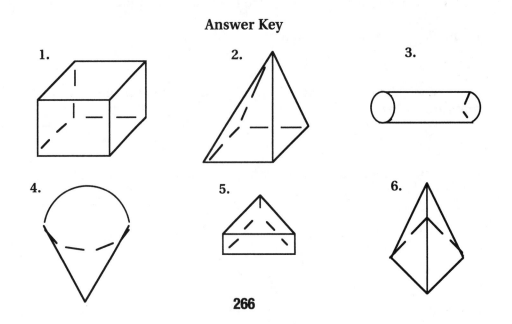

266

Name _____ Date _____ Section _____

5–9 Drawing Three-dimensional Figures

Being able to draw three-dimensional figures is an important skill, especially if you need to copy a diagram or make a sketch to help you illustrate or solve a problem. Study the four examples that show how to draw a cube, cylinder, pyramid, and cone. Then draw the three-dimensional figures according to the instructions that follow. Use graph paper for your drawings.

EXAMPLE 1: TO DRAW A CUBE . . .

▲ Draw the face located at the top of the cube.

▲ Draw three line segments to represent the three edges that are visible.

▲ Draw a face congruent to the face drawn in the first step. The solid lines are in front. The broken lines represent the edges that are hidden from view.

▲ Connect the vertices that are hidden by using a broken line segment.

EXAMPLE 2: TO DRAW A CYLINDER . . .

▲ Draw an oval base.

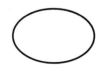

▲ Draw two line segments.

▲ Draw an oval that is congruent and parallel to the base. Use a solid line to represent the part that is showing and a broken line to represent the part that is hidden from view.

EXAMPLE 3: TO DRAW A PYRAMID . . .

▲ Draw a base using solid lines to represent edges that can be seen. Use broken lines to represent edges that are hidden from view.

▲ Choose a point above the base.

▲ Draw solid lines to show the edges that can be seen. Use broken lines to represent the edges that are hidden from view.

EXAMPLE 4: TO DRAW A CONE . . .

▲ Draw an oval base. Use a solid line to show the part that you can see. Use a broken line to represent the part that is hidden from view.

▲ Choose any point above the base.

▲ Draw two solid lines from the point to the base.

Now Use Graph Paper to Draw the Following:

1. A rectangular prism. The bases appear to be parallelograms.

2. A rectangular pyramid. The base appears to be a parallelogram.

3. A cylinder shaped like a long tube. The bases appear to be ovals.

4. A cone resembling an ice-cream cone. The base appears to be an oval.

5. A triangular prism. The bases are triangles.

6. A pyramid whose base is a square. The base appears to be a rhombus.

ROTATIONS OF PLANE FIGURES AROUND A LINE

Objective: Students will visualize the three-dimensional figures formed by rotating a square, right triangle, rectangle, and semicircle around a line. Students should work individually to complete this activity.

Special Materials: four 12-inch pipe cleaners per student, protractors, rulers

TEACHING NOTES

Although our world is a three-dimensional one, students often have a hard time visualizing three-dimensional figures. With a little imagination and helpful props, your students can sharpen their visualization skills and enhance their understanding of geometry.

1. Introduce this activity by explaining that a figure with three dimensions possesses length, width, and height. Illustrate these dimensions with a box, book, or similar object. Explain that in this activity students will use pipe cleaners to construct models of plane figures, fasten them to a pipe cleaner (which will represent a line), rotate the pipe cleaner, and determine what three-dimensional figure would be formed.

2. Distribute copies of Worksheet 5–10 and review the instructions with your students. Remind them to follow the instructions carefully and record the name of each figure.

Answer Key

1. cylinder; **2.** cylinder, cylinder; **3.** cone; **4.** sphere

5–10   Rotations of Plane Figures Around a Line

We live in a three-dimensional world of length, width, and height. Follow the instructions below and try to imagine which three-dimensional figure is formed when a plane figure is rotated around a line.

1. Connect two pipe cleaners and shape them into a square.

   ▲ Use a ruler to make sure that the sides of the square are equal in length.

   ▲ Use your protractor to make sure that the angles of your square are 90°.

   ▲ Connect a straight pipe cleaner by "snaking" it in and out along one side of the square. (Your pipe cleaners should look something like a square flag on a pole.)

   ▲ Slowly rotate the straight pipe cleaner. As it turns, the square will turn, too. Use your imagination to visualize what figure the square outlines as it rotates.

   ▲ This figure is a _____.

2. Take your square apart and reshape the pipe cleaners into a rectangle.

   ▲ Use a ruler to make sure that the opposite sides of the rectangle are equal in length.

   ▲ Use your protractor to make sure that the angles of your rectangle are 90°.

   ▲ Connect a straight pipe cleaner to one of the shorter sides of the rectangle by snaking the straight pipe cleaner in and out.

   ▲ Slowly rotate the straight pipe cleaner and try to visualize what figure the rectangle outlines.

   ▲ This figure is a _____.

   ▲ Now connect the rectangle at one of its longer sides to the straight pipe cleaner.

   ▲ Slowly rotate the straight pipe cleaner and try to visualize what figure the rectangle outlines.

   ▲ This figure is a_____.

3. Take your rectangle apart and reshape the pipe cleaners into a right triangle.

   ▲ Use your protractor to make sure that the right angle of your triangle is 90°.

   ▲ Connect your right triangle to the straight pipe cleaner so that the right angle is next to the straight pipe cleaner.

▲ Slowly turn the straight pipe cleaner and try to visualize what figure the right triangle outlines.

▲ This figure is a _____.

4. Take your right triangle apart and reshape the pipe cleaners into a semicircle.

▲ Connect your semicircle to the straight pipe cleaner so that the curve is opposite the straight pipe cleaner.

▲ Slowly turn the straight pipe cleaner and try to visualize what figure the semicircle outlines.

▲ This figure is a _____.

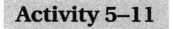

TYPES OF SOLIDS

Objective: Students will identify prisms, pyramids, cylinders, cones, and spheres. Students should work individually to complete this activity.

Special Materials: models of three-dimensional figures

TEACHING NOTES

In this activity students are given illustrations of three-dimensional figures that they must identify. To complete the activity successfully, students should know the following:

▲ Both prisms and pyramids are named by the type of bases. For example, if a prism has a triangular base, it is called a triangular prism. If a pyramid has a pentagonal base, it is called a pentagonal pyramid.

▲ Prisms have two bases and pyramids have one.

▲ Cylinders have two congruent circular bases and cones have one circular base.

▲ Spheres have no bases.

1. Introduce this activity and explain that it focuses on different solids. Show your students models of three-dimensional figures, and, if necessary, review the prerequisite skills.

2. Hand out copies of Worksheet 5–11 and review the instructions with your students. Emphasize that every name will be used, and that some will be used more than once.

Answer Key

SOLIDS ARE NOT PLANE.

5–11   Types of Solids

A solid is a three-dimensional figure. Write the letter of the name of each solid in the space below the figure. Correct answers will reveal a message.

rectangular pyramid—A	cone—D
triangular prism—E	rectangular prism—I
pentagonal prism—L	cube—N
triangular pyramid—O	pentagonal pyramid—P
hexagonal pyramid—R	cylinder—S
sphere—T	

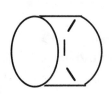

_____   _____   _____   _____
   1   2   3   4

_____   _____   _____   _____
   5   6   7   8

_____   _____   _____   _____
   9   10   11   12

_____
13

_____
14

_____
15

_____
16

_____
17

A CROSSWORD PUZZLE OF SOLID FIGURES

Objective: Students will create a crossword puzzle using a list of geometric terms relating to solid figures. Students should work individually or in pairs to complete this activity.

Special Materials: rulers, graph paper; *optional*—computers with software capable of generating crossword puzzles, printers

TEACHING NOTES

This activity serves as an excellent review of solid figures. Prior to the activity you may wish to collect crossword puzzles from newspapers and magazines to hand out to students as examples.

1. Introduce this activity by explaining that students are to create a crossword puzzle about solids, or three-dimensional figures. Ask students to name some three-dimensional figures and terms associated with them.

2. Hand out copies of Worksheet 5–12 and review the instructions with your students. Provide students with at least two sheets of graph paper, one on which they may design their puzzle and another for the final copy. Suggest that students do the rough copies in pencil.

3. If students have access to computers that possess software capable of creating crossword puzzles, suggest that they complete the activity using their computers. Although the software will design the puzzle, students still must write the clues for the answers.

4. Accept any reasonable crossword puzzles upon conclusion of the activity. Consider making copies of the puzzles and distributing them to the class.

5–12   A Crossword Puzzle of Solid Figures

Using the words below for the answers, create a crossword puzzle of solid figures. The following suggestions will help you to create your puzzle.

1. Arrange the answers of your puzzle in the boxes of the graph paper so that there is one letter per box. Be sure to place answers down and across, trying to have approximately the same number of down and across answers.

2. Write lightly in pencil so that it is easier to erase any mistakes you might make. Keep revising the structure of your puzzle until you find a form you like.

3. Make sure you spell all words correctly.

4. After you are satisfied with the way your puzzle looks, write a small number in the first box of each answer. Number the answers consecutively, one set of numbers for the down answers and another set for the across answers.

5. On a separate sheet of paper, write clues, or definitions, for your answers. Be sure that your facts about solids are correct.

6. Double-check your work, and create a final copy of your puzzle on a new piece of graph paper. Draw heavy lines on the boxes of your answers to make your answers stand out. Put the clues below the puzzle or on a separate sheet of paper.

Use the following words for the answers in your puzzle.

cone	triangular prism
sphere	regular dodecahedron
rectangular solid	regular icosahedron
Euler's Formula	regular pyramid
regular hexahedron	face
regular tetrahedron	edge
cube	prism
cylinder	polyhedra
Platonic Solids	pyramid
vertex	right prism

Part 6

APPLICATIONS OF GEOMETRY

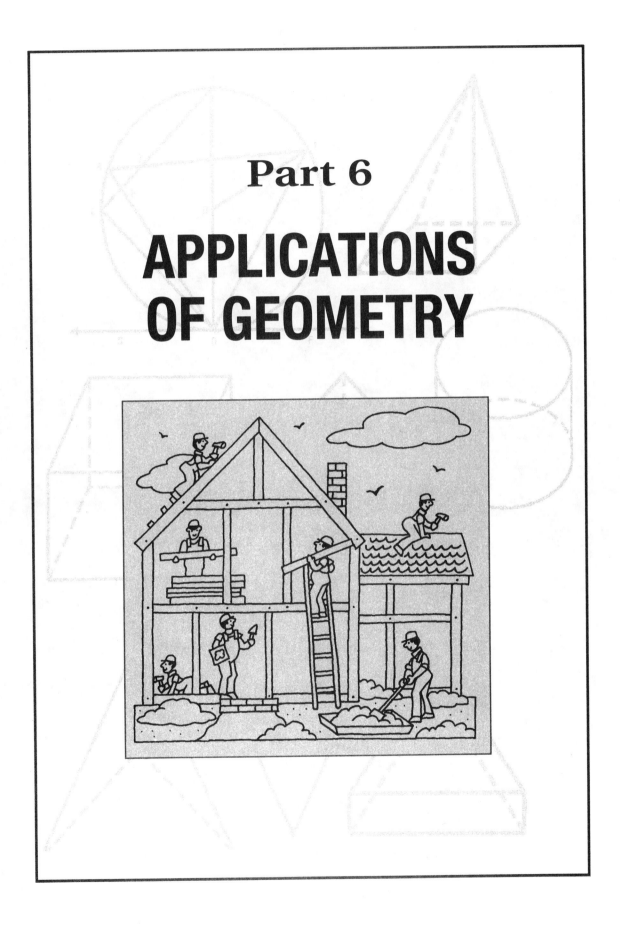

WORKING WITH A SCALE

Objective: Students will find the length of an object by using a scale. Students should work individually to complete this activity.

Special Materials: none; *optional*—calculators, a scale model of a car (or truck, train car, or similar item)

TEACHING NOTES

Scale is a difficult concept for many students. Even though they may understand that scale relates to measurement, they may not realize that scale functions as a precise ratio.

1. An excellent way to introduce this activity is to show the class a scale model. (Many hobby and toy stores sell inexpensive cars and trucks that are manufactured to scale.) Explain the concept of a scale by stating that a scale is used to create a miniature version of a large object. For example, if one inch on a scale model equals 20 feet, then that one-inch length would be equivalent to 20 feet in real life. A scale helps us to understand size and distance, as well as the relative size of objects.

2. Distribute copies of Worksheet 6–1 and review the instructions with your students. Emphasize that they are to calculate the actual dimensions of each object. Encourage them to create a scale problem of their own that they can share with classmates.

Answer Key

1. 7,200 ft.;   **2.** 36 ft.;   **3.** 84 ft.;   **4.** 112 ft. $\times$ 42 ft. $\times$ 23 $\frac{1}{3}$ ft.;   **5.** Accept any reasonable problems.

6–1   Working with a Scale

A *scale* is a ratio or comparison of two numbers. If a scale model of a car is 1 inch to 2 feet, and the model is 7 inches long, the length of the real car would be 14 feet. Some dimensions of scale models are noted below. Calculate the actual size of each.

1. A model of a volcano has a scale of 2.5 inches to 1,000 feet. If the model is 18 inches high, find the height of the volcano. _____

2. An HO model railroad car has a scale of 1 inch to 87 inches. Find the length of the rail-road car if the model is 5 inches long. (Round your answer to the nearest foot.) _____

3. A model of a brontosaurus has a scale of $\frac{1}{2}$ inch to 7 feet. From the tip of the nose to the end of the tail, the model is 6 inches long. Find the length of the brontosaurus from the tip of its nose to the end of its tail. _____

4. A model of an office building (with a flat roof) has a scale of 3 inches to 21 feet. If the model is 16 inches long, 6 inches wide, and $3\frac{1}{3}$ inches high, find the dimensions of the actual building. _____

5. Create a word problem of your own using a scale and share it with some of your class-mates. Be sure that you make an answer key and that your math is correct!

© 2000 by The Center for Applied Research in Education

FINDING PERIMETER—FENCING A YARD

Objective: Students will find the perimeter to determine the amount of fencing required to enclose a yard. Students should work individually to complete this activity.

Special Materials: none; *optional*—calculators

TEACHING NOTES

While most geometry students know the concept of perimeter and can easily find the perimeter of basic geometric figures, real-life applications of perimeter are not usually so simple. This activity gives students a chance to work with perimeter in a realistic example.

1. Introduce this activity by asking students how they would determine the amount of fencing required to enclose a yard. There are two ways. You can physically measure the distance or you can determine the distance from a plot plan of the yard. While fencing installers will, of course, measure a yard when they provide their estimate, the wise homeowner knows in advance about how much fencing he or she will need before the installer arrives.

2. Distribute copies of Worksheet 6–2 and review the instructions with your students. Encourage them to study the diagram carefully and note that only the backyard is to be fenced in. Remind students that they are to leave space for a four-foot wide gate (which is a separate item and should be deducted from the total length of fencing). Emphasize that students will need to find any missing lengths from the lengths that are provided on the diagram. To find the length of the back property line, students should use the Pythagorean Theorem. (If your students haven't studied the theorem, you may provide them with the length, which is 100 feet.)

Answer Key

345 ft.

283

6–2   Finding Perimeter—Fencing a Yard

Imagine that you are to help a friend enclose his backyard with a fence. Before he contacts fence installers, your friend wishes to have an estimate of how much fencing he will need. Since you don't have a trundle wheel or other measuring instrument that will allow you to easily find the length of the fence needed, you decide to estimate the length by using geometry.

Study the diagram below. Only the backyard is to be fenced in. Finding the perimeter of the backyard, excluding the back of the house and the 4-foot wide gate, will provide you with an accurate estimate of how much fencing your friend should order. Use the dimensions given to determine any missing dimensions you will need. Round your answer to the nearest foot.

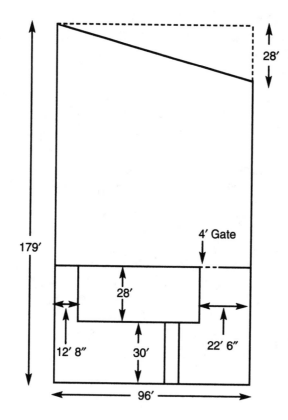

The amount of fencing needed is about _____.

FINDING AREA—PAINTING A ROOM

Objective: Students will find the area and determine the amount of paint required to paint a room. Students should work individually to complete this activity.

Special Materials: none; *optional*—calculators

TEACHING NOTES

At one time or another most people either have painted or will paint a room in their home. Being able to determine how much paint is necessary can not only save money by reducing the chances of buying too much, but can also save the aggravation of having to return to the paint store in the middle of the job.

1. Introduce this activity by asking how many of your students have ever helped parents or friends paint a room or rooms in their homes. Ask them how they determined how much paint they would need. Explain that people frequently under- or overestimate how much paint they require because they do not take the time to measure the room. The best way to determine the amount of paint needed is to find the area of the surface they wish to paint and then check the label on the can, which provides coverage information.

2. Hand out copies of Worksheet 6-3 and review the instructions with your students. Instruct them to study the diagram of the room carefully and note the dimensions of the walls, doors, windows, and height of the room. Emphasize that they are to paint the room (four walls) and ceiling the same color, and that they are not to paint the window, closet door, or the door to the room. If necessary, review the formula for finding the area of a rectangle, A = l x w.

Answer Key

1. 640 sq. ft.; **2.** 52.5 sq. ft.; **3.** 587.5 sq. ft.; **4.** 2 gal.

6–3   Finding Area—Painting a Room

Assume you are to paint a room and must determine how much paint you are to buy. You want to paint all four walls and the ceiling the same color. You are not to paint the doors, door frames, or window frames, which are finished with wood stain. (The dimensions shown for the doors and windows include their frames.) Study the diagram and then answer the questions below.

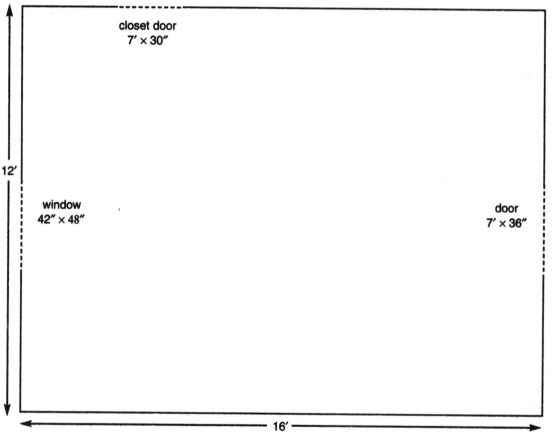

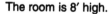

The room is 8′ high.

1. What is the total area of the walls and ceiling? (Before the area of the windows and door are subtracted.) _____

2. What is the total area covered by the window and doors? _____

3. What is the area of the room that must be painted? _____

4. Assume that a gallon of paint covers 300 to 400 square feet. How many gallons should you buy for one coat of paint? _____

FINDING AREA—TILING A FLOOR

Objective: Students will find the area to determine the number of tiles necessary to cover a kitchen floor and also calculate the cost. Students should work individually or in pairs to complete this activity.

Special Materials: none; *optional*—calculators.

TEACHING NOTES

Determining how much vinyl floor covering, tiles, or carpeting is needed to cover a floor is a practical skill. Miscalculate and you'll either buy too much or not enough.

1. Introduce this activity by asking students if they have ever helped their parents or a friend remodel a room. If they have, they probably have an idea of the importance of determining the proper amount of materials and supplies. Tell your students that for this activity they are to assume they are planning to buy new tiles for a kitchen floor.

2. Distribute copies of Worksheet 6–4 and review the instructions with your students. Instruct them to carefully study the diagram and note the dimensions of the floor. They are not to tile under cabinets, beneath the island, or under the stove. The areas of these places must be deducted from the overall area of the kitchen floor. (They must tile the space under the refrigerator.) If necessary, review the formula for finding the area of a rectangle, $A = l \times w$.

3. Emphasize that once students find the area to be covered, they are to determine how many 12-inch by 12-inch tiles will be needed, and also the cost. (You might mention that if they were to actually tile a floor, they should consider buying a few extra tiles in case they make a mistake cutting tiles.)

Answer Key

1. 352 sq. ft.; 2. $108 \frac{2}{3}$ sq. ft.; 3. $243 \frac{1}{3}$ sq. ft.; 4. $243 \frac{1}{3}$ tiles; 5. 6 boxes;
6. $269.70

6–4 Finding Area—Tiling a Floor

Imagine you are to help your parents, a relative, or friend tile a kitchen floor. Before beginning the job, you should determine the number of tiles you will need and calculate the cost. Study the diagram. Use the dimensions given to determine any missing dimensions you will need, then answer the questions that follow.

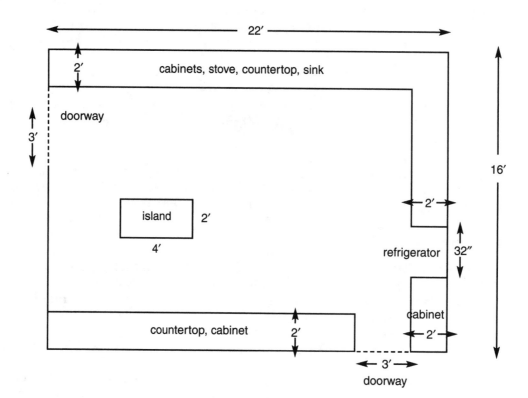

© 2000 by The Center for Applied Research in Education

1. What is the total area of the kitchen floor? _____

2. What is the area covered by cabinets, the stove, sink, and the island? _____ This area is not to be tiled.

3. Subtract the area that is not to be tiled from the total area. What is the area that must be tiled? _____

4. If the size of the tiles are 12 inches by 12 inches, how many will you need? _____

5. If the tiles are packaged in boxes of 45, how many boxes will you need? _____

6. The cost of a box containing 45 tiles is $44.95. What is the total cost? (Assume that sales tax is not required.) _____

FINDING AREA—FERTILIZING A LAWN

Objective: Students will find the areas of rectangles and circles to determine how much fertilizer is required for a lawn; they are also to calculate cost and decide which bag of fertilizer is the better buy. Students should work individually or in pairs to complete this activity.

Special Materials: none; *optional*—calculators

TEACHING NOTES

Sometimes seemingly simple tasks such as buying fertilizer for a lawn can be rather complicated, especially when a lawn is dotted with flower beds, decks, and sheds. The area of such things must be deducted from the overall area of the yard if one is to buy the right amount of fertilizer.

1. Introduce this activity by asking students how many of them help their parents or friends with yard work, particularly working on the lawn. Explain that in this activity students are to assume they are buying fertilizer for a yard, and they must determine how much to purchase and what size bags of fertilizer represent the better buy.

2. Hand out copies of Worksheet 6–5 and review the instructions with your students. Direct them to study the diagram carefully and note that areas of the yard covered by the house, garage, driveway, deck, shed, hedges, and flower gardens are to be deducted from the total area of the yard. If necessary, remind them of the formulas for finding the area of a rectangle, $A = l \times w$, and the area of a circle, $A = \pi \times r^2$. Caution them that although all of the dimensions they will need are not labeled, the missing measures can be determined from the dimensions that are given.

Answer Key

1. 15,000 sq. ft.;   **2.** 3,731 sq. ft.;   **3.** 11,269 sq. ft.;   **4.** One bag that covers 15,000 sq. ft. for $47.99. Although there will be leftover fertilizer, buying two bags that cover 5,000 sq. ft. will not be enough, and three small bags would cost $59.97.

6–5 Finding Area—Fertilizing a Lawn

Imagine you are to buy fertilizer for a lawn. Determining the area of the yard that is to be fertilized will help you to buy the appropriate amount. Study the diagram below and then answer the questions that follow. You will have to find missing dimensions from the dimensions that are given.

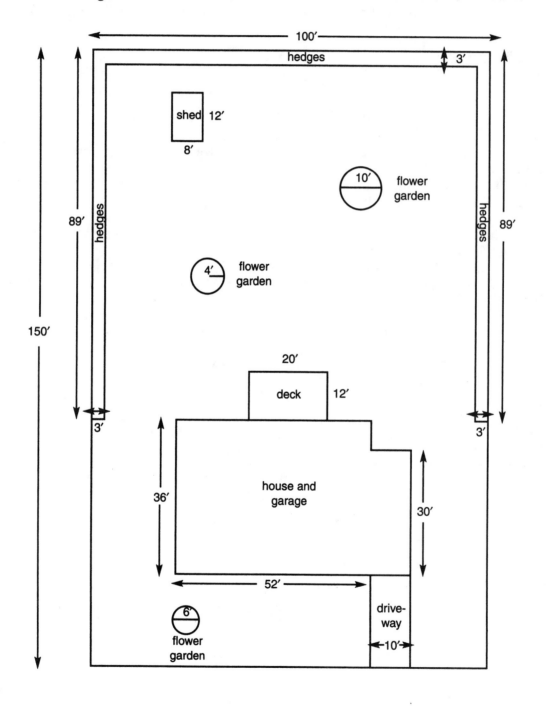

© 2000 by The Center for Applied Research in Education

1. What is the total area of the yard? _____

2. What is total area of the yard that is covered by the house, deck, garage, driveway, hedges, shed, and flower gardens? Round your answer to the nearest square foot. _____

3. Assuming that the rest of the yard is covered with grass, find the area that must be fertilized. _____

4. Fertilizer can be purchased in bags that cover 5,000 square feet for $19.99, and bags that cover 15,000 square feet for $47.99. Which bag or bags would be the better buy? Explain your answer. (Assume that sales tax is not required.) _____

   _____

   _____

   _____

   _____

Activity 6–6

COMPARING AREAS

Objective: Students will construct and compare the areas of a square, rectangle, triangle, parallelogram, trapezoid, and circle. Students should work in pairs to complete this activity.

Special Materials: rulers, protractors, compasses, unlined paper; *optional*—calculators

TEACHING NOTES

When comparing the areas of geometric figures simply by sight, appearances can be deceiving. What appears to be the larger figure may in fact not have the larger area. This activity gives students the chance to draw and compare the areas of various figures.

1. Introduce this activity by asking students to define or explain the concept of area. Area, of course, refers to the region inside specific boundaries. The area of a square, for example, is the region within the sides of the square.

2. Hand out copies of Worksheet 6–6 and review the instructions with your students. Emphasize that they are to do the first problem before computing the areas. Make sure they understand how to use the formulas, and caution them to follow the directions of the worksheet carefully.

Answer Key

1. Answers will vary.

2. square, $6\frac{1}{4}$ sq. in.; rectangle, $6\frac{7}{8}$ sq. in.; triangle, $6\frac{3}{4}$ sq. in.; parallelogram, $8\frac{1}{4}$ sq. in.; circle, $7\frac{13}{200}$ sq. in.; trapezoid, $7\frac{7}{8}$ sq. in.

3. parallelogram, trapezoid, circle, rectangle, triangle, square

4. Answers will vary; accept all reasonable explanations.

6–6 Comparing Areas

The *area* of a geometric figure is the region inside the figure. Follow the directions below to draw a square, rectangle, triangle, parallelogram, trapezoid, and circle. Then answer the questions.

> ▲ Draw a square with sides of 2.5 inches.
>
> ▲ Draw a rectangle with a length of $5\frac{1}{2}$ inches and width of $1\frac{1}{4}$ inches.
>
> ▲ Draw a right triangle with a base of 3 inches and a height of $4\frac{1}{2}$ inches.
>
> ▲ Draw a parallelogram with a base of $2\frac{3}{4}$ inches and a height of 3 inches.
>
> ▲ Draw a circle with a diameter of 3 inches.
>
> ▲ Draw a trapezoid with parallel bases of $2\frac{1}{2}$ and $2\frac{3}{4}$ inches and a height of 3 inches.

1. Look at your drawings closely. Without actually finding the areas, which do you think has the largest area? _____ Which has the smallest area? _____ List the names of the figures in order from largest to smallest based on your observation.

   _____

   _____

   _____

2. Calculate the area of each figure. Use the formulas below.

   Area of a square: s × s = _____

   Area of a rectangle: l × w = _____

   Area of a triangle: $\frac{1}{2}$ bh = _____

   Area of a parallelogram: bh = _____

   Area of a circle: πr^2 = _____

   Area of a trapezoid: $\frac{1}{2}$ h(b$_1$ + b$_2$) = _____

3. List the names of the figures in order from largest to smallest according to their areas.

   _____

   _____

   _____

4. Were your lists the same? _____ If not, explain why you think they varied.

   _____

   _____

   _____

   _____

   _____

SURFACE AREA AND WRAPPING PAPER

Objective: Students will find the cost of wrapping gift boxes. Students should work in pairs to complete this activity.

Special Materials: various shirt-sized boxes, scissors, ribbon, 1 roll of wrapping paper, tape, calculators

TEACHING NOTES

This activity relates the concept of surface area to wrapping gifts. Prior to beginning the activity, collect about four or five shirt-sized boxes to use as models for students to refer to as they work on this activity. To successfully complete the activity, students should be familiar with the concepts of area and surface area, and length and width of the faces of a prism.

1. Introduce this activity by finding the dimensions of a shirt-sized box. Find the surface area of the box as a class exercise. Then place the box on a roll of wrapping paper and determine where to cut the paper so that it wraps around the box. Explain that some of the paper must overlap if you are to cover the box completely. Demonstrate the way the ribbon is to be tied, horizontally and vertically, with some extra on each piece of ribbon to tie a bow.

2. Distribute copies of Worksheet 6–7 and review the instructions with your students. Note that students should follow the directions carefully. You may wish to provide extra gift boxes for students who work more efficiently with a model.

Answer Key

1. 12,420 sq. in. or 86.25 sq. ft.;   **2.** 366 sq. in.;   **3.** 23 in. by 24 in.; 552 sq. in.;   **4.** 22; explanations may vary;   **5.** 34 in., 46 in.;   **6.** 9 packages;   **7.** three rolls, two packages; **8.** $17.44

6–7 Surface Area and Wrapping Paper

The *surface area* of a box is the sum of the areas of every rectangle of the box: two sides, front and back, and top and bottom. These rectangles are called *faces*. Whenever you wrap a gift, or cover a box, you are using the concept of surface area.

The dimensions of a gift box, wrapping paper, ribbon, and bows are provided below. Also included are the costs. Use the information to answer the questions that follow.

▲ 1 gift box measuring 9 inches by 15 inches by 2 inches

▲ 1 jumbo roll of wrapping paper, 23 inches by 45 feet that costs $7.99

▲ 1 roll of ribbon, 66 feet per roll that costs $1.49

▲ 1 package of 12 bows that costs $2.49

© 2000 by The Center for Applied Research in Education

1. What is the area of the wrapping paper? _____

2. What is the surface area of the gift box? _____

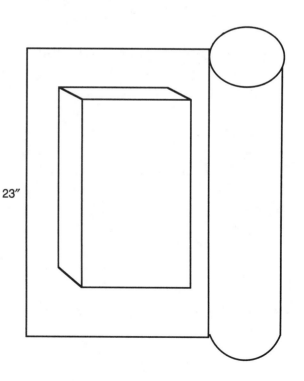

3. If a box is placed on the wrapping paper as illustrated on the right and a two-inch strip of paper overlaps, find the dimensions of the sheet of wrapping paper required to wrap the entire box. (Do not cut the roll above or below the box. Only cut to the right of it.)

Record the dimensions and find the area.

_____

_____

4. How many gift boxes could be wrapped using the jumbo roll? _____ Explain why this answer differs from dividing the area of the roll by the surface area of the box.

_____

_____

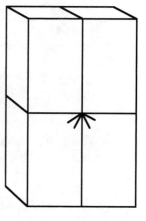

5. To wrap the package with ribbon, two pieces are required per box. One piece is tied horizontally and one extra foot is required to tie a knot. Another piece is tied vertically, and one extra foot is required to tie a knot. The finished wrapped box is pictured at the right.

   Find the length of each piece of ribbon. _____

   _____

6. How many packages can be tied using one roll of ribbon? _____

7. Refer to the answer to problem 4. How many rolls of ribbon are required to wrap this number of boxes? _____ How many packages of bows are required? (Assume one bow is placed on every package.) _____

8. Find the cost of wrapping the number of packages found in problem 4. _____

Activity 6–8

VOLUMES OF CONTAINERS

Objective: Students will find the volume of common prisms and cylinders. Students should work individually to complete this activity.

Special Materials: none; *optional*—calculators, a container with which you can demonstrate volume

TEACHING NOTES

When most students hear the word "volume," they think of their stereo or sound system. In this activity students will find the volume of various containers found in the typical kitchen.

1. Introduce this activity by discussing volume with your students. If you have a container such as a cardboard box or empty cylinder, explain that the volume is the space inside the container.

2. Hand out copies of Worksheet 6–8 and review the instructions with your students. Note that they are to find the volume of the items listed. If necessary, review the formulas for finding the volume of prisms and cylinders.

Answer Key

1. 20 cu. in.; **2.** 30 cu. in.; **3.** 22 cu. in.; **4.** 40 cu. in.; **5.** 70 cu. in.; **6.** 25 cu. in.;
7. 13 cu. in.; **8.** 25 cu. in.

6–8 Volumes of Containers

The prisms and cylinders listed below may be found around the kitchen. The items and their dimensions are given. Try to picture each item in your mind and then find the volume by using the correct formula.

The volume of a prism: V = lwh

The volume of a cylinder: $V = \pi r^2 h$

Use 3.14 or $\frac{22}{7}$ as the value of pi and round your answer to the nearest cubic inch. Place your answer in the space provided. Note that two containers have the same volume.

1. 12-oz. package of cheese slices: 3.5 in. × 3.25 in. × 1.75 in. _____

2. 12-fl. oz. can of soda: 5 in. high with a 2.75-in. diameter. _____

3. $10\frac{3}{4}$ -oz. can of soup: 4 in. high with a $2\frac{5}{8}$ -in. diameter. _____

4. 75-sq. ft. roll of aluminum foil: 2 in. × 2 in. × 10 in. _____

5. 1 box of 3 packages of microwavable popcorn: $6\frac{1}{4}$ in. × $4\frac{1}{2}$ in. × $2\frac{1}{2}$ in. _____

6. 11-oz. can of corn: $3\frac{1}{2}$ in. high with a 3-in. diameter. _____

7. 3.4-oz. box of instant pudding: 3.25 in. × 2.75 in. × 1.5 in. _____

8. 6-oz. can of cooking spray (including cap): 8 in. high with a 2-in. diameter. _____

Activity 6–9

SURFACE AREA AND VOLUME OF A RECTANGULAR PRISM

Objective: Students will calculate the surface area and volume of a rectangular prism. They will also make and test a conjecture about the relationship of surface area and volume. Students should work individually or in pairs to complete this activity.

Special Materials: rulers, empty cardboard boxes (such as cereal boxes, pasta boxes, and similar boxes that might be found in a kitchen cabinet); *optional*—calculators

TEACHING NOTES

In this activity students will explore the concepts of surface area and volume using boxes that are commonly found around the home. Prior to the activity, ask students to bring in empty boxes, like the kind that contain cereal, pasta, microwavable popcorn, cake mix, pudding, etc. Request only boxes that contained dry goods and avoid boxes that contained detergents, cleaners, or toxic materials. To ensure that you have enough boxes on the day of the activity, you might collect some of your own and also ask colleagues to donate some of their used boxes. Have extras ready in case some students forget to bring in a box.

1. Introduce this activity by discussing surface area and volume. Hold up a box and identify it as a rectangular prism. Explain that the surface area is the area of all faces and that the volume is the space inside.

2. Distribute copies of Worksheet 6–9 and review the instructions with your students. Make sure they understand the concepts of surface area and volume, and caution them to closely follow the directions on the worksheet.

Answer Key

Answers may vary. One acceptable answer is that boxes with a larger surface area do not necessarily have a larger volume.

6–9 Surface Area and Volume of a Rectangular Prism

A *rectangular prism* is a three-dimensional figure whose flat surfaces, called faces, are rectangles. Boxes are examples of rectangular prisms. Follow the instructions below to find the surface area and volume of a box. Answer the questions and compare the surface area and volume.

1. Examine the box. Note that it has six rectangular faces: front, back, two sides, and top and bottom. There are three pairs of congruent rectangles, and together the six rectangles form a rectangular prism.

2. Find the surface area of the box. First measure the length and width of each rectangle, then find the area of each rectangle. Add the areas of the rectangles to find the surface area. (Another way to find the surface area is to multiply the area of the top by two, the area of the front by two, and the area of one side by two and then add the products.)

    Surface Area = _____

3. Find the volume of the box. Multiply the area of the bottom of the box by the height of the box. (Another way to do this is to multiply *length* times *width* times *height*.)

    Volume = _____

4. Compare the surface area and volume of your box with the findings of five other students in class. Does the box with the larger surface area always have the larger volume?

    _____

    What conclusions can you draw about surface area and volume?

    _____

    _____

    _____

    _____

    _____

    _____

CREATING A POSTER OF APPLICATIONS AND DEFINITIONS

Objective: Students will create a poster on which they define and provide an example for various geometric terms and figures as they are applied. Students should work individually or in pairs to complete this activity.

Special Materials: rulers, compasses, protractors, scissors, markers, poster paper, old magazines, glue sticks or glue, and geometry books; *optional*—geometry references

TEACHING NOTES

It is often the case in geometry class that students work more with figures and shapes than they do with words. This activity gives students the opportunity to emphasize words and relate them to applications in geometry.

Since students will require pictures that demonstrate geometry being applied, you should gather old magazines prior to assigning this activity. General interest and mathematic magazines are likely to have many potential pictures, but other magazines will also be helpful. Ask colleagues and students to bring in old magazines that you can use for this activity.

1. Distribute copies of Worksheet 6–10 and review the instructions with your students. Explain that students are to define or explain the 15 terms and also provide a picture, example, or sketch of each that shows the term in a real-life situation. For example, for a sphere, students might select a picture of a basketball from a magazine or draw a picture of the moon. They are to design a poster to display their definitions and illustrations. Suggest that students conduct their research first, using their geometry texts or other references. Caution them to map out their poster lightly in pencil to make sure that all of their information will fit before they use markers for highlighting. Encourage them to be creative and colorful.

2. Accept any reasonable posters that accurately define or describe the terms. You may like to display the posters upon completion of the activity.

Name _____ **Date** _____ **Section** _____

6–10   Creating a Poster
of Applications and Definitions

The words below often appear in the practical applications of geometry. Using your geometry book or other references, define or explain each word. Then design a poster highlighting the word and its meaning. Illustrate the term in a real-life situation with a picture, drawing, or example.

1. Square _____

2. Rectangle _____

3. Triangle _____

4. Parallelogram _____

5. Trapezoid _____

6. Rhombus _____

7. Circle _____

8. Cylinder _____

9. Cube _____

10. Sphere _____

11. Area _____

12. Perimeter _____

13. Circumference _____

14. Surface Area _____

15. Volume _____

CREATING PROBLEMS AND APPLYING FORMULAS

Objective: Students will demonstrate their proficiency at using formulas by creating problems and supplying the answers. Students should work individually or in pairs to complete this activity.

Special Materials: rulers, paper, compasses, protractors; *optional*—computers with software capable of creating geometric figures, printers

TEACHING NOTES

This activity provides practice in applications by applying formulas. Using a reference sheet that summarizes formulas for area, perimeter, volume, and surface area, students will create their own problems, which they will then exchange with their classmates. The formulas included in this activity are standard for middle school math, and the problems students create can be used as a review.

1. Introduce this activity by explaining that students are to create problems for their classmates to solve. This, of course, requires that students fully understand the applications they use in the problems they create.

2. Hand out copies of Worksheet 6–11 and review the instructions with your students. Make sure students understand the formulas on the worksheet. Note that students should create at least one problem for each figure, resulting in a total of at least ten problems. Remind them that all figures and dimensions, including the units, must be accurate, and they must also supply an answer key. Encourage them to create word problems. If students have access to computers with software capable of drawing geometric figures, consider having them create their problems using the equipment.

3. Accept any reasonable problems. Encourage students to exchange their problems with other members of the class and try to solve each other's problems.

Name _____ **Date** _____ **Section** _____

6–11   Creating Problems and Applying Formulas

Create problems for your classmates to solve. Create at least one problem for each of the ten figures below, including any necessary diagrams and all information that is required to solve the problems. Write your problems on a separate sheet of paper, and place an answer key on another sheet. Use the formulas for reference.

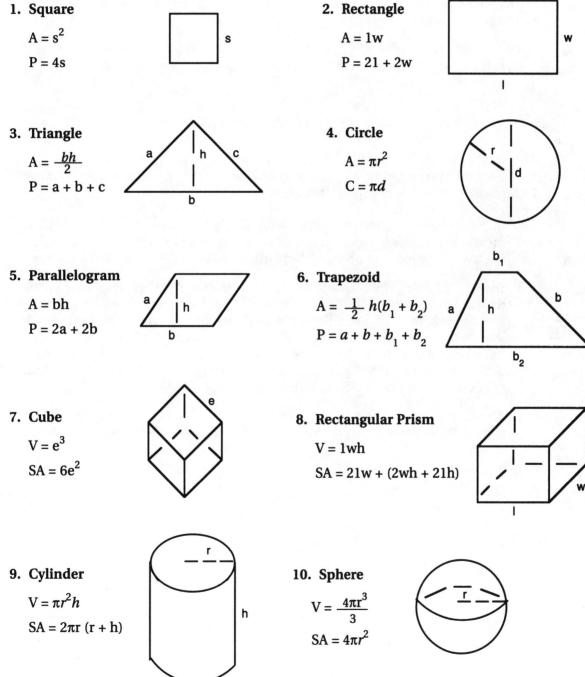

1. **Square**

   $A = s^2$

   $P = 4s$

2. **Rectangle**

   $A = lw$

   $P = 2l + 2w$

3. **Triangle**

   $A = \dfrac{bh}{2}$

   $P = a + b + c$

4. **Circle**

   $A = \pi r^2$

   $C = \pi d$

5. **Parallelogram**

   $A = bh$

   $P = 2a + 2b$

6. **Trapezoid**

   $A = \dfrac{1}{2} h(b_1 + b_2)$

   $P = a + b + b_1 + b_2$

7. **Cube**

   $V = e^3$

   $SA = 6e^2$

8. **Rectangular Prism**

   $V = lwh$

   $SA = 2lw + (2wh + 2lh)$

9. **Cylinder**

   $V = \pi r^2 h$

   $SA = 2\pi r\,(r + h)$

10. **Sphere**

    $V = \dfrac{4\pi r^3}{3}$

    $SA = 4\pi r^2$

CREATING PROBLEMS AND
APPLYING FORMULAS (ADVANCED)

Objective: Students will demonstrate their proficiency at using formulas by creating problems and supplying answers. Students should work individually or in pairs to complete this activity.

Special Materials: rulers, paper, compasses, protractors; *optional*—computers with software capable of creating geometric figures, printers

TEACHING NOTES

This activity is similar to Activity 6–11, however, the formulas students are required to use are more appropriate for a high school geometry class. This activity contains 20 formulas, out of which students are required to create 10 problems.

1. Introduce this activity by telling students that they are to create geometry problems for their classmates to solve. In the process they will be demonstrating their knowledge of geometry and also providing the class with a review.

2. Distribute copies of Worksheet 6–12 and review the instructions with your students. If necessary, review the formulas. Remind students that they are to create 10 problems. Because the formulas vary in difficulty, you may require students to use two or three specific formulas and then allow them to choose from among the others. Encourage them to design word problems. Note that they must include any diagrams and supply the proper measurements that are needed to solve their problems; they must also provide an answer key.

3. Accept any reasonable problems. Encourage students to exchange their problems with other members of the class and try to solve each other's problems.

© 2000 by The Center for Applied Research in Education

Name _____ Date _____ Section _____

6–12 Creating Problems and Applying Formulas (Advanced)

Create problems for your classmates to solve. Create at least 10 problems, including all necessary diagrams and information that is required to solve the problems. Write your problems on a separate sheet of paper, and place an answer key on another sheet. Use the formulas for reference. (*Note*: "B" stands for the area of the base. "P" stands for the perimeter of the base.)

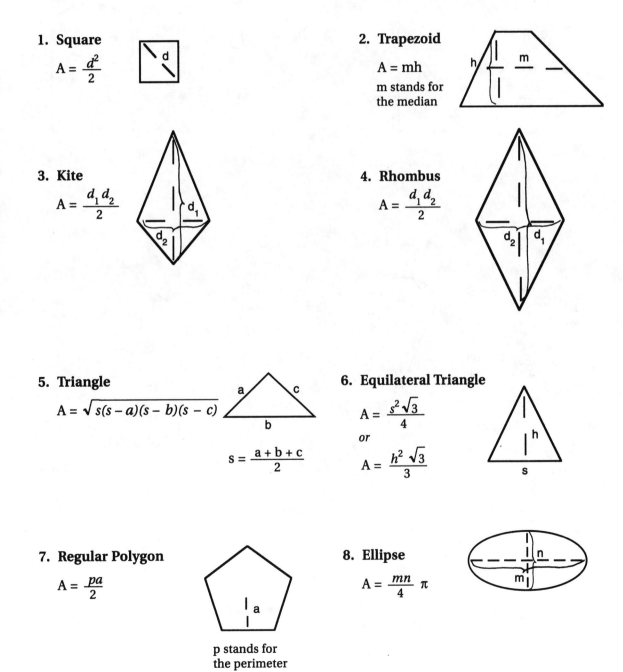

1. Square

$$A = \frac{d^2}{2}$$

2. Trapezoid

$$A = mh$$

m stands for
the median

3. Kite

$$A = \frac{d_1 d_2}{2}$$

4. Rhombus

$$A = \frac{d_1 d_2}{2}$$

5. Triangle

$$A = \sqrt{s(s-a)(s-b)(s-c)}$$

$$s = \frac{a+b+c}{2}$$

6. Equilateral Triangle

$$A = \frac{s^2 \sqrt{3}}{4}$$

or

$$A = \frac{h^2 \sqrt{3}}{3}$$

7. Regular Polygon

$$A = \frac{pa}{2}$$

p stands for
the perimeter

8. Ellipse

$$A = \frac{mn}{4} \pi$$

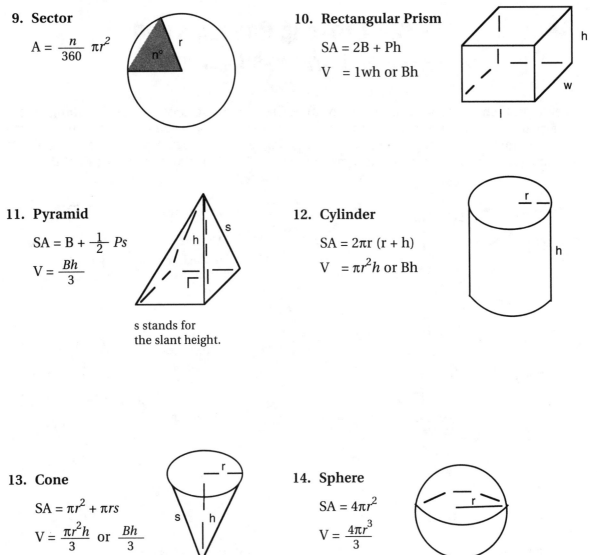

9. Sector

$$A = \frac{n}{360} \; \pi r^2$$

10. Rectangular Prism

SA = 2B + Ph

V = 1wh or Bh

11. Pyramid

$$SA = B + \frac{1}{2} \; Ps$$

$$V = \frac{Bh}{3}$$

s stands for
the slant height.

12. Cylinder

SA = 2πr (r + h)

V = $\pi r^2 h$ or Bh

13. Cone

$$SA = \pi r^2 + \pi rs$$

$$V = \frac{\pi r^2 h}{3} \; \text{ or } \; \frac{Bh}{3}$$

s stands for
the slant height.

14. Sphere

$$SA = 4\pi r^2$$

$$V = \frac{4\pi r^3}{3}$$

Part 7

A POTPOURRI OF GEOMETRY

A BIOGRAPHICAL SKETCH
OF A FAMOUS GEOMETER

Objective: Students will select a mathematician who has contributed to the advancement of geometry, research this individual, and write a biographical sketch. Students should work individually to complete this activity.

Special Materials: various reference sources; *optional*—computers, printers

TEACHING NOTES

Too often when students study geometry, they learn concepts and ideas, but only occasionally do they learn much about the men and women who have contributed to the study and advancement of geometry. Yet, many of these people have led fascinating lives. This activity enables students to select a mathematician who has excelled in geometry, research his or her life, and write a biographical sketch that highlights this person's contributions to geometry.

Note that this activity contains two worksheets, 7–1A and 7–1B. The first worksheet guides students in their research; the second provides a list of famous geometers.

1. Introduce this activity by explaining that a biography is an account of a person's life, written by another individual. A biographical sketch is a short biography that usually focuses on some of the achievements of the subject's life.

2. Hand out copies of Worksheet 7–1A and review the instructions with your students. Note that the worksheet will help guide students in their research efforts. You might also wish to distribute copies of Worksheet 7–1B, which is a list of mathematicians noted for their work in geometry. Explain that this list is only a start. Encourage students to consider other individuals for their biographical sketches. If students have access to computers, suggest that they write their biographical sketches on their computers.

3. As a way to encourage students to concentrate their efforts on the most important details of their subject's life, you might want to put a limit of two to three pages on their biographical sketches. Remind students to be accurate in their research and highlight the person's contribution to geometry. Suggest that they consult reference materials in the library as well as on-line sources.

4. At the end of the activity, display the biographical sketches or publish them in a collection.

7–1A   A Biographical Sketch of a Famous Geometer

A *biographical sketch* is a short biography that usually focuses on the subject's most important achievements. In researching an individual, you should consult various sources. Answering the following questions can help you to develop a biographical sketch about an individual who contributed to the study and advancement of geometry.

1. Who is your subject? _____

2. When was he/she born? _____ Where? _____

   Where and when did he/she die? _____

   What was the cause of death? _____

3. Include the following details:

   Childhood and schooling: _____
   _____
   _____
   _____

   Professional life: _____
   _____
   _____
   _____

   Personal life: _____
   _____
   _____
   _____

4. What was this person's contribution to geometry? _____
   _____
   _____

5. Include your sources. Consult your English text or a writer's style book for the correct formats.

7–1B   Famous Geometers

Many mathematicians throughout history have contributed much to the study and advancement of geometry. Following are some of the more famous. Note that many of these men and women have also contributed greatly to other branches of mathematics.

Ahmes (about 1650 B.C.), Egypt

Pythagoras (about 585–507 B.C.), Greece

Thales of Miletus (about 580 B.C.), Greece

Leno of Elea (about 450 B.C.), Greece

Plato (429–347 B.C.), Greece

Aristotle (384–322 B.C.), Greece

Euclid (about 365–300 B.C.), Greece

Archimedes (about 297–212 B.C.), Greece

Appollonius (about 260 B.C.), Greece

Eratosthenes (276–194 B.C.), Greece

Heron of Alexandria (about 50–100), Greece

Hypatia (370–415), Greece

Brahmagupta (about 600), India

Omar Khayyam (1048–1131), Persia

Leonardo da Vinci (1452–1519), Italy

Pierre de Fermat (1601–1665), France

Mei Wending (1633–1721), China

Adrien-Marie Legendre (1752–1833), France

Sophie Germain (1776–1831), France

Carl Friedrich Gauss (1777–1855), Germany

Grace Chisholm Young (1868–1944), England

Albert Einstein (1879–1955), Germany

Maurits Cornelis Escher (1898–1971), Holland

THE GEOMETRY TEACHER

Objective: Students will develop and present a geometry lesson to the class. Students should work individually, in pairs, or small groups to complete this activity.

Special Materials: along with providing materials of their own, students may require the use of an overhead projector, manipulatives, rulers, protractors, compasses, etc.

TEACHING NOTES

This activity allows students to assume the role of the teacher. In creating a geometry lesson students will need to select a topic, learn the material, organize their information, and present the lesson to the class.

You can conduct this activity in several ways. You might prefer to set aside a few class periods and have each student present a lesson, or you may select some students to prepare and give a lesson each quarter. You may permit students to choose from a variety of topics for their lessons, or you may direct them to a specific unit, chapter, or topic. A good time to have students present lessons on a chapter is near the end so that the student lessons will also serve as a review.

Note that this activity contains two worksheets, 7–2A and 7–2B. The first worksheet provides guidelines on how students may develop a lesson for the class, while the second highlights the elements of an effective lesson.

1. Introduce this activity by explaining that students will have the opportunity to present a lesson to the class. To generate topics, brainstorm with the class. After giving students the general parameters of the activity (for example, they are to use material from Unit 3 or Chapter 7), ask students to suggest possible topics for lessons. List these on the board or an overhead projector. Keep brainstorming until you have listed several topics. Afterward, see if the class can expand some of the topics and generate more.

2. Distribute copies of Worksheets 7–2A and 7–2B and review them with your students. Be sure to stress the importance of mastering their subject matter, and developing, organizing, and planning their lesson.

3. We recommend a time limit of about 10 minutes for lessons presented by an individual; a bit longer for pairs or groups. Any handouts or worksheets students create and distribute should likewise be limited to a few problems or examples. Consider permitting a question-and-answer session after each lesson.

4. Schedule students for the day they are to present their lesson and remind them to hand in a written plan of their lesson at least one week before they are to present it. They should also include a list of materials they will need. Review their lesson plans; if you see a weakness, meet with students to improve them.

5. Evaluation of students' lessons can be based on the overall effectiveness of their lesson, including topic, materials, and presentation.

7–2A   The Geometry Teacher

In order to teach a subject to others, a teacher must understand the material completely. In addition, the information must be organized and presented clearly. For this activity, you are to assume the role of a geometry teacher, and prepare and present a lesson to the class. Following are some suggestions.

1. Select a topic in geometry you would like to teach.

2. A good lesson is the result of several factors:

   Research—You must know your material.

   Organization—You must present your material in a clear, logical manner.

   Visual aids—Transparencies, models, charts, posters, graphs, etc., can help students understand your lesson.

   Activities for the learners—Worksheets, sample problems, making diagrams, or creating puzzles can help students master the concepts and skills of your lesson.

3. Write out your plan.

4. Practice giving your lesson so that you are able to present it smoothly. Speak clearly and don't rush your words.

5. Give clear directions for any activities you plan.

6. Try to anticipate questions you might be asked and be ready to answer them during your presentation.

7–2B   The Geometry Teacher—Lesson Plan Guide

Following is a common format for lesson plans.

OBJECTIVE

Every plan has an objective or goal. The objective is what the students should learn from the lesson.

MATERIALS

To teach some lessons only a textbook or an overhead projector is needed. Others may require a lot of materials such as protractors, graph paper, compasses, rulers, etc.

METHOD

The method of a lesson plan is how the lesson will be taught. There are many ways to teach a lesson in geometry. You might:

▲ Show examples on the chalkboard.

▲ Use transparencies to show examples on an overhead projector.

▲ Use a model to illustrate a geometric concept.

▲ Use a table, chart, or graph to demonstrate an idea.

▲ Offer students a problem that they must solve.

▲ Distribute a worksheet with examples of problems.

PROCEDURE

In this part of your lesson plan, you decide how you will present your material. What will you do first? What comes next? How will you finish?

EVALUATION

Evaluation is your way of finding out if students learned what you hoped to teach them. You might give a quiz, a homework sheet, or simply ask students questions about the material you taught.

Activity 7–3

A GEOMETRY NEWSLETTER

Objective: Students will create and publish a geometry newsletter. While students may contribute individual work to a newsletter, they may also work in groups to complete this activity.

Special Materials: black pens, rulers, protractors, compasses, correction fluid, white tape, scissors, transfer letters, clip art, graph paper, glue, stapler; *optional—* computers, printer, photocopier

TEACHING NOTES

Creating and publishing a newsletter can be an excellent project for your geometry class. This activity will provide students with an opportunity to work together on topics in geometry in an environment that goes beyond the typical classroom setting. The activity provides for the integration of mathematics and writing in a meaningful manner. Producing a geometry newsletter is not so much work as you may think and the rewards are wonderful. Newsletters of outstanding quality can be produced using word processors, personal computers, and photocopiers.

Because the activity combines math and writing, you may consider working with your students' English teacher. While he or she helps students with the actual writing of the newsletter, you manage the math and production. A newsletter of four pages (two photocopied pages back to back) will be big enough to contain several articles yet remain small enough to be manageable. Once you have gained experience in producing newsletters, you may wish to expand the length.

Before beginning this activity, decide what kinds of articles the newsletter will contain. You might make these decisions yourself, or you might discuss them with your students. All of the material should have a geometry "angle."

There are many ways to conduct this activity. You may divide students into groups of four or five and have each group produce its own newsletter, or you may have a different group produce a newsletter each month or each quarter. If you wish to involve everyone with the same newsletter, you may have different groups work on different parts of the newsletter. For example, Group 1 might be responsible for writing the articles. Group 2 might create mind-bending puzzles. Group 3 may handle artwork, headlines, design, and layout. Group 4 might be the proofreaders and checkers of the math. If you prefer, you may simply have individual students contribute articles to the newsletter and organize a group of volunteers to produce it.

1. Introduce this activity by explaining to your students that a newsletter is a publication that contains information about a specific subject or topic. The purpose of the articles in a newsletter is to provide the reader with information. Most of the articles are short and are written in a clear, straightforward style. If you have copies of newsletters from past groups, distribute them as samples so that your students have an idea of what a geometry newsletter can be.

Activity 7–3   *(Cont'd)*

2. Distribute copies of Worksheet 7–3 and review the guidelines with your students. While they may use ideas from the list of possible topics, encourage them to brainstorm to come up with even more potential ideas. Remind them that their work must be accurate.

3. If you have access to computers, word processors, and printers, use this equipment to produce high-quality newsletters. Remind students to run their spelling and grammar checkers (if their word processors contain these applications).

4. Many word-processing programs include clip art. If students have access to clip art via their computers, use the art to highlight and add interest to your newsletter. If you have access to software with geometry capabilities, your students will be able to add precise geometric figures and designs to the newsletter. The figures created with such software, in many cases, can be easily transferred (or imported) into word-processing files. Perhaps your school's computer specialist can help you if you have questions about software.

5. Instead of computer clip art, students may illustrate their newsletter with hand-drawn line pictures. Any hand-drawn illustrations should be kept simple and contain dark lines for photocopying. Caution students that complex drawings with a lot of shading don't reproduce well on many photocopiers. Rather than having students draw illustrations on printed pages, which they might ruin if they make a mistake, have them do their drawings on plain white paper. Cut out the finished illustrations and paste or tape them to the printed page. Titles and headlines can be created on graph paper with stencils or transfer letters. Your school's art teacher can be a source of materials and advice here.

6. Be sure to set deadlines so that your newsletter can be published on time. Set reasonable deadlines for the various tasks that will go into completing your newsletter.

7. When your newsletter is done, have proofreaders and checkers review the work once more to catch any remaining oversights. Once the newsletter is deemed finished, have it photocopied. By photocopying on both sides of a page, you will save paper and produce a more attractive newsletter. Be sure to produce enough copies for each student as well as a few extra for display in your class or the school library.

8. Consider going really high tech. Produce your newsletter as a computer file and e-mail it to students. For most systems, an easy way to do this would be via an e-mail attachment.

9. Evaluation should focus on individual or group contributions to the newsletter.

7–3   A Geometry Newsletter

A *newsletter* is a publication that provides readers with information about a specific subject or topic. For this activity you will help to create and produce a geometry newsletter. Following are some helpful tips.

1. Your newsletter should contain interesting articles about geometry.

2. Some topics may require research. Be sure that your geometry and math facts are correct.

3. Write clearly and use correct grammar and punctuation.

4. Use headlines to capture the reader's attention.

5. Illustrate your newsletter with clip art or line drawings.

6. Design your newsletter in an attractive layout.

7. If possible, use computers and printers to produce your newsletter.

8. After producing your newsletter, be sure to share it with others.

   Here are some possible topics for articles. Brainstorm to identify more.

   Famous Mathematicians and Geometry

   Self-help Articles for Learning Geometry

   Games and Puzzles

   Shortcuts for Solving Geometry Problems

   Geometry Trivia

   Little-Known Facts in Geometry

   Interviews with Students about Geometry

   Suggestions for Geometry Projects

   Articles about Geometry in Real Life

   Escher and Geometry

GEOMETRY REBUSES

Objective: Students will create rebuses using terms in geometry. Students should work individually or in pairs to complete this activity.

Special Materials: none

TEACHING NOTES

A rebus is a puzzle made of words, syllables, symbols, and pictures. Because creating rebuses can be challenging and fun, rebuses can make an excellent geometry activity.

1. Distribute copies of Worksheet 7–4 and review the instructions with your students. Explain what a rebus is and review the three examples. Instruct students to create three to five rebuses of their own. Suggest that they create puzzles on scrap paper first, and then put them on the worksheet.

2. After students have completed their rebuses, you may have them exchange puzzles with other groups (or individuals). You might like to select some of the best and produce a collection of class rebuses.

7–4   Geometry Rebuses

A *rebus* is a puzzle made of words, syllables, and pictures. Following are three examples of simple rebuses.

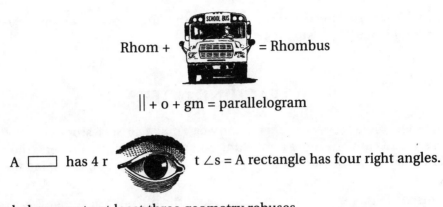

Mid + • = Midpoint

Rhom + [bus] = Rhombus

‖ + o + gm = parallelogram

A ▭ has 4 r [eye] t ∠s = A rectangle has four right angles.

In the space below, create at least three geometry rebuses.

CREATING A GEOMETRY POSTER

Objective: Students will create a poster that highlights a concept or theme in geometry. Students should work individually or in pairs to complete this activity.

Special Materials: poster paper, rulers, protractors, compasses, markers; *optional—*drafting materials, T-squares

TEACHING NOTES

Posters that convey ideas about geometry can make any classroom more attractive. When students are given the opportunity to make geometry posters, they are able to share ideas about geometry and brighten the classroom at the same time.

1. Introduce this activity by explaining that the purpose of a poster is to share an idea. Effective posters attract a person's attention with catchy headlines, vivid colors, and interesting pictures or photos. If you have samples, show them to your students, noting the different features.

2. Hand out copies of Worksheet 7–5 and review the guidelines with your students. Using the possible topics listed as a starting point, brainstorm more topics, which you may list on an overhead projector or the board.

3. If students have access to digital cameras and computers with software for processing photos, they might like to create photos for their posters. Printing the photos on a color printer can result in exceptional posters.

4. Emphasize that students should create a poster that shares an observation, idea, or theme in geometry. At the end of the activity, display the completed posters in the classroom.

7–5   Creating a Geometry Poster

The purpose of creating a poster is to share ideas. Posters are often used in advertising or as a display to attract attention. Following are some tips how you can create a geometry poster.

1. Think of a concept or theme in geometry that you can communicate in a poster. Consider the examples at the bottom of this page and also consult your math text for possible ideas.

2. Focus your topic so that you can share it in the form of a poster. The message of your poster should be clear.

3. Do a rough sketch (or several sketches if necessary) of your poster. Bright, attractive illustrations or photos and catchy headlines can capture a viewer's attention. Avoid cluttering your poster with too many pictures or too much lettering. Too many clashing colors can make your poster difficult to read. Borders can help focus attention.

4. Highlight main ideas with color, underlining, or arrows or dots.

5. Try to make sure that your poster is balanced. All words, pictures, and colors should support your idea. No part of your poster should outweigh another. Strive for symmetry.

6. Be neat. Lines should be straight, letters should be clear, and pictures should be as precise as possible.

POSSIBLE POSTER IDEAS

▲ Geometry Will Give You the Angle on Life

▲ Geometry Is Not Square

▲ Pythagoras—Number One Geometer of Ancient Greece

▲ The Circle Goes Round and Round

▲ The Circle—Symbol of Infinity

▲ The Circle—No Beginning, No End

▲ Geometry in Nature

▲ Geometry—More Than Lines and Circles

▲ Geometry Is All Around You

▲ Geometry—Language of the Universe

A GEOMETRY COMIC STRIP

Objective: Students will create a comic strip that communicates an idea about geometry. Students should work individually or in pairs to complete this activity.

Special Materials: pens, rulers, plain white paper, samples of comic strips; *optional*—colored pencils, crayons, markers

TEACHING NOTES

Too many students view geometry as abstract and mundane. Asking students to create a comic strip in which a geometry idea, fact, or theorem is communicated is an excellent way to stimulate interest in and reflection on geometry.

Before starting this activity, collect examples of various comic strips and share them with your students. Note their structure, particularly their frames. Local newspapers are a good source of comic strips.

1. Introduce this activity by asking your students if they read the comics. Most probably do, and many likely have their favorites. Explain that in this activity students are to create a comic strip that shares an idea about geometry.

2. Distribute Worksheet 7–6 and review the guidelines with your students. Emphasize that students must decide on an idea they wish to communicate (the theme of the comic strip) and then develop the comic strip around this idea. Suggest that they try to limit their comic strips to between one and four frames. More than four might become difficult to handle. Mention that they will probably need to sketch rough copies before they are ready to do a final version of their comic strip.

3. At the end of the activity, display the comic strips.

7–6   A Geometry Comic Strip

Comic strips are found in most newspapers. While most are designed to make readers chuckle, many also share a message. Use the following information to create a comic strip that shares a concept, fact, or insight about geometry.

ELEMENTS OF A COMIC STRIP

1. The story, called a *narrative*, is told on frames. *Frames* are also called *panels*.

2. Characters may be human or nonhuman. They should be interesting.

3. The story is told in captions, which may be either at the top of the frame or the bottom.

4. Dialogue is written in "speech" balloons.

5. Art helps to tell the story.

6. The idea that communicates the message the writer hopes to share is called the *punchline*. It may be delivered in the form of a joke, an observation, a play on words, or an amusing situation.

TIPS FOR CREATING A GEOMETRY COMIC STRIP

1. Think about a concept, fact, or insight about geometry you would like to share.

2. Think of how you can share this idea in the form of a story. Create interesting characters to help tell your story.

3. Decide how many frames you will need to tell your story.

4. Develop your narrative. Remember that you have to tell your story in a limited amount of space.

5. Develop your punchline out of your story.

6. Sketch rough copies of your comic strip. As you do, pay attention to the relationships between characters and setting. Try to balance your comic strip.

7. Be neat. Use rulers for straight lines. Words and art should be clear.

THE GEOMETRY GAME

Objective: Students will create questions for a game about geometry and then play the game. Students should work in groups of four or five to complete this activity.

Special Materials: at least 20 3″ × 5″ note cards per group

TEACHING NOTES

Most students like games. Playing a game can make for a challenging, exciting, and enjoyable geometry class. Since students will be writing questions about geometry for the game, as well as playing the game, this activity is best conducted over two class periods.

Before beginning the activity, you should select the general content on which you wish students to concentrate. You might focus this activity on a chapter, a unit, or several chapters of your text.

1. Introduce this activity and divide your students randomly into teams of four or five. Explain that teams will compete against each other in a round-robin tournament. Four teams or six teams are ideal, because these even numbers will make a good round robin. If necessary explain that in a round robin, Team A competes against Team B, and Team C competes against Team D. The winners of the two matches then compete, while the runners-up play against each other. The team with the most wins after all teams play is declared the champion.

2. Distribute copies of Worksheet 7–7 and review the instructions with your students. The worksheet details the rules of the game. Emphasize that students can compose their questions only from the material you have designated. Stress that their questions must be clear and answers must be correct. Students may use scratch paper to reason out their answers.

3. Before beginning any game, you should read through the questions and answers students have written to make sure they are appropriate and the level of difficulty is acceptable. Discard questions that are too difficult. During the match, if you judge any question unclear, or if the answer provided by the writers of the question proves to be wrong, the team answering the question is automatically awarded two points.

4. When playing the game, have the competing teams sit at the front of the room. Arrange desks or tables so that the teams face each other. Other students remain at their seats as the audience.

Activity 7–7   *(Cont'd)*

5. Since you should act as the judge, it is usually best that you have only one competition at a time. Having several simultaneous competitions can be hard to manage.

6. To move the match along, be sure to set a time limit. Five or ten minutes generally works well for a match, or you might simply run the match until all the questions are asked. You might also put a 15- or 20-second time limit on answering questions; however, in most cases a time limit on answers is not needed.

7. You may keep score, or ask for a student volunteer to keep a tally of correct answers. Have a few questions of your own ready in case the score is tied at the end of the match. Correct answers to your questions can be the tie-breaker.

8. Like most games, the geometry game can be fun. Even more important, it will help students to reinforce their skills and understanding of geometry.

7–7   The Geometry Game

Most people like to play games. Here is how you can play the "Geometry Game."

Work with your team and follow the steps below to prepare for the game.

1. Using the topics and material your teacher has assigned, write 20 questions and their answers.

2. Write each question on one side of a note card and the answer for that question on the back of the card. When you are done, you will have 20 cards.

3. Be sure your questions are clear and your answers are correct.

RULES FOR PLAYING THE GAME

1. Team A plays against Team B. Each team will select a host who will ask the other team questions that the host's group wrote. The host will ask all of the team's questions or as many as time permits.

2. For our example, we will assume that Team A will be the team that answers the questions.

3. The host of Team B should shuffle the question cards so that questions come up randomly.

4. After the Team B host asks the question, the members of Team A will have an opportunity to answer. Team members may confer. A correct answer results in two points and an incorrect answer receives zero.

5. A time limit for the game should be set in advance. Ten minutes is a good limit.

6. After time runs out for Team A, its score should be tallied.

7. A host for Team A then asks questions of Team B, following the same procedure. At the end of the round, the team with the higher score is the winner.

8. If there are more teams, Team A might then compete against Team C and Team B might compete against Team D. The winners would then compete against each other, and the runners-up of that round would compete. At the end of the round, a champion is declared based on the most wins.

A GEOMETRY PRESENTATION

Objective: Students will select a topic in geometry and present information about it to the class. Students should work individually, in pairs, or in small groups to complete this activity.

Special Materials: 4″ × 6″ note cards, reference books; other materials will vary based on the content of the students' presentations, but might include overhead projectors, transparencies, rulers, protractors, compasses, displays, and graphs

TEACHING NOTES

Preparing and presenting information on a topic in geometry is a comprehensive activity that provides various skills: identifying a topic, focusing a topic, researching, organizing information, and, of course, presenting to an audience. This activity can add much to a geometry class. It can also be an excellent interdisciplinary activity. While you handle the mathematics of the presentation, your students' English teacher may work with students toward the development of their topic.

Before assigning this activity, decide what kinds of topics students may select. You may direct students to choose topics from a unit or, if you assign this activity toward the end of the year, several units. You may leave the topic selections wide open and permit students to choose any topic related to geometry. The activity can be implemented in various ways, and you should select the format with which you feel most comfortable and you feel will be of most benefit to your class.

1. Introduce the activity by explaining to students that they are to select a topic in geometry, which they will research and present to the class. Set deadlines: one for topic selection, one for research to be completed, and a final due date.

2. Distribute copies of Worksheet 7–8 and review the guidelines with your students. Emphasize the importance of selecting an interesting topic and conducting thorough research. If necessary, schedule time in your school's library for students to conduct research. Also suggest that students consult on-line sources. There are many excellent websites for geometry. Searching a topic's key words should lead to many potential sources of information. (Depending on your students, you might wish to review their topics before they begin in-depth research.) Remind students to include their sources. (Bibliographic formats can be obtained from students' English books, research guides, or writer's style books.) Note that students who will need special materials or equipment for their presentations—such as an overhead projector or photocopied handouts—should inform you well in advance.

3. Suggest that students' presentations range between three to five minutes. This is usually sufficient for solid presentations without the activity becoming overwhelming. You should provide time for a question-and-answer session after each presentation.

7–8   A Geometry Presentation

Following are some guidelines that will help you prepare and present your topic on geometry.

PREPARATION

1. Choose a topic. Selecting a topic that interests you will likely interest your audience. Do some preliminary research to gain an understanding of your topic's scope. Avoid choosing a topic that may not have enough substance for your presentation. Likewise, avoid choosing a topic that may be too complex.

2. Focus your topic. Try to zero in on what your topic is *really* about. Identify what is most important about your topic and be sure to include these points in your presentation.

3. Research your topic thoroughly. Consult reference books in the library, if necessary, and also check on-line sources about your topic. Use key words to conduct a search for useful websites. Look for ways ideas relate to other ideas.

4. Organize your information. Begin your presentation with an *introduction*, arrange your main points and details in a *body*, and make your final point or summary in a *conclusion*. Write notes clearly on 4″ × 6″ note cards, to which you can refer during your presentation. Include a list of your references. If there is to be a question-and-answer session after your presentation, try to anticipate the types of questions you may be asked. This will help you prepare for them.

5. Decide what types of support materials you will require to present your topic. These might include an overhead projector, charts, handouts, etc. Arrange for these in advance.

6. Practice your presentation. Stand in front of a mirror, give your presentation to a friend or partner, or perhaps even tape or videotape it. Be sure to time your presentation.

GIVING YOUR PRESENTATION

1. Before you give your presentation, be sure your note cards are in order and that you have any special materials or equipment you need. Make sure you have enough materials and your equipment is working.

2. When your turn comes, take a deep breath and step before your audience. Place your notes on a podium or table.

3. Stand straight, place your weight evenly on both feet, and look at your audience. Make eye contact. Avoid looking over the heads of people or sweeping your eyes around the room. Also, avoid looking at just one or two people.

4. It is natural to feel nervous. Try to remain relaxed and comfortable. If you know your material well and have prepared, your presentation will be fine.

5. Speak clearly and in your natural voice.

6. When you finish your presentation, don't rush away. Be prepared to answer questions. Answer any questions politely and completely. After the session is done, pick up your notes and any materials and return to your seat.

A GEOMETRY POEM

Objective: Students will write poems on topics in geometry. Students should work individually to complete this activity.

Special Materials: none; *optional*—computers, printers

TEACHING NOTES

Poetry is found in virtually every culture around the world. There are many kinds of poems. Although many students associate poetry with rhythm and rhyme, most poems don't have a musical quality of stressed and unstressed syllables nor do they utilize rhyme. Poems can express ideas on just about anything, including geometry.

1. Introduce this activity and explain that students are to select a topic, issue, or idea in geometry and write a poem expressing their thoughts or feelings about it. You may permit students to write on any topic in geometry, or direct them to use topics that you have covered in a unit or chapter. Giving students wide latitude in the selection of topics helps to ensure that everyone can come up with something to write about.

2. You may wish to conduct a brainstorming session to identify possible topics. Ask students to volunteer topics and write them on the board or an overhead projector. Some sample topics for geometry include:

   ▲ Studying for Geometry Tests

   ▲ A Tribute to Euclid

   ▲ It's Tough Being Square

   ▲ Would the World Be Round without Geometry?

   ▲ Angles, Angles Everywhere

3. Suggest that students think of a topic, idea, or feeling they have about geometry and develop their poem from there. Emphasize that while they may wish to write poems with rhythm and rhyme, these poetic devices are not necessary.

4. Distribute copies of Worksheet 7–9 and discuss the guidelines with your students. Remind them that while they certainly have "poetic license" for this activity, all facts about geometry should be accurate.

5. At the end of the activity, have a poetry reading session where student volunteers read their poems to the class, or perhaps display the poems on a bulletin board. You may prefer to collect the poems and publish them in a class anthology of *Geometry Poems*.

7–9   A Geometry Poem

A *poem* is a form of writing in which the poet expresses an idea with powerful images or emotions. For this activity you are to write a poem about geometry. Answering the questions below will help you write your poem.

1. What is the topic or subject of your poem? _____

   _____

   _____

2. Briefly describe what your poem will be about. _____

   _____

   _____

   _____

3. To express ideas vividly, poets often use figures of speech such as *similes*, *metaphors*, and *personification*. A simile uses the words *like*, *as*, or *than* to make a comparison. A metaphor makes a comparison without using such signal words. Personification gives human traits to nonhuman things. Following is an example of each.

   Simile: Her smile was like a semicircle.

   Metaphor: He was a square.

   Personification: The happy kite soared in the sky.

   Write three figures of speech you might use in your poem.

   _____

   _____

   _____

4. What is the most important idea you wish to express in your poem? _____

   _____

   _____

   _____

   _____

WRITING CONCRETE POEMS IN GEOMETRY

Objective: Students will write concrete poems expressing an idea or concept in geometry. Students should work individually to complete this activity; however, if you have reluctant "poets," you may let them work in pairs.

Special Materials: pens, rulers, protractors, compasses, plain white paper; *optional*—markers or colored pencils

TEACHING NOTES

Concrete poems take the shape of their subject. A concrete poem about a tree is written in the shape of a tree. A concrete poem about a circle is written in the form of a circle. Although many people believe that concrete poems are a relatively modern form of poetry, the first concrete poem, "The Altar," was written by English poet George Herbert in the seventeenth century.

1. Introduce this activity by explaining what concrete poems are. While it is likely that your students will be familiar with this poetic form, you may wish to show them some examples. Concrete poems can be found in many books and anthologies of poetry. Two excellent sources are *Concrete Poetry*, edited by Mary E. Solt and Willis Barnstone (Indiana University Press, 1969), and *An Anthology of Concrete Poetry*, edited by Emmett Williams (Something Else Press, 1967).

2. Hand out copies of Worksheet 7–10 and review the guidelines with your students. While students can do the obvious—for example, write a poem about a square in the shape of a square—encourage them to utilize their creativity for this activity.

3. After students have completed their poems, display them or publish them in a class collection of Concrete Poems.

7–10   Writing Concrete Poems in Geometry

A *concrete poem* takes the shape of its subject. For example, a concrete poem about a square is written in the shape of a square. The following guidelines will help you to write a concrete poem on a topic or idea in geometry.

1. Select a topic or idea in geometry that can be illustrated. Some topics and ideas will be easy to develop as concrete poems, while others will be more difficult. Use your creativity.

2. Decide how you will illustrate your poem.

3. Because the words of a concrete poem must be arrange to fit a specific figure, try to estimate how many words you can have in your poem.

4. Decide whether or not your poem will rhyme.

5. When writing your poem, first write your draft. Use vivid words that paint pictures in the minds of your reader.

6. After you have written your poem, revise it.

7. After your poem is revised, redo it in the form of the illustration that represents its topic or idea. When drawing the shape of your poem, use a pencil and make your lines light. The lines will guide you in writing the words in the form that illustrates your ideas.

A GEOMETRY HANDBOOK

Objective: Students will write a handbook of geometry that highlights important concepts or facts. Students should work in groups of three or four to complete this activity.

Special Materials: lined paper, construction paper, black pens, rulers, protractors, compasses, markers, scissors, glue, stapler; *optional*—computers, printers, photocopier

TEACHING NOTES

Having students write a handbook of geometry can serve as an excellent review of concepts, terms, and facts. The activity should be spread over a few days with students working in class as well as out of class.

You have many options in developing this activity. You may suggest that students focus their efforts on a specific chapter, unit, or several chapters of their text. You may have them write a handbook for their class, or encourage them to write a handbook for younger students. (In this case, you might wish to arrange time for your students to present their handbook to students in lower grades.)

1. Introduce this activity by explaining that a handbook is a short manual that provides specific information on a subject. Tell your students that they will create a handbook about geometry in this activity.

2. Hand out copies of Worksheet 7–11 and review the instructions with your students. Suggest that they select major concepts or ideas from a chapter or unit, summarize them for their handbook, and provide any examples, figures, or illustrations that are necessary. Students should limit their handbook to two to four sheets of paper (four to eight pages).

3. If students have access to computers, they should use their computers for the writing of their handbooks. Many software programs have drawing capabilities that will allow students to easily illustrate their handbooks with simple figures such as lines, squares, rectangles, and circles. Most art and drawing programs are compatible with major word-processing programs, and figures and illustrations can usually be imported to the word-processing file. Your school's computer teacher can probably offer you help with this. If not, a call to the software producer's technical support can provide the help you need.

4. If students are to highlight their handbooks with drawings done by hand, suggest that they do their illustrations on a separate piece of paper and then cut and paste the drawing onto the finished page. This will reduce the chances that mistakes with art will ruin printed pages.

5. Upon conclusion of the activity, you may display the handbooks or have photocopies made and distribute them to students.

7–11   A Geometry Handbook

Following are suggestions for creating a geometry handbook.

1. Select topics, concepts, or facts that you would like to include in your handbook.

2. Focus your topics. "Geometry Figures" is too broad. It can include many topics. "Quadrilaterals" is more focused. To give your handbook a sense of unity, select topics that are related.

3. Write clearly. When describing mathematical procedures, write them in order.

4. Be sure your math and geometry facts are accurate.

5. Include examples, figures, or illustrations where necessary.

6. When designing, or laying out, your handbook, keep spacing and balance in mind. Avoid trying to put too much information on a page because this will result in clutter. In arranging your material, make sure examples are placed in the proper place. Try different layouts until you find the one you feel is best.

7. Create an attractive cover.

8. If you have access to computers and printers, use the equipment to write and produce your handbook. Many word-processing programs include art and drawing components that will permit you to create geometric figures.

9. Proofread your writing. Double-check all math and geometry facts and figures for accuracy.

10. After your handbook is completed, share your work with others. Perhaps you can have copies made.

IN SUPPORT OF GEOMETRY—
A PERSUASIVE ESSAY

Objective: Students will write a persuasive essay about geometry. Students should work individually to complete this activity.

Special Materials: lined paper, pens; *optional*—computers, printers

TEACHING NOTES

In recent years it has become clear that the learning of mathematics can be enhanced and supported through writing. Many of the skills necessary for effective writing—clear thinking, organization, and analysis—are essential to mathematics. This activity combines both math and writing in a way that your students will likely find interesting and challenging.

1. Introduce this activity and discuss with your students the elements of a persuasive essay. Sometimes referred to as editorials or opinion pieces, a persuasive essay is a type of writing in which the author writes about a topic and offers his or her opinion about it. The purpose of such pieces is to inform readers about the topic and persuade readers to accept and support the writer's position. Persuasive essays are often contained in newspapers and magazines in the editorial, opinion, or "Letters to the Editor" pages. Since geometry is often misunderstood or minimized, the topic is an excellent one for a persuasive essay.

2. Distribute copies of Worksheet 7–12 and review the guidelines with your students. Note that the purpose of this activity is to write a persuasive essay in support of geometry. Depending upon your class, you might have some students who will ask you if they can write an essay that questions the value of geometry. If you are confronted by this type of question, simply say that geometry has great value in our society. It is the student's task to recognize that value and write an essay in support of it.

3. After students have written their persuasive essays, display the essays or publish them in a class collection.

7–12   In Support of Geometry— A Persuasive Essay

Persuasive essays, sometimes called *editorials* or *opinion pieces*, express an author's opinion about a topic or issue. The following guidelines will help you to write a persuasive essay entitled "Why Geometry Is Important."

1. Most persuasive writing follows the structure of an *introduction*, *body*, and *conclusion:*

   ▲ The *introduction* should contain a strong opening sentence that hooks the reader and explains the topic.

   ▲ The author develops his or her position in the *body*. Facts, examples, and explanations are used to support the author's ideas. Depending on the topic or issue, the body may be one or many paragraphs long.

   ▲ In the *conclusion*, the author encourages the reader to accept or support the author's ideas.

2. Persuasive essays are written in a clear style. Facts must be accurate.

3. Write an opening sentence that explains your topic.

   _____

   _____

4. List some facts, examples, or details you will use in the body of your essay.

   _____

   _____

   _____

   _____

   _____

   _____

   _____

5. What final point will you make in your conclusion?

   _____

   _____

A COLLAGE OF GEOMETRY CAREERS

Objective: Students will create a collage highlighting a career or careers in which geometry plays an important role. They will write an explanation of how geometry is vital to the professions or occupations represented by their collages. Students should work individually, in pairs, or in small groups to complete this activity.

Special Materials: large poster paper, rulers, lined paper, pens, markers, scissors, glue or glue sticks, old magazines

TEACHING NOTES

A major complaint of some geometry students is that they don't see the relevance of geometry in their lives. This activity enables students to explore professions and occupations in which geometry is essential.

Before beginning the activity, collect old magazines that students can use in creating their collages. Mathematics, science, architectural, gardening, and home-improvement magazines will offer some of the best pictures, though even general-interest publications often contain pictures that relate to geometry. You might ask students, as well as colleagues, to bring in old magazines.

1. Introduce the activity by asking students to think of professions or occupations in which geometry is important. List these on the board or an overhead projector. You may prefer to have students focus on one profession for their collage, or you may encourage them to create collages that include many professions.

2. Distribute copies of Worksheet 7–13 and review the instructions with your students. Emphasize that students should include a written explanation of how geometry plays a vital role in the professions or occupations represented in their collages.

3. Display the collages upon completion of the activity. You might use them to launch a discussion of the many types of jobs in which the understanding of geometry is essential.

7–13   A Collage of Geometry Careers

Geometry plays an important role in many professions and occupations. Use the following guidelines to create a collage that shows a career(s) in which knowledge of geometry is a necessary skill.

1. List professions or occupations in which geometry plays a key role. Conduct research, if necessary, to identify these careers and jobs.

2. Using old magazines, select pictures that show how geometry is used in the workplace. Combine different pictures to express ideas.

3. After collecting an assortment of pictures, place them on poster paper to create images that express your ideas. Pay attention to design, especially spacing.

4. Try to make your collage pleasing to the eye. Be neat. Use color, but remember that too much color can make it hard for your ideas to stand out. Strive for unity and balance.

5. Once you have found a satisfying arrangement for your pictures, paste or glue the pictures onto the poster paper. Avoid using too much glue or paste, which will smudge or build up underneath the pictures and make them wavy.

6. Write an explanation of your collage, describing how geometry is important to the professions or occupations represented on your collage. Attach your explanation to the side of your collage.

Activity 7–14

GEOMETRY IN NATIVE AMERICAN CULTURES

Objective: Students will research examples of geometry in a Native American culture and present an oral report to the class. They are also to make a model or illustration of an example of geometry in the culture they select. Students should work in pairs or small groups to complete this activity.

Special Materials: 4″ × 6″ inch note cards, poster paper, rulers, protractors, compasses, markers; students may require other materials for models they wish to make in support of their presentation

TEACHING NOTES

Many students think of geometry as being merely a subject of mathematics. They don't realize that geometry is found in cultures throughout the world—and not just as a part of math. By exploring geometry in Native American cultures students will gain a greater understanding and significance of geometry.

Geometric symbols and figures are found in the art and traditions of many Native American cultures. The Mission Indians of California frequently wove intertwining star shapes into their baskets; many tribes of the Pacific Northwest included geometric designs in their woodworking and totem poles; Indians of the Plains painted geometric decorations on their clothing, weapons, shelter, and bodies; and the Navajo, known for seeing creative beauty in all life, used intricate geometric shapes in their basketry, pottery, and weaving.

While many good books on Native American cultures are available, an excellent series is the *Native American Resource Library*, a four-volume set written by Dana Newmann (The Center for Applied Research in Education, 1995, 1996, 1997). The series focuses on the Indians of North America and includes: *Desert Indians*; *Plains Indians*; *Coastal Indians*, and *Woodlands Indians*.

1. Introduce this activity by explaining to students that geometry is found throughout the world. Tell them that for this activity, they will work in groups and research geometry in Native American cultures.

2. Distribute copies of Worksheet 7–14 and review the guidelines with your students. Note that many Native American groups made extensive use of geometric figures and designs in their art, pottery, weaving, and basket-making. Suggest that students first conduct general research about Indian cultures in different regions—for example, the woodlands, plains, Pacific Northwest, or southwest desert—and select one that used geometry in their art or traditions. Students should then thoroughly research this group and organize their material for an oral presentation. Encourage students to make models or illustrations of the geometry found in their Indian group's culture. To help students in their research efforts, you might schedule class time in your school's library. Remind students to consider using on-line sources as well.

3. Provide time for the presentations. Display any models or pictures students create.

7–14   Geometry in Native American Cultures

Many Native American cultures used geometric figures and designs in their art, weaving, basketry, and even body paint. Research a Native American group and present an oral presentation to the class explaining how geometry was used in their culture. The following guidelines will help you to organize and present your material.

1. Conduct background research on various Native American cultures. Numerous Indian groups lived in woodlands, on the plains, the Pacific northwest coast, and southwestern desert. Each had distinctive customs and traditions, and many used geometry.

2. Select one Native American culture to be the focus of your report.

3. Find examples of geometry in this culture. Try to answer these questions:

   ▲ What types of geometric symbols, figures, or designs were used?

   ▲ What were the symbols, figures, or designs used for?

   ▲ Did these geometric signs have any special significance? What was this significance?

   ▲ Did the making of these geometric signs require any special talent? If yes, what type?

4. After completing your research, organize your material and write main points and details on note cards.

5. Make models or illustrations that show the geometric patterns used in the Indian culture you researched.

6. Determine how you will present your material. Will each member of your group speak or will one member assume the role of spokesperson?

7. Practice your presentation so that it will be effective.

GEOMETRY IN SPORTS

Objective: Students will select a sport in which geometry is important, make a scale diagram or model that shows how geometry is used in the sport, and present their work to the class. Students should work in groups of three or four to complete this activity.

Special Materials: poster paper, rulers, protractors, compasses, graph paper, pens, markers, and other materials students might require to make models

TEACHING NOTES

Most students are sports fans. While they probably know the rules by which their sports are played, many are unaware that their favorite sports are played on fields or courts that are designed with geometry. Without geometry, most sports would be quite different.

To ensure that various major sports are covered in this activity, require each group to select a different sport. While geometry is apparent in most sports, the following are particularly good choices: baseball, football, soccer, hockey, basketball, and tennis. Geometry also plays a major role in billiards, but not many students are familiar with this game.

1. Introduce this activity by asking students to name some favorite sports. Ask them to consider how geometry is important to these sports. You might generate a brief discussion to encourage students' ideas.

2. Distribute copies of Worksheet 7–15 and review the guidelines with your students. Note that creating a diagram or model is an essential part of the activity. Emphasize the importance of scale and instruct students to establish a workable scale. Depending on your class, you may need to demonstrate how students can set up a scale for a drawing or model.

3. Since students will require the dimensions of various fields and courts, you might schedule a class session in the library. One period should be sufficient for research. Students should work on diagrams and models in class or after school.

4. At the end of the activity, allow time for the presentations, diagrams, and models. You might also like to display the diagrams and models.

7–15 Geometry in Sports

Geometry is important to most sports. Playing fields and courts, equipment, and sometimes even strategies are based on geometry. For this activity you are to:

▲ Select a sport.

▲ Research how geometry is used in this sport.

▲ Draw a diagram or create a model showing the use of geometry in the sport.

▲ Present your findings to the class.

Use the following guidelines to help you in your work.

1. Determine which sport you will research. Be sure that geometry plays an important part in it. Possible choices include baseball, football, soccer, basketball, hockey, and tennis.

2. Describe how geometry is used in the sport. For most sports, geometry is apparent in the way the field or court is set up. Look for lines, line segments, angles, rectangles, squares, circles, and half-circles. What significance do geometric figures have in the sport?

3. Create a diagram or plan a model that will demonstrate how geometry is used in your sport.

4. In drawing a diagram or designing a model, pay close attention to scale. Your model or diagram should be accurate. For example, you might find that a scale of 1 in. = 10 ft. will work well for your representation.

5. Write an explanation of how geometry plays a vital role in your sport and present your findings to the class.

GEOMETRY IN NATURE

Objective: Students will research an example of geometry in nature, and create a model or illustration of their subject for display. Students should work individually, in pairs, or small groups to complete this activity.

Special Materials: poster paper, markers, pens, rulers. Students who choose to do a model will likely need additional materials—encourage them to obtain their own materials if possible, or you might be able to supply what they need from your school's general supplies

TEACHING NOTES

Examples of geometry are found throughout nature. Snowflakes and honeycombs are hexagons, diamonds are octahedrons, and the shell of the chambered nautilus (snail) is a spiral. These are just some examples. From the smallest diatoms, which are circles, to galaxies that are spiral or elliptical, geometry is everywhere. Unfortunately, many students are unaware of the preponderance of geometry. This activity will give them an opportunity to explore geometry throughout Earth and beyond.

1. Introduce the activity by conducting a short discussion of instances of geometry in nature. Ask students to volunteer some examples. Typical responses will likely include starfish (pentagons), snowflakes (hexagons), and planets and moons (which students may describe as circles but are actually spheres).

2. Distribute copies of Worksheet 7–16 and review the examples of geometry found in nature with your students. You might wish to discuss how geometric patterns often provide more balance and stability compared with random ones.

3. Instruct students to select one of the examples of geometry in nature provided on the worksheet, or find another if they wish. Explain that they are to create a model or detailed illustration on poster paper. If they select an organism, they should also research how the geometric pattern is beneficial to the organism. For example, an earthworm's cylindrical shape makes it easier to slither through the soil. If they select a mineral, planet, galaxy, or other example, they should research why the object has taken that geometric pattern. An example here is a planet. When a planet forms from super hot gases and dust particles, gravity causes the material to collapse, resulting in a sphere.

4. Provide time for presentations and display of students' models or illustrations at the end of the activity.

7–16   Geometry in Nature

Examples of geometry are found throughout nature. The list below contains some of the more common examples. Select one of the following (or conduct research and choose another example), then create a model or illustration that shows your subject's geometric characteristics. Be prepared to present your work to the class.

chambered nautilus (snail)—spirals

common starfish—pentagons

daisy head—spirals

diamond—octahedron

diatoms—circles

earthworms—cylinders

flowers—often ovals, star-shaped, circular

galaxies—spirals and ellipticals; some galaxies have no specific shape and are classified as irregular

honeycomb—hexagons

human beings and many other animals—symmetry

moons—solid spheres

morning glory buds—spirals

orbits of comets—elliptical or parabolic

orbits of planets—most often circular with slight variations

pine-cone scales—spirals

planets—solid spheres

quartz—hexagons

salt—cubic crystals

snowflakes—hexagons

stars—gaseous spheres

sulfur (an element)—rhombic prism

tourmaline (a mineral)—internal structure in the shape of triangles

tree trunks—lines or cylinders

GEOMETRY IN BUILDINGS AND ARCHITECTURE

Objective: Students will find examples of geometry in the architecture of their homes and neighborhoods. Students should work individually to complete this activity.

Special Materials: none

TEACHING NOTES

Geometry is truly all around us. Taking the time to see examples of geometry that they encounter every day will help students gain an appreciation of just how significant geometry is in their lives.

1. Introduce this activity by pointing out some examples of geometry in your classroom—a circular clock, square ceiling or floor tiles, rectangular windows, the line segments where walls and ceiling meet. Emphasize that examples of geometry are just about everywhere in buildings.

2. Distribute copies of Worksheet 7–17 and review the instructions with your students. Encourage students to list at least two to three examples for each of the geometric terms.

3. At the end of the activity, discuss your students' findings. Accept any reasonable answers.

7–17   Geometry in Buildings and Architecture

The buildings and structures in which we live, work, and play contain countless examples of geometry. Use your home and neighborhood to find examples of the following. (Try to find more than one example for each.)

1. point _____

2. line segment _____

3. right angle _____

4. acute angle _____

5. obtuse angle _____

6. triangle _____

7. square _____

8. rectangle _____

9. rhombus _____

10. parallelogram _____

11. trapezoid _____

12. parallel line segments _____

13. perpendicular line segments _____

14. intersecting lines _____

15. circle _____

16. semicircle _____

17. concentric circles _____

18. diameter _____

19. radius _____

20. arc _____

21. ellipse _____

22. pentagon _____

23. hexagon _____

24. octagon _____

25. rectangular prism _____

GEOMETRY AND THE INTERNET

Objective: Students will find three websites that focus on geometry and write a review of each. Students should work individually or in pairs to complete this activity.

Special Materials: computers with Internet access

TEACHING NOTES

Computers play a major part in the lives of many people these days, and they will only become more important in the future. One place the growing importance of computers is clearly reflected is the Internet, which is a marvelous resource that contains information on countless topics. Although many students enjoy Internet access and surf the net, many lack proficient skills in finding information. In most cases it is not a question of finding enough material, but of finding too much which makes for a massive task of separating the "stuff" from the "fluff."

This activity will not only give students practice in using the Internet for finding information, but will require them to find and investigate three websites in geometry. While you may permit students to work in pairs for this activity (particularly if computer access is difficult to arrange), students will benefit most by working individually.

If your school has a computer room with Internet access, consider scheduling time there for students to complete this activity. If students have Internet access at home, you might permit them to do the activity there. Some public libraries provide Internet access, which might be an option for some students.

1. Introduce this activity by asking students how many of them have ever used the Internet. It's likely that most have. Explain that for this activity students are to use the Internet to locate three websites on geometry, for which they will write reviews.

2. Distribute copies of Worksheet 7–18 and review the guidelines with your students. In particular, discuss how they can find information on the Internet. Explain that search engines—Excite, Lycos, Infoseek, Yahoo, Snap, and HotBot are some examples—can enable them to find the information they require. Using key words will help them in their search. For example, if they are searching for information about "right triangles," searching under the key word "geometry" will result in thousands of websites that may not offer much about right triangles. Using right triangles as a key word, however, will identify sites that are more likely to contain useful information.

3. Suggest that students visit several sites before selecting the ones they wish to review. Some sites will undoubtedly be better than others.

4. At the end of the activity, conduct a discussion in which students share their findings. You might like to compile a list of the websites students reviewed and make them available to the class. The list can become a fine source of information about geometry. *A word of caution here:* Before you make the list available to the class, you should visit each website yourself to make sure questionable material is not included.

7–18   Geometry and the Internet

Thousands of websites about geometry can be accessed on the Internet. For this activity you are to conduct a search for websites about geometry, visit several of these sites, and select three for which you will write a review.

Include the following information in your review:

1. Write the complete Internet address, known as the URL (Uniform Resource Locator), of each website.

2. Briefly summarize the information the site contains. Try to answer questions such as the following:

   ▲ Who is the sponsor, or owner, of this site?

   ▲ What is the focus of the site?

   ▲ What are its major topics?

   ▲ Is the information presented in a clear manner?

   ▲ Did you learn anything new from the site?

   ▲ What did you like most about the site?

   ▲ What, if anything, did you find uninteresting?

3. Investigate some of the site's links. Are they worthwhile? Which one did you find most interesting? Why?

4. Offer your opinion of this website. Be sure to back up your opinion with reasons and details.

5. After reviewing three websites, rank them 1, 2, and 3 with the best being number 1.

A GEOMETRY SCAVENGER HUNT

Objective: Students will find at least 25 examples of geometry in their environment (both natural and artificial). Students should work individually to complete this activity.

Special Materials: none

TEACHING NOTES

In an attempt to demonstrate to students that geometry is truly all around them, send them on a geometry scavenger hunt. For this activity students are to find at least 25 examples of geometry in their environment, home, and school.

1. Introduce this activity by discussing with your students how common geometry is in both the natural and manmade worlds. Ask for volunteers to offer some examples of geometry they find in everyday life.

2. Distribute copies of Worksheet 7–19 and review its instructions with your students. To encourage students to make a good effort at finding examples of geometry, perhaps you can offer a prize—a homework pass—for students who find the most examples or the most unusual example of geometry.

3. Upon completion of the activity, discuss their findings.

7–19   A Geometry Scavenger Hunt

Whether you live in a city, the suburbs, or on a farm, examples of geometry are all around you. For this activity, find at least 25 examples of geometry and write them down. If necessary, continue your list on another sheet of paper. Be sure to write down the object and geometric figure or concept it represents; for example: Main Street Intersection—perpendicular lines.

1. _____
2. _____
3. _____
4. _____
5. _____
6. _____
7. _____
8. _____
9. _____
10. _____
11. _____
12. _____
13. _____
14. _____
15. _____
16. _____
17. _____
18. _____
19. _____
20. _____
21. _____
22. _____
23. _____
24. _____
25. _____

A GEOMETRY BOARD GAME

Objective: Students will invent a board game that focuses on information or some aspect of geometry. Students should work in groups of three or four to complete this activity.

Special Materials: will vary according to student needs, but will likely include oaktag, poster paper, sheets of cardboard, rulers, protractors, compasses, markers, dice, scissors, glue, thumbtacks (for spinners), note cards

TEACHING NOTES

This activity can be an excellent group effort that allows students to employ the full range of their creativity. It can also reinforce important concepts in geometry.

1. When introducing the activity, ask students to name some board games with which they are familiar. Discuss the elements of common board games. For example, in many games two to six players can play at once, movement over the board is determined by dice or spinners, and the object of the game might be to accumulate the most money, find a treasure, or win a race. Explain that students are to design a board game of their own that in some way includes facts or information about geometry.

2. Distribute copies of Worksheet 7–20 and review the guidelines with your students. Emphasize the importance of providing instructions or rules for their game. While you can provide class time for students to work on their game, particularly at the start of the activity, you might also suggest that they work to complete their games outside of class.

3. At the end of the activity, set aside time to play the games.

7–20   A Geometry Board Game

Board games are popular pastimes. It is likely that you have some favorite board games that you enjoy playing with friends and relatives. For this activity you are to create a board game that in some way includes geometry facts or ideas. The following suggestions will help you to design your board game of geometry.

1. Think of board games with which you are familiar. Consider how they are designed. What is their appeal? What is the object of playing? How do players move along the board? How do you win?

2. Think of ways you might design your board game. Consider the following—

   ▲ *Players:* How many people will be able to play?

   ▲ *Objective:* What is the goal or purpose?

   ▲ *Movement:* Will you use dice, spinners, or cards to move across the board? How will you design the pathway?

   ▲ *Penalties:* Will players ever lose a turn or have to move backward? Why? How?

   ▲ *Bonuses:* Will players ever take an extra turn or move forward extra spaces? Why? How?

3. Consider the design of your board. Will you use oaktag or cardboard? If you intend to use spinners, where will they be located? Will your pathway be square, rectangular, circular, or wind its way around the board?

4. Will you use cards for information? If yes, what kind of information? How will players obtain a card?

5. Design your board. Sketch an example of it first. You may need to try several different arrangements.

6. When you produce your board, be neat. For example, use rulers for measuring and making straight lines. Use markers for highlighting. Print clearly.

7. Write clear instructions for your game.

8. Share your game with others and have fun!

Activity 7–21

GEOMETRY AND GALILEO

Objective: Students will write their interpretation and reaction to a quote about geometry attributed to Galileo. Students should work individually to complete this activity.

Special Materials: none

TEACHING NOTES

Sometimes a single quote can capture the essence of a complex concept or subject. Galileo Galilei (1564–1642), the famous Italian scientist and astronomer, in speaking of understanding the universe said: ". . . it is written in the language of mathematics, and its characters are triangles, circles, and other geometrical figures." With those words, Galileo expressed his understanding that geometry is a fundamental mathematical subject that is at the very nature of existence.

1. Introduce this activity by sharing Galileo's words about geometry with your students. Encourage them to reflect upon the words and interpret them in the light of their own experiences and ideas.

2. Distribute copies of Worksheet 7–21 and review the guidelines with your students. Note that completing the worksheet will help students clarify and formulate their thoughts.

3. At the end of the activity, conduct a discussion of Galileo's words and invite students to share their interpretations and impressions.

7–21   Geometry and Galileo

Galileo Galilei (1564–1642) was a famous Italian scientist and astronomer. In speaking of understanding the universe, Galileo said: ". . . it is written in the language of mathematics, and its characters are triangles, circles, and other geometrical figures."

Do you agree with Galileo? Why or why not? Explain your thoughts in an essay. To help you clarify and develop your thoughts, answer the following questions.

1. What do you think Galileo meant when he said that the universe is "written in the language of mathematics"? _____

_____

_____

_____

2. To what might "characters" refer? _____

_____

_____

_____

3. What "other geometrical figures" might Galileo have seen in the universe?

_____

_____

_____

4. Do you agree with Galileo? Why or why not? _____

_____

_____

_____

5. What quote of your own about geometry might you share with others?

_____

_____

_____